W9-BWY-417

DISCARDED

$Do\ 73585$

$1-8-01$

Brooks - Cork Libr

DISCARDED

Brooks - Cork Library
Shelton State
Community College

Religion and the New Republic

Faith in the Founding of America

Edited by
James H. Hutson

ROWMAN & LITTLEFIELD PUBLISHERS, INC.
Lanham • Boulder • New York • Oxford

ROWMAN & LITTLEFIELD PUBLISHERS, INC.

Published in the United States of America
by Rowman & Littlefield Publishers, Inc.
4720 Boston Way, Lanham, Maryland 20706
http://www.rowmanlittlefield.com

12 Hid's Copse Road
Cumnor Hill, Oxford OX2 9JJ, England

Copyright © 2000 by Rowman & Littlefield Publishers, Inc.

All rights reserved. No part of this publication may be reproduced,
stored in a retrieval system, or transmitted in any form or by any
means, electronic, mechanical, photocopying, recording, or otherwise,
without the prior permission of the publisher.

British Library Cataloguing in Publication Information Available

Library of Congress Cataloguing-in-Publication Data

Religion and the new republic : faith in the founding of America /
    edited by James H. Hutson.
        p.   cm.
    Includes bibliographical references and index.
    ISBN 0-8476-9433-X (cloth : alk. paper).—ISBN 0-8476-9434-8
(paper : alk. paper)
    1. United States—Religion—to 1800. 2. Church and State—United
States—History—18th century. 3. United States—Religion—19th
century. 4. Church and state—United States—History—19th century.
    I. Hutson, James H.
    BL2525.R4623 2000
    200'.973'09033—dc21   99-26705
                                                                       CIP

Printed in the United States of America

♾™ The paper used in this publication meets the minimum requirements of
American National Standard for Information Sciences—Permanence of Paper
for Printed Library Materials, ANSI/NISO Z39.48–1992.

Contents

Editor's Preface

The essays presented in this volume are revisions of papers prepared by the authors for delivery at a Library of Congress symposium, "Religion and the Founding of the American Republic," June 18–19, 1998, with one exception: Professor Mark Noll has substituted an entirely new paper for the one he delivered at the symposium.

The papers are all concerned, in varying degrees, with the relation of government to religion in the Founding Period. Three of the papers examine this issue at the state level, by considering the situation in Massachusetts and Virginia, the two most important states in the revolutionary era, which adopted opposite approaches to the problem. The remaining papers consider the issue on the national level or examine special topics (i.e., the status of women evangelists) in the national period.

One of the contributors, Professor Jon Butler, observes that because of current debates about the relation of government to religion in which appeals are frequently made to examples in the Founding Period, "it is no longer possible for historians . . . to pretend that any judgment about this question is merely an exercise of abstract scholarship. The questions of the last three decades have inevitably politicized scholarship in this area."

Since this observation is, regrettably, true, sponsors of scholarly programs about government and religion are obliged to ensure that a variety of views are represented in their presentations and that all participants, however different their convictions may be, adhere to the most rigorous canons of scholarship. The authors of the essays presented here do, in fact, have fundamental disagreements about the role of religion in the American Founding, but they make their cases by scrupulously using evidence and by adhering to all conventions of scholarship. The essays that they have presented will challenge readers to reflect once again about the relevance of the Founding Period to current issues and about the complexity of those issues as they emerged in both the eighteenth and twentieth centuries.

The Library of Congress deeply appreciates grants from Mr. and Mrs. Henry J. (Bud) Smith of Dallas, Texas, the Pew Charitable Trusts of Philadelphia, Pennsylvania, and the Lilly Endowment of Indianapolis, Indiana, for supporting the exhibition, "Religion and the Founding of the American Republic," the symposium of the same name and this publication, which issued from it.

James H. Hutson
Library of Congress

1

"A Most Mild and Equitable Establishment of Religion" John Adams and the Massachusetts Experiment

John Witte, Jr.

I. TWO MODELS OF RELIGIOUS LIBERTY

Thomas Jefferson once described the 1779 Bill for the Establishment of Religious Freedom in Virginia as a "fair" and "novel experiment" in religious liberty for all.[1] This bill, declared Jefferson, defied the millennium-old assumptions of the West—that one form of Christianity must be established in a community, and that the state must protect and support it against all other religions. Virginia would no longer suffer such governmental prescriptions or proscriptions of religion. All forms of Christianity must now stand on their own feet and on an equal footing with the faiths of "the Jew and the Gentile, . . . the Mahometan, the Hindoo, and Infidel of every denomination."[2] Their survival and growth must turn on the cogency of their word, not the coercion of the sword, on the faith of their members, not the force of the law.[3]

Jefferson's lifelong friendly rival, John Adams, wrote with equal enthusiasm about the "completely successful" "political experiment" in religious liberty engineered by the 1780 Massachusetts Constitution. "[I]t can no longer be called in question," he wrote, that "authority in magistrates and obedience of citizens can be grounded on reason, morality, and the Christian religion, without [succumbing to] the monkery of priests or the knavery of politicians"—or other forms of "ecclesiastical or civil tyranny."[4] The Massachusetts Constitution guarantees that "all men of all religions consistent with morals and property . . . enjoy equal liberty [and] security of property . . . and an equal chance for honors and power."[5] Yet, at the same time, the Constitution institutes a "most mild and equitable establishment of religion" featuring special state protections and privileges for preferred forms of Christian piety, morality, and charity.[6]

Here are two models of religious liberty offered by two of the greatest luminaries of the American founding era.[7] Both Jefferson and Adams were self-consciously engaged in a new experiment in religious liberty. Both started with the credo of the American Declaration of Independence, which they drafted—that "all men are created equal" and that they have "certain unalienable rights." Both insisted upon bringing within the mantle of constitutional protection every recognized religion of the day—Christian and Jew, Muslim and Hindu, infidel and pagan alike. Both advocated guarantees of "essential rights and liberties of religion" for all.[8] Both cast their views in enduring legal forms in 1779—Jefferson in his draft bill, which became the law of Virginia seven years later, and Adams in his draft Constitution, which was ratified by the people of Massachusetts in 1780.

Jefferson and Adams, however, cast these common principles into their own models of religious liberty, with their own distinctive legal emphases and applications. Jefferson thought that true religious liberty required both the disestablishment and the free exercise of all religions. The state, he insisted, should give no special aid, support, privilege, or protection to any religion—through special tax subsidies and exemptions or through special criminal protections and special forms of religious incorporation. The state should predicate no laws or policies on explicitly religious grounds or arguments, or draw on the services of religious officials or bodies to discharge its functions. The state should refrain "from intermeddling . . . with religious institutions, their doctrines, discipline, or exercises . . . and from the power of effecting any uniformity of time or manner among them."[9] The state should respect the liberty of conscience and free exercise of all its subjects, which are "the most inalienable and sacred of all human rights."[10] "Almighty God hath created the mind free," Jefferson wrote. "[A]ll attempts to influence it by temporal punishments, or burthens, or by civil incapacitations, tend only to beget habits of hypocrisy and meanness, and are a departure from the plan of the holy author of our religion. . . ." "[N]o man shall be compelled to frequent or support any religious worship, place, or ministry whatsoever, nor shall be enforced, restrained, molested, or burthened in his body or goods, nor shall otherwise suffer, on account of his religious opinions or belief; but that all men shall be free to profess, and by argument to maintain, their opinion in matters of religion, and that the same shall in no wise diminish, enlarge, or affect their civil capacities."[11] Such views, which

Jefferson wrote into his famous 1779 Bill, would have a profound influence on the religious liberty experiment not only of Virginia, but eventually of the entire nation.[12]

Adams thought that true religious liberty required the state to balance the establishment of one "Publick religion"[13] with the freedom of many private religions. On the one hand, he said, every polity must establish by law some form of public religion, some image and ideal of itself, some common values and beliefs to undergird and support the plurality of private religions. The notion that a state and society could remain neutral and purged of any religion was, for Adams, a philosophical fiction. Absent a commonly adopted set of values and beliefs, politicians would invariably hold out their private convictions as public ones. It was thus essential for each community to define the basics of its public religion. In Adams's view, the creed of this public religion was honesty, diligence, devotion, obedience, virtue, and love of God, neighbor, and self.[14] Its icons were the Bible, the bells of liberty, the memorials of patriots, and the Constitution.[15] Its clergy were public-spirited ministers and religiously devout politicians.[16] Its liturgy was the public proclamation of oaths, prayers, songs, and election and Thanksgiving Day sermons.[17] Its policy was state appointment of chaplains for the legislature, military, and prison; state sanctions against blasphemy,[18] sacrilege, and iconoclasm; and state sponsorship of religious societies, schools, and charities.[19]

On the other hand, Adams argued, every civil society must countenance a plurality of forms of religious exercise and association—whose rights could be limited only by the parallel rights of juxtaposed religions, the concerns for public peace and security, and the duties of the established public religion. The notion that a state could coerce all persons into adherence to a common public religion alone was, for Adams, equally a philosophical fiction. Persons would make their own private judgments in matters of faith, for the rights of conscience are "indisputable, unalienable, indefeasible, [and] divine."[20]

Moreover, the maintenance of religious pluralism was essential for the protection of religious and other forms of liberty. As Adams put it in a letter to Jefferson: "Roman Catholics, English Episcopalians, Scotch and American Presbyterians, Methodists, Moravians, Anbabtists [sic], German Lutherans, German Calvinists, Universalitists, Arians, Priestlyians, Socinians, Independents, Congregationalists, Horse Protestants and House Protestants, Deists and Atheists and Protestants qui ne croyent rien [who believe nothing] are . . . [n]ever the less all Educated in the general Principles of Christianity: and the general Principles of English and American liberty."[21] "Checks and balances, Jefferson"—in the political as well as the religious sphere—Adams went on in another letter, "are our only Security, for the progress of Mind, as well as the Security of Body. Every Species of these Christians would persecute Deists, as [much] as either Sect would persecute another, if it had unchecked and unballanced Power. Nay, the Deists would persecute Christians, and Atheists would persecute Deists, with as unrelenting Cruelty, as any Christians would persecute them or one another. Know thyself, Human nature!"[22]

The 1780 Massachusetts Constitution, which John Adams in large measure drafted, struck this balance between the establishment of one public religion and the freedom of all private religions. The Constitution's most controversial provisions on religious test oaths and tithes were outlawed by amendments of 1821 and 1833. The harder edges of religious establishment were further blunted by judicial interpretation and legislative innovation.[23] But the basic model of religious liberty, constructed by John Adams and his colleagues, has remained unchanged in fundamentals until today. Over the past two centuries, this Massachusetts model has gathered its own substantial following, not only among other New England states but also among various courts interpreting the First Amendment to the United States Constitution.[24] Indeed, while Jefferson's model lies at the heart of modern theories of separationism and religious individualism, Adams's model lies at the heart of modern theories of accommodationism and religious communitarianism.

In this chapter, I explore Adams's model of religious liberty, as it was adopted and adapted in Massachusetts. Section II summarizes the events and texts leading to the formation of the Massachusetts Constitution. Section III explores the juxtaposed provisions on the establishment of a public religion and the freedom of private religions, and the considerable controversy surrounding the definition and defense of the same. The Conclusion harvests some of the lessons from the Massachusetts experience for the ongoing experiment in religious liberty in America.

II. THE FORMATION OF THE MASSACHUSETTS CONSTITUTION

The Massachusetts Constitution of 1780 is "the oldest written organic law still in operation anywhere in the world."[25] The original document, running thirty-three 6" x 9" printed pages, has a preamble and two main parts. Part One is a Declaration of Rights of the Inhabitants of the Commonwealth in thirty articles. Part Two is a Frame of Government in six chapters. The Constitution has been amended 117 times since its ratification. But the original terms and terminology remain mostly in place.

The Failed 1778 Constitution

The 1780 Constitution replaced the 1691 Provincial Charter, issued by the British Crown as the organic law of the colony of Massachusetts-Bay. The charter had ruled continuously until June 17, 1774, when the last General

Court called by the royal governor adjourned. During the first rumblings of the American Revolution in 1774 and 1775, the colonists formed three successive Provincial Congresses. In July 1775, they elected their own representative General Court—for the first time without royal permission and without compliance with the procedures of the Provincial Charter. The General Court, in turn, elected a Council and vested it with legislative and executive powers, and appellate jurisdiction over the lower courts. The Council was transformed into a constitutional convention in June 1777. John Adams, who was serving at the time in the Continental Congress and in Europe, did not participate in these convention or ratification debates.

On February 28, 1778, the Council submitted a draft constitution for popular ratification. The draft was largely a bare-bones blueprint of government. It seemed calculated more to respond to immediate concerns of representation of the townships than to the enduring needs of the commonwealth. Most of its thirty-six articles concerned the rights and restrictions of popular suffrage and regional representation, and the powers and procedures of the executive, legislative, and judicial offices of the commonwealth. Article XXXII simply confirmed as presumptively constitutional all colonial laws, including the laws on religion—"such parts only excepted as are repugnant to the rights and privileges contained in this Constitution." Few such "rights and privileges" were set forth. Article XXXII guaranteed for all "the inestimable right of trial by jury." Two other articles confirmed the traditional privileges and protections of Protestants: Article XXIX stated: "No person unless of the Protestant religion shall be Governor, Lieutenant Governor, a member of the Senate or of the House of Representatives, or hold any judiciary employment within this State." Article XXXIV provided: "The free exercise and enjoyment of religious profession and worship shall forever be allowed to every denomination of Protestants within this State."[26] For the rest, the document was silent on religious and civil rights.

The 1778 draft constitution was roundly rejected by the people of Massachusetts. A leading opponent of ratification was Theophilus Parsons, a young lawyer from Newburyport, who would later figure prominently in the formation and enforcement of the religion clauses of the 1780 Massachusetts Constitution. In his *Essex Result,* a pamphlet that both galvanized and systematized popular objections to the draft constitution, Parsons singled out for special criticism the absence of a declaration of civil rights and the deliberate abridgment of religious rights. "[T]he rights of conscience are not therein clearly defined and ascertained," he wrote. "We have duties, for the discharge of which we are accountable to our Creator and benefactor, which no human power can cancel. What those duties are, is determinable by right reason, which may be, and is called, a well-informed conscience. What this dictates as our duty, is so; and that power which assumes a controul over it, is an usurper; for no consent can be pleaded to justify the controul, as any consent in this case is void." Moreover, "the free exercise and enjoyment of religious worship is there said to be allowed to all protestants of the State, when in fact, that free exercise and enjoyment is the natural and uncontrollable right of every member of the State."[27]

"A Company of Earthly Hosts" on Religious Liberty

On February 20, 1779, the House of Representatives called for a new constitutional convention, and "lawfully warned" the "Selectmen of the several Towns" to deliberate their concerns and to instruct their delegates.[28] The constitutional protection of religious liberty figured prominently in these deliberations and instructions, with the townships revealing wide-ranging concerns. The township of Stoughton, for example, instructed its delegate:

> You are directed to use and employ your assiduous Endeavours as Soon as the Convention meets that a Bill of Rights be in the first place compiled, wherein the inherent and unalienable Rights of Conscience and all those alienable rights are not necessary to be given up in the hands of government . . . shall be clearly, fully and unequivocally defined and explained.[29]

The delegate of Pittsfield came armed with a recommended provision:

> every man has an unalienable right to enjoy his own opinion in matters of religion, and to worship God in that manner that is agreeable to his own sentiments without any control whatsoever, and that no particular mode or sect of religion ought to be established but that every one be protected in the peaceable enjoyment of his religious persuasion and way of worship.[30]

The township of Sandisfield instructed its delegate to seek protection of both local control over the establishment of Protestantism and guarantees of toleration for other faiths:

> [Y]ou will Endeavour in the forming of the Constitution that the Free Exercise of religious principles or Profession, worship and Liberty of Conscience shall be for ever Secured to all Denominations of Protestants—and Protestant Disenters of all Denominations within the State, without any Compulsion whatever. Always allowing the Legislative Body of this State the Power of Toleration to other Denominations of Christians from time to time as they Shall see Cause, at the same time, Reserving to our Selves, the Right of Instructions to our Representatives Respecting Said Toleration as well as in other Cases.[31]

Delegates who were not furnished with explicit directives from the townships could draw inspiration and instruction from the scores of sermons and pamphlets on the constitutional protection of religious liberty that circulated in Massachusetts in the later 1770s.[32] The intense volume and volatility of these writings led Adams later to quip: "A whole company of earthly hosts hath debated these heavenly things with an hellish intensity."[33]

The oft-printed pamphlet, *Worcestriensis Number IV* of 1776, offered a typical moderate position, defending both the generous toleration of all religions and the gentle establishment of the Protestant religion. The pamphlet began with a defense of liberty of conscience and religious pluralism.

> In a well regulated state, it will be the business of the Legislature to prevent sectaries of different denominations from molesting and disturbing each other, to ordain that no part of the community shall be permitted to perplex and harass the other for any supposed heresy, but that each individual shall be allowed to have and enjoy, profess and maintain his own system of religion, provided it does not issue in overt acts of treason undermining the peace and good order of society. To allow one part of a society to lord it over the faith and consciences of the other, in religious matters, is the ready way to set the whole community together by the cars.[34]

State officials thus had an important role to keep the common peace among the plural faiths of the community. State officials were also empowered, however, "to give preference to that profession of religion which they take to be true," the author of *Worcestriensis* insisted. State officials could not command citizens to conform to this preferred religion, nor could they subject nonconformists "to pains, penalties, and disabilities."

> The establishment contended for in this disquisition, is of a different kind, and must result from a different legal Procedure. It must proceed only from the benign principles of the legislature from an encouragement of the General Principles of religion and morality, recommending free inquiry and examination of the doctrine said to be divine; using all possible and lawful means to enable its citizens to discover the truth, and to entertain good and rational sentiments, and taking mild and parental measures to bring about the design; these are the most probable means of bringing about the establishment of religion.[35]

State officials could thus "exert themselves in favor of one religion over the other." They could extract religious oaths from their officials, "for there is no stronger cement of society." They could punish profanity, blasphemy, and debauchery, all of which "strike a fatal blow at the root of good regulation, and well-being of the state." They could provide "able and learned teachers [that is, ministers] to instruct the people in the knowledge of what they deem the truth, maintaining them by the public money, though at the same time they have no right in the least degree to endeavor the depression of professions of religious denomination."[36]

Phillips Payson, an influential congregationalist minister, laid greater stress on the need for a public religious establishment, warning against "dangerous innovations" in the inherited colonial patterns. To be sure, Payson wrote, "religious or spiritual liberty must be accounted the greatest happiness of man, considered in a private capacity."[37] But, he insisted:

> [R]eligion, both in rulers and people [is] . . . of the highest importance to . . . civil society and government, . . . as it keeps alive the best sense of moral obligation, a matter of such extensive utility, especially in respect to an oath [of office], which is one of the principal instruments of government. The fear and reverence of God, and the terrors of eternity, are the most powerful restraints upon the minds of mind; and hence it is of special importance in a free government, the spirit of which being always friendly to the sacred rights of conscience, it will hold up the Gospel as the great rule of faith and practice. Established modes and usages in religion, more especially the public worship of God, so generally form the principles and manners of a people that changes or alterations in these, especially when nearly conformed to spirit and simplicity of the Gospel, may well be deemed very dangerous experiments in government. For this, and other reasons, the thoughtful and wise among us trust that our civil fathers, from a regard to gospel worship and the constitution of these churches, will carefully preserve them, and at all times guard against every innovation that might tend to overset the public worship of God. . . . Let the restraints of religion once broken down, as they infallibly would be, by leaving the subject of public worship to the humours of the multitude, and we might well defy all human wisdom and power, to support and preserve order and government in the State.[38]

Isaac Backus, the most learned and articulate Baptist voice of the day, laid greater stress on the protection of private religious liberty, warning against the "hypocrisy" and "futility" of public religious establishments. In a series of pamphlets in the 1770s, he charged that the Massachusetts authorities were "assuming a power to govern religion, rather than being governed by it."[39] "I am as sensible of the importance of religion and of the utility of it to human society, as Mr. Payson is," Backus wrote. "And I concur with him that the fear and reverence of God and the terrors of eternity are the most powerful restraints upon the minds of men. But I am so far from thinking with him that these restraints would be broken down if equal religious liberty was established. . . . "[40] Look at the long history of Christian establishment, Backus wrote. It has led not to pure religion; instead "tyranny, simony, and robbery came to be introduced and to be practiced under the Christian name."[41] Look at the city of Boston, which has had no religious establishment of late; there religion, state, and society all flourish without fail.[42] Look at the principles of the American Revolution; "all America is up in arms against taxation without representation." But just as certainly as we Americans were not represented in the British Parliament, so we religious dissenters are not represented among the established civil authorities. Yet we are still subject to their religious taxes and regulations.[43] Look at the principles of the Bible:

God has expressly armed the magistrate with the sword to punish such as work ill to their neighbors, and his faithfulness in that work and our obedience to such authority, is enforced [by the Bible]. But it is evident that the sword is excluded from the kingdom of the Redeemer. . . . [I]t is impossible to blend church and state without violating our Lord's commands to both. His command to the church is, Put away from among yourselves that wicked person. His command to the state is, Let both grow together until the harvest. But it has appeared for these thousand years that pure Gospel discipline in the church is very little if at all known in state establishments of religion and that instead of letting conformists thereto, and dissenters therefrom, grow together to enjoy equal worldly privileges, the sword has been employed to root up, and to prepare war against all such as put not into the mouths of the established teachers who are the means of upholding such rulers pervert all equity.[44]

Religion and the Formation of the 1780 Constitution

Such were some of the discordant sentiments on religious liberty on the eve of the second constitutional convention in Massachusetts. It was clear that the congregationalists would insist on some form of establishment. As John Adams put it: "We might as soon expect a change in the solar system as to expect they would give up their establishment."[45] It was equally clear that religious dissenters, and more liberal congregationalists, would insist on the disestablishment and free exercise of religion—particularly since several other states had already granted such liberties.[46] Some via media between these competing perspectives would have to be found.

On September 1, 1779, 293 delegates gathered in Boston to draft a new constitution.[47] Included in the convention were most of the leading lights of Massachusetts—39 merchants, 31 lawyers, 22 farmers, 21 clergy, 18 physicians, and 18 magistrates.[48] Most delegates were Puritan Congregationalists. Five delegates were Baptists. A few others were suspected to be quiet Quakers, Anglicans, or Catholics.[49]

On September 4, 1779, the constitutional convention elected a committee of 27 members—later augmented by four others—to prepare a draft declaration of rights and a frame of government. This committee, in turn, delegated the drafting to a three-member subcommittee of James Bowdoin, Samuel Adams, and John Adams. John Adams, widely respected for his legal and political acumen, was selected to push the pen for the subcommittee. He completed his work in mid-October. First the three-member subcommittee, then the full drafting committee made some modest alterations to Adams's draft.[50] The committee's draft was submitted to the full convention for debate on October 28, 1779.[51] The convention debated the draft constitution until November 12; Adams participated in this session of the debate, but set sail immediately thereafter for France. The convention completed its deliberations from January 27 to March 1, 1780, now without Adams.

The convention chose to vote separately on each article of the Declaration of Rights and each chapter of the Frame of Government in Adams's draft constitution. Ten provisions of the draft dealt with matters of religion and religious liberty—the preamble, Articles I, II, III, VII, and XVIII of the Declaration of Rights, and Chapters I, II, V, and VI of the Frame of Government. Five of these ten provisions were approved without comment, controversy, or change.

Four of the remaining provisions on religion in Adams's draft garnered modest discussion and revision in the constitutional convention. In Article II, Adams had written: "It is the Duty of all men in society, publickly, and at stated seasons to worship the SUPREME BEING, the great Creator and preserver of the Universe." After brief discussion, the convention amended this to say: "It is the right as well as the duty of all men" so to worship.[52] In Chapter I of the Frame of Government, Adams had stipulated that no person was eligible to serve in the House of Representatives, "unless he be of the Christian religion." The convention struck this provision—though it left untouched the next Chapter, where Adams imposed the same religious conditions upon the offices of governor and lieutenant governor.[53] In the same spirit, Adams had proposed in Chapter VI that all state officials and appointees swear the same religious test oath: "that I believe and profess the Christian religion and have a firm persuasion of its truth." The convention insisted on a slightly reworded such oath only for elected executive and legislative officers, requiring all others simply to declare their "true faith and allegiance to this Commonwealth." After several delegates argued for a more specifically Protestant test oath, the convention added to both oaths a transparently anti-Catholic provision, which Adams and others protested without success: "I do renounce and abjure all allegiance, subjection and obedience to . . . every . . . foreign Power whatsoever: And that no foreign . . . Prelate . . . hath, or ought to have, any jurisdiction, superiority, pre-eminence, authority, dispensing, or other power, in any matter, civil, ecclesiastical or spiritual within this Commonwealth. . . . "[54] Adams's draft oath had concluded: "So help me God," but had then made specific provision "that any person who has conscientious scruples relative to taking oaths, may be admitted to make solemn affirmation" by other means. After some delegates protested that so generic an exemption might be subject to abuse, the convention restricted the exemption to Quakers only.[55] An 1821 amendment to the Constitution expunged the religious test oath for political office altogether.[56]

Article III, stipulating the payment of religious taxes in support of congregational ministers, was by far "the most controversial one in the whole draft constitution," occupying more than a third of the convention debate.[57] Given the heat of the religious liberty debate on the eve of the convention, the controversy was not unexpected. Adams chose not to draft Article III himself. "I could not satisfy my own Judgment with any Article that I thought would be accepted," he later wrote. "Some of the Clergy, or older and graver Persons than myself would be more likely to hit the Taste of the Public."[58] Adams did, however, approve without recorded reservation a draft that came out of the full drafting committee and, as we shall see in a moment, incorporated establishment provisions elsewhere in the constitution.

The first draft of Article III, submitted to the convention on October 28, 1779, read thus:

> Good morals, being necessary for the preservation of civil society; and the knowledge and belief of the being of GOD, His providential government of the world, and of a future state of rewards and punishment, being the only true foundation of morality, the legislature hath, therefore, a right, and ought to provide, at the expense of the subject, if necessary, a suitable support for the public worship of GOD, and of the teachers of religion and morals; and to enjoin upon all the subjects an attendance upon these instructions, at stated times and seasons; provided there be any such teacher, on whose ministry they can conscientiously attend.
>
> All monies, paid by the subject of the public worship, and of the instructors in religion and morals, shall, if he requires it, be uniformly applied to the support of the teacher or teachers of his own religious denomination, provided there be any on whose instructions he attends; otherwise it may be paid towards the support of the teacher or teachers of the parish or precinct in which the said moneys are raised.[59]

The first paragraph of this draft Article III, stipulating the necessity and utility of public worship and religious instruction, was a common sentiment and not particularly controversial. The second paragraph, however, mandating the collection of religious tithes to support the same, was a matter of great controversy.

It takes a bit of historical imagination and explication to appreciate the controversy over state collection of church tithes. Article III was designed to raise to constitutional status a colonial pattern of church–state relations, introduced by a law of 1692, and amended several times thereafter.[60] This law blended church and state for purposes of taxation. It designated one territory as both a "parish" and a "township" under the authority of one city council. (In large townships that had more than one church, the multiple "parishes" were called "precincts," and each of these likewise was subject to the same council's authority.) To be a member of the township was automatically to be a member of a parish (or precinct). Each of the c. 290 parish-townships in Massachusetts was required to have at least one congregationalist "teacher of religion and morality" (that is, a minister). This minister would lead the local community not only in public worship but often in education and charity as well. The community was required to provide him with a salary, sanctuary, and parsonage. Funds for this came from special religious taxes (usu-

ally called tithes, sometimes called church, parish, or religious rates). These
were collected from all subjects in the township, who were by statutory definition also members of the parish.[61]

This tithing system worked rather well when all subjects within the same
township were also active members of the same church. It did not work so
well for persons who were religiously inactive or were members of a non-
congregationalist church, whether Baptist, Quaker, Anglican, or Catholic. As
the number of such dissenting churches grew within the townships of Massachusetts, so did the protests to paying these mandatory taxes in support of
the congregationalist ministers and churches. During the eighteenth century,
colonial Councils and courts eventually carved out exceptions for some religious dissenters, allowing them to pay their tithes to support their own dissenting ministers and churches. Such dissenters, however, were required to
register each church as a separate religious society and to demonstrate their
own faithful attendance at the same. Not all dissenting churches were able
or willing to meet the registration requirements, and not all townships co-
operated in granting the registrations or tithe exemptions.[62] If the dissenting
church was too small to have its own full-time minister, registration was routinely denied or rescinded. If the dissenting church was conscientiously opposed to legal incorporation and registration, as were the Baptists after 1773,
their members could not be exempt from taxation. If a member of a registered dissenting church was too lax in his attendance of public worship, he
could still be denied exemption from the congregationalist tithe. And if a
town treasurer was too pressed for revenue, or too prejudiced against a certain group, he could refuse to give dissenting ministers their share of the
tithes. In many of these cases, the Massachusetts courts proved notably
churlish in granting standing, let alone relief, to groups or individuals who
protested such inequities.[63]

It was this century-long system of religious taxes that the cryptic provisions
of Article III were designed to perpetuate. And it was this feature of the inherited tradition of religious establishment that caused such controversy at the
convention. The initial reaction to the draft of Article III was so heated that
convention members voted to put off debate until November 1. They also
voted to suspend the rule that no member could speak twice to the same issue,
without requesting special privilege from the chair. Rancorous debate over the
article broke out immediately on November 1—some condemning the provision as "too pale an approximation of a proper establishment," others calling
for abolition of the article altogether, still others decrying the insufficient recognition of the concessions that dissenters had arduously won over the years.
When matters deadlocked on November 3, the delegates appointed a seven-
member ad hoc committee of distinguished delegates, chaired by the Baptist
delegate Rev. Noah Alden of Bellingham, to redraft the controversial Article
III.[64] On November 6, this ad hoc committee put a new draft Article III before

the convention, which spelled out the prevailing religious tax system in more detail. This new draft was debated intermittently for the next four days, and modest word changes were approved.[65] On November 10, a motion to abolish the article altogether was defeated. A slightly amended draft of the article was passed the following day. The final text of Article III reads thus:

> As the happiness of a people, and good order and preservation of civil government, essentially depend upon piety, religion, and morality; and as these cannot be generally diffused through a Community, but by the institution of publick Worship of God, and of public instructions in piety, religion, and morality: Therefore, to promote the happiness and to secure the good order and preservation of their government, the people of this Commonwealth have a right to invest their legislature with power to authorize and require . . . the several Towns, Parishes, precincts and other bodies politic, or religious societies, to make suitable provision, at their own Expence, for the institution of the Public worship of GOD, and for the support and maintenance of public protestant teachers of piety, religion and morality, in all causes which provision shall not be made Voluntarily.—And the people of this Commonwealth have also a right to, and do, invest their legislature with authority to enjoin upon all the Subjects an attendance upon the instructions of the public teachers aforesaid, at stated times and seasons, if there be any on whose instructions they can Conscientiously and conveniently attend—PROVIDED, notwithstanding, that the several towns, parishes, precincts, and other bodies politic, or religious societies, shall, at times, have the exclusive right of electing their public Teachers, and of contracting with them for their support and maintenance.—And all monies, paid by the Subject of the support of the public teacher or teachers of his own religious sect or denomination, provided there be any on whose institution he attends; otherwise it may be paid towards the support of the teacher or teachers of the parish or precinct in which the said monies are raised—And every denomina[t]ion of christians, demeaning themselves peaceably, and as good Subjects of the Commonwealth, shall be equally under the protection of the Law: And no subordination of any one sect or denomination to another shall ever be established by law.[66]

This final text routinized, and raised to constitutional status, the traditional tithing system, and outlawed some of the hard-fought concessions that Baptists, Anglicans, and other dissenters had secured through litigation in the prior decades. As Samuel Eliot Morison writes in his definitive early study: "Article III was even less liberal than [the colonial] system, for instead of exempting members of dissenting sects from religious taxation, it merely gave them the privilege of paying their taxes to their own pastors. Unbelievers, non-church-goers, and dissenting minorities too small to maintain a minister had to contribute to Congregational worship. The whole Article was so loosely worded as to defeat the purpose of the fifth paragraph [guaranteeing the equality of all sects and denominations]. Every new denomination that entered the Commonwealth after 1780, notably the Universalists and Methodists, had to wage a long and expensive lawsuit to obtain recognition as a religious sect. . . . [A] subordination of sects existed in fact."[67]

Article III was not without its own concessions, however. The tithe collection system was now to be local and "voluntary" rather than statewide—allowing Boston and, later, other townships to forgo mandatory tithing and have churches muster their own support through tithes, tuition, or pew rents. Religious societies could now contract individually with their own ministers—presumably allowing them to pay their tithes directly to their chosen ministers rather than to a potentially capricious town treasurer. Local townships and religious societies could now participate in the choice of their community minister, rather than be automatically saddled with a congregationalist minister. This provision "had some unexpected results. Several of the towns and parishes, which thereby were given the exclusive right to elect their ministers . . . were converted to Unitarianism and settled Unitarian pastors over old Calvinist churches."[68] And the provision that no religious sect or denomination was to be subordinated to another was the first formal statement in Massachusetts history of religious equality before the law not only for individuals but also for groups.

On March 2, 1780, the convention put the final draft of the constitution before the people for ratification. Eighteen hundred copies of the constitution were printed and sent out—and were read from pulpits and lecterns, and posted in town halls throughout the state. Surprisingly, no newspaper of the day ran copies of the draft constitution, a familiar technique used by other states to ensure wide dissemination. The convention also sent out a committee report that explained the rationale of the constitution and encouraged the people's ratification of the same. The committee report dealt directly with Article III, saying:

> [W]e have, with as much Precision as we were capable of, provided for the free exercise of the Rights of Conscience: We are very sensible that our Constituents hold those Rights infinitely more valuable than all others; and we flatter ourselves, that while we have considered Morality and Public Worship of GOD, as important to the happiness of Society, we have sufficiently guarded the rights of Conscience from every possible infringement. This Article underwent long debates, and took Time in proportion to its importance; and we feel ourselves peculiarly happy in being able to inform you, that the debates were managed by persons of various denominations, it was finally agreed upon with much more unanimity than usually takes place in disquisitions of this Nature. We wish you to consider the Subject with Candor, and Attention. Surely it would be an affront to the People of Massachusetts-Bay to labour to convince them, that the Honor and Happiness of a People depend upon Morality; and that the Public Worship of GOD has a tendency to inculcate the Principles thereof, as well as to preserve a people from forsaking Civilization, and falling into a state of Savage barbarity.[69]

The people of Massachusetts did give the draft their full "Candor and Attention." Those who voted for ratification—constituting less than 5 percent of the population[70]—rejected the controversial Article III on religious taxes, and perhaps Chapters II and VI on religious test oaths as well, while approving the rest of the constitution. Of the 290 eligible townships, 188 sent in their returns.[71] The clerks kept close tallies on the votes for Article III. Article III "fell some 600 votes short of the necessary two-thirds majority for ratification"—with the popular vote in favor standing at 8,865-6,225.[72] Though the individual township tallies were less closely kept for other provisions, it appears that the provisions of Chapters II and VI, requiring the governor to be a Christian and to profess his adherence to the same in a solemn oath, also did not garner sufficient two-thirds support.[73] Nevertheless, members of the convention—out of ignorance of the exact numbers of votes, or out of manipulation of the same—treated the constitution as fully ratified.

On June 16, 1780, James Bowdoin, the president of the Convention, announced, without caveat, that the entire Constitution had garnered the requisite two-thirds vote. On October 25, 1780, the Constitution went into effect, with the first day of General Court after ratification. Among the first acts of the General Court was to pledge its support for religious liberty: "Deeply impressed with a sense of the importance of religion to the happiness of men in civil society to maintain its purity and promote this efficacy, we shall protect professors of all denominations, demeaning themselves peaceably and as good subjects of the Commonwealth, in the free exercise of the rights of conscience."[74]

III. JOHN ADAMS AND THE MASSACHUSETTS MODEL OF RELIGIOUS LIBERTY

John Adams was both eclectic and pragmatic in crafting the religion clauses of the Massachusetts Constitution. This was part of the reason for his success. Though a devout Christian of Puritan extraction, Adams eschewed rigorous denominational affiliation or rigid doctrinal formulation.[75] While in Philadelphia for the sessions of Congress, for example, Adams attended services in Presbyterian, Anglican, Catholic, Quaker, Baptist, and Methodist churches alike.[76] When Benjamin Rush later pressed him about his religious affiliation, Adams wrote: "Ask me not . . . whether I am a Catholic or Protestant, Calvinist or Arminian. As far as they are Christians, I wish to be a fellow-disciple with them all."[77] Though a fierce American patriot, Adams knew the value of history and comparative politics. Much of his three-volume *Defense of the Constitutions of Government in the United States of America* (1788), among other political writings, was devoted to sifting ancient, medieval, and early modern Western polities for useful lessons on the best construction of authority and the best protection of liberty. Many of his letters and other informal writings are chock full of favorable references to Greek, Roman, Catholic, Protestant, and Enlightenment writers alike. Though a vigorous moralist, Adams offered his constitutional formulations without "a pretence of miracle or mystery." Any persons "employed in the service of forming a constitution," he wrote, cannot pretend that they "had interviews with the gods, or were in any degree under the inspiration of Heaven." "[G]overnments [are] contrived merely by the use of reason and the senses." Constitutions "are merely experiments made on human life and manners, society and government."[78] There will always be "a glorious uncertainty in the law."[79]

In his constitutional experiment, Adams chose to balance the establishment of a public religion with the freedom of many private religions. This was, in part, a pragmatic choice. Adams knew that the congregationalists would insist on their establishment, and that the dissenters would insist on their freedom. He sought to respect and protect both interests by combining what he called a "tempered" religious freedom with a "slender" religious establishment.[80] But this was also, in part, a principled choice. Adams was convinced that the establishment of one common public religion among a plurality of freely competing private religions was essential to the survival of society and the state. We must certainly begin "by setting the conscience free," Adams wrote. For "when all men of all religions consistent with morals and property, shall enjoy equal liberty, . . . and security of property, and an equal chance for honors and power . . . we may expect that improvements will be made in the human character, and the state of society."[81] But we must just as certainly begin by "setting religion at the fore and floor of society and government," Adams wrote. "Statesmen may plan and speculate for liberty, but it is religion and morality alone which can establish the principles upon which freedom can securely stand."[82] A common "religion and virtue are the only foundation, not only of republicanism and of all free government, but of social felicity under all governments and in all the combinations of human society."[83] "Without religion, this world would be something not fit to be mentioned in polite company—I mean hell."[84]

The Liberty of Private Religions

In the 1780 Massachusetts Constitution, Adams dealt rather briefly with the guarantees of liberty of conscience and the free exercise of religion. He had already stated several times his devotion to the protection of such private religious rights, calling them "indisputable, unalienable, indefeasible, [and] divine."[85] He had praised the sagacity and sacrifice of his Protestant forebearers in securing such rights for themselves and their posterity.[86] And he saw both the necessity and utility of the continued protection of these rights for all religious groups. As he wrote in the spring of 1780, "our honest and pious Attention to the unalienable Rights of Conscience is our best and most refined Policy, tending to conciliate the Good Will, of all the World, preparing an Asylum, which will be a sure Remedy against persecution in Europe, and drawing over to our Country Numbers of excellent Citizens."[87]

In the preamble to the 1780 Massachusetts Constitution, Adams spoke of "the power of the people of enjoying in safety and tranquility their natural rights, and the blessings of life," and "the right of the people to take measures necessary for their safety, prosperity and happiness." These words were largely repeated in Article I of the Declaration of Rights: "All men are born free and equal, and have certain natural, essential, and unalienable rights; among which may be reckoned the right of enjoying and defending their Lives and Liberties; that of acquiring, possessing and protecting property; in fine, that of seeking and obtaining their safety and happiness."[88]

In Article II, Adams tendered more specific protections of religious liberty. "It is the [right as well as the] duty of all men in society, publickly, and at stated seasons to worship the SUPREME BEING, the great Creator and preserver of the Universe. No subject shall be hurt, molested, or restrained, in his person, Liberty, or Estate, for worshipping GOD in the manner and season most agreeable to the Dictates of his own conscience, or for his religious profession or sentiments; provided he doth not Disturb the public peace, or obstruct others in their religious Worship." Article III, at least tacitly, recognized the right to form religious associations, to select one's own minister, and to pay tithes directly to him. Chapter VI included within the ambit of religious freedom the right of Quakers to claim an exemption from the swearing of oaths to which they were "conscientiously opposed."

The freedom of religion, as Adams defined it, was thus rather closely circumscribed. It was, in effect, the right of each individual to discharge divine duties—which duties the Constitution helped to define. "It is the right as well as the duty" of each person to worship, Article II states. While a person could worship in "the manner and season most agreeable to the Dictates of his own conscience," such worship, per Article II, had to be directed to God, defined as "the SUPREME BEING, the great Creator and preserver of the Universe." Moreover, such worship, per Article III, had to include "conscientious and convenient" "attendance upon the instructions of ministers" "at stated times and seasons." If a person's conscience dictated another object, order, or organization of worship, it was by definition neither religious nor protected as a constitutional right.

This right to religion was further limited by social demands. Neither the Preamble nor Article I lists religion among the "natural rights," those rights held prior to society in the state of nature. Instead, Article II emphasized the social character of religious rights—they are held by "all men in society" and involve "public worship." Each individual's religious rights are limited by the needs of society—by the need for public peace and for protection of the worship of others, as Article II puts it. And each individual's religious rights are subject to the "rights" and "powers" of society—to mandate church attendance, tithe payments, Christian affiliation, and oath swearing, as Article III and Chapters II and VI put it.[89]

By comparison with other state constitutions of the day, the Massachusetts Constitution was rather restrained in its protection of religious freedom. Other states defined liberty of conscience expansively to include the right to choose and change religion, to be free from all discrimination on the basis of religion, to be exempt from a number of general laws that prohibited or mandated conduct to which a religious party or group had scruples of conscience. Many states also defined free exercise rights expansively to include freedom to engage in religious assembly, worship, speech, publication, press, education, travel, parentage, and the like, without political or ecclesiastical conditions or controls.[90] Few such protections appear in the 1780 Massachusetts Constitution.

Adams was convinced that such a "tempered" form of religious freedom would bring the best "improvements to the character of each citizen."[91] On the one hand, he believed, following conservative conventions of the day, that to grant too much freedom of religion would only encourage depravity in citizens.[92] "Man is not to be trusted with his unbounded love of liberty," one preacher put it, "unless it is under some other restraint which arises from his own reason or the law of God—these in many instances would make a feeble resistance to his lust or avarice; and he would pursue his liberty to the destruction of his fellow-creature, if he was not restrained by human laws and punishment."[93] The state was thus required to "take mild and parental measures" to educate, encourage, and emulate a right belief and conduct.[94] On the other hand, Adams believed, following more liberal conventions of the day, that "[c]ompulsion, instead of making men religious, generally has a contrary tendency, it works not conviction, but most naturally leads them into hypocrisy. If they are honest enquirers after truth; if their articles of belief differ from the creed of their civil superiors, compulsion will bring them into a sad dilemma" of choosing between a feigned and firm faith.[95] The state was thus required to refrain from dictating the exact doctrines, liturgies, and texts of a right religion. This was the balance of religious freedom that Adams struck in crafting the Constitution.

The Establishment of Public Religion

Adams further balanced this "tempered" liberty of private religion with a "slender" establishment of public religion. Adams had nothing but contempt for the harsh establishments of earlier centuries—those featuring state prescriptions of religious doctrines, liturgies, and sacred texts; state controls of religious properties, polities, and personnel; state persecution of religious heresy, blasphemy, and nonconformity. His 1774 *Dissertation on the Canon and Feudal Law* was a bitter invective against the "civil and ecclesiastical tyranny" of earlier Catholic and Protestant establishments. His 1788 *Defense of the American Constitutions* devoted several long chapters to digesting critically the horrors of religious wars, crusades, inquisitions, and pogroms, and the sorry plight of some of his Protestant forebearers.

The established public religion that Adams had in mind was much more "slender," "moderate and equitable" in form—tempered by its own provisions, and by the juxtaposed guarantees of religious freedom for all. As Adams set out his views in the Constitution, the public religion was to be established (1) ceremonially; (2) morally; and (3) institutionally. It was only the third dimension of the public religious establishment, its institutionalization, that drew controversy.

Ceremonial Establishment

The establishment of public religious ceremonies is reflected especially in the Preamble. The Preamble refers to the constitution as "a covenant" or "compact" between the people and God: "[T]he whole people covenants with each Citizen, and each Citizen with the whole people, that all shall be governed by certain Laws for the Common good." And again, "the people of Massachusetts, acknowledging, with grateful hearts, the goodness of the Great Legislator of the Universe, in affording us, in the course of his Providence, an opportunity, deliberately and peaceably, without fraud, violence, or surprize, o[f] entering into an Original, explicit, and Solemn Compact with each other; and of forming a New Constitution of Civil Government for ourselves and Posterity; and devoutly imploring His direction in so interesting a Design, DO agree upon, ordain and establish the following Declaration of Rights and Frame of Government. . . . "

This is a covenant ceremonial liturgy, rooted in the Hebrew Bible and in a New England tradition going back to the Mayflower Compact of 1620.[96] The nature of the constitution is made clear: it is a "solemn" covenant, with God invoked as witness, judge, and participant. The purpose of the covenant is set forth—to create and confirm the identity of the people (the "peoples" and "citizens of Massachusetts"), their common morals and mores (a devotion to the "common good"), and their cardinal institutions (their rights and frame of government). The ethic of the covenant is defined—featuring "gratitude," "peacefulness," integrity ("without fraud, violence, or surprize"), and prayerful devotion ("devoutly imploring His direction in so interesting a Design").

A variant of this covenant ceremony was the oath-swearing ritual of state officials. Adams wrote into Chapter VI of the Frame of Government the requirement that all state officials must swear a full oath to the constitution and the commonwealth—not just privately, but before the people and their representatives in full assembly. "I, A.B., do declare, that I believe the christian religion, and have a firm persuasion of its truth . . . ; and I do swear, that I will bear true faith and allegiance to the said Commonwealth . . . so help me God." Adams's insistence on such oaths reflected the conventional view that the oath was "a cement of society" and "one of the principal instruments of government," for it invoked and induced "the fear and reverence of God, and the terrors of eternity."[97] This provision also reflected Adams's view that the oath of office was a public confirmation of the covenant among God, the people, and their rulers.

These preambulary and oath swearing provisions were not merely a bit of hortatory throat-clearing that preceded the real business of constitutional government. They established favorite ceremonies of the traditional public religion of Massachusetts. In the minds of more conservative Puritan sermonizers and subjects of the day, they raised the image of Massachusetts being "under a solemn divine Probation,"[98] and the image of the magistrate as God's vice-regent, called to exemplify and enforce a godly life. Traditionally, the New England Puritans stressed ambition, austerity, frugality and other virtues because the covenant rendered them agents of God, instruments of God's providential plan. For them to be lax in zeal, loose in discipline, or sumptuous in living would be a disservice to God, a breach of their covenant. Such a breach would inevitably bring divine condemnation on the community in the form of war, pestilence, poverty, and other forms of *force majeure*. Traditionally, the New England Puritans' belief in a "solemn divine probation" also rendered the reformation of society a constant priority. They had to ensure that all institutions and all aspects of society comported with the covenantal ideal. Thus, Puritan sermonizers urged their listeners: "Reform all places, all persons and all callings. Reform the benches of judgment, the inferior magistrates. . . . Reform the universities, reform the cities, reform the counties, reform inferior schools of learning, reform the Sabbath, reform the ordinances, the worship of God. Every plant which my Father hath not planted shall be rooted up."[99] It was this tradition, albeit in a less denominationally and doctrinally rigorous form, that Adams established in the constitution.

Beyond the preamble and the provisions on oath-swearing, the Constitution had a few more scattered evidences of a ceremonial establishment. God is invoked, by name or pseudonym (the "Great Legislator of the Universe," and "Supreme Being") a dozen times. References to the "common" or "public good" appear four more times, as do two further references to divine "blessings" and "privileges." These provisions establishing the public religious ceremonies of Massachusetts are more overt and detailed than those of any other state constitution of the day. All these provisions, save the oath provision, were passed without controversy, or even recorded comment. And they remain unchanged to this day.

Moral Establishment

The moral dimensions of the public religious establishment, implicated by the use of covenant and oath-swearing ceremonies, are set out clearly elsewhere in the 1780 Constitution. Article II of the Declaration of Rights, as Adams formulated it, states: "It is the Duty of all men in society, publickly, and at stated seasons to worship the SUPREME BEING, the great Creator and preserver of the Universe." Article III follows with the reason for this duty: "the happiness of a people, and good order and preservation of civil government, essentially depend upon piety, religion, and morality; and . . . these cannot be generally diffused through a Community, but by the institution of publick Worship of God, and of public instructions in piety, religion, and morality. . . . "[100]

Adams did not consider these constitutional endorsements of religious morality to be mere platitudes. In Article XVIII of the Declaration of Rights, he rendered adherence to these moral duties integral to the character of public offices and public officials:

> A frequent recurrence to the fundamental principles of the constitution, and a constant adherence to those of piety, justice, moderation, temperance, industry, and frugality, are absolutely necessary to preserve the advantages of liberty, and to maintain a free government. The people ought, consequently, to have a particular attention to all those principles, in the choice of their Officers and Representatives, and they have a right to require of their lawgivers and magistrates, an exact and constant observance of them, in the formation and execution of the laws necessary for the good administration of the Commonwealth.

For, as Article VII of the Declaration puts it: "Government is instituted for the Common good; for the protection, safety, prosperity, and happiness of the people."

Adams rendered these same moral qualities essential ingredients of education within the state. Chapter V of the Frame of Government provides: "Wisdom, and knowledge, as well as virtue, diffused generally among the body of the people, [is] necessary for the preservation of their rights and liberties." It is thus "the duty of Legislatures and Magistrates in all future generations of the Commonwealth to cherish the interests of literature and sciences, and all seminaries of them; . . . to encourage private societies and public institutions, rewards and immunities, for the promotion of [education] . . . ; to countenance and inculcate the principles of humanity and general benevolence, public and private charity, industry and frugality, honesty and punctuality in their dealings, sincerity, good humour, and all social affections, and generous sentiments among the people." The same Chapter V confirmed and commended the incorporation of Harvard College, since "the encouragement of arts and sciences, and all good literature, tends to the honor of God, the advantage of the christian religion, and the great benefit of this and other United States of America."

None of these provisions establishing a public religious morality triggered much debate during the constitutional convention, and none of these provisions was amended or emended thereafter. Indeed, the famous Eleventh

Amendment of 1833 that purportedly "disestablished religion" in Massachusetts simply repeated the mantra of the moral establishment: that "the public worship of GOD and instructions in piety, religion and morality, promote the happiness and prosperity of a people and the security of a Republican Government."

To this day, the Massachusetts Constitution on its face establishes both religious ceremonies and religious morality. To be sure, this language has become largely a dead letter in recent generations—its legal revival stymied by a political climate that is indifferent, if not hostile, to public religion, and by a First Amendment interpretation that discourages, if not prohibits, the state's implementation of these provisions.[101] But even in this climate, the Massachusetts courts have recently used these provisions to uphold the constitutionality of state funding of legislative chaplains and of political oaths ending in "so help me God."[102] Today, with the center of gravity of the American religious liberty experiment slowly shifting from the courts to the legislatures, and from the federal government to the states, these long-dormant constitutional provisions might well find new life.

Institutional Establishment

It was the third dimension of the established public religion—Article III's establishment of specific religious institutions supported by public taxes—that drew fire in the convention and ratification debates and eventually was outlawed by the Eleventh Amendment in 1833. Here, critics charged, the balance between private religious freedom and a public religious establishment tilted too much toward the latter.

It was one thing for the Constitution to establish general public religious ceremonies and to define basic public morals and mores—to encourage "piety, religion, and morality," to endorse the public worship of God, to list the "moral virtues" necessary in a good ruler, to commend schools and colleges that offered religious and moral education, to limit breaches of the peace and interference in another's religious rights, all on the assumption that "the happiness of a people, and the good order and preservation of civil government" depended upon the same.[103] Such provisions at least left a good deal of religious expression and participation open to voluntary choice and individual accent.

It was quite another thing, however, for the Constitution to institute religious practices by law—to require persons to attend a preferred form of public worship, to compel them to pay tithes in support of ministers and teachers, to force them to incorporate themselves into state-registered religious societies, and to require them to be faithful in their attendance at worship lest their tithes be diverted or their societies dissolved. For many, such an establishment crossed the line from gentle patronage to odious persecution.

Criticisms—During the constitutional ratification debates in 1780, critics issued a torrent of objections against Article III.

A large group of critics charged that Article III's establishment of public religious institutions contradicted the liberties of private religions guaranteed in Article II.[104] The Return of the Town of Dartmouth put it thus:

> It appears doubtful in said Articles whether the Rights of Conscience are sufficiently secured or not to those who are really desirous to, and do attend publick Worship, and who are not limited to any particular outward Teacher. . . . we humbly conceive it intirely out of the power of the legislature to establish a way of Worship that shall be agreable to the Conceptions and Convictions of the minds of the individuals, as it is a matter that solely relates to and stands between God and the Soul before whose Tribunal all must account each one for himself.[105]

A second group of critics retorted that the happiness of a people and the good order and preservation of civil government did not, as a matter of historical fact, depend upon piety, religion, and morality.[106] The Return of the Town of Natick put it well:

> When both antient History and modern authentik information concur to evince that flourishing civil Governments have existed and do still exist without the Civil Legislature's instituting the publick Christian worship of God, and publick Instruction in piety and the Christian,—but that rather wherever such institutions are fully [executed] by the civil authority have taken place among a people instead of essentially promoting their happiness and the good order and preservation of Civil Government, it has We believe invariably promoted impiety, irreligion, hypocrisy, and many other sore and oppressive evils.[107]

A third group of critics acknowledged the public utility of piety, morality, and religion, but thought that such an institutional establishment would jeopardize both religion and the state. The Return of the Town of Petersham put it thus:

> We grant that the Happiness of a People and the good Order and preservation of Civil Government Greatly Depends upon Piety, Religion, and Morality. But we Can by no Means Suppose that to Invest the Legislature or any Body of men on Earth with a power absolutely to Determine For others What are the proper Institutions of Divine Worship and To appoint Days and seasons for such Worship With a power to impose and Indow Religious Teachers and by penalties and punishments to be able to Enforce an Attendance on such Publick Worship or to Extort Property from any one for the Support of what they may Judge to be publick Worship Can have a Tendency to promote true piety Religion or Morality But the Reverse and that such a Power when and where Ever Exercised has more or Less Been an Engine in the Hands of Tyrants for the Destruction of the Lives Liberties and Properties of the People and that Experience has abun-

dantly Taught Mankind that these are Natural Rights which ought Never to be Delegated and Can with the greatest propriety be Exercised by Individuals and by every Religious Society of men.[108]

A fourth group of critics believed that to institute such a mild establishment would inevitably lead to more odious forms. A pamphleteer named Philanthropos puts this "slippery slope" argument well:

> Perhaps it will be said that the civil magistrate has a right to oblige the people to support the ministers of the gospel, because the gospel ministry is beneficial to society. [But if so] it will follow, by the same law, that he may adopt any of the maxims of the religion of Christ into the civil constitution, which he may judge will be beneficial to civil society . . . if magistrates may adopt any the least part of the religion of Christ into their systems of civil government, that supposes magistrates to be judges what parts shall be taken, and what left; power, then which nothing be more dangerous, [be] lodged in the hands of weak and fallible men.[109]

A fifth group of critics repeated and amplified Isaac Backus's charge that Article III constituted another species of taxation without representation—now in the religious sphere. As the Return of Ashby put it: "Relegeous Societys as such have no voice in Chusing the Legeslature, the Legeslature therefore have no right to make law binding on them as such; every religeous Society, as such, is intirely independent on any body politick, the Legeslature having therefor no more right to make laws Binding on them, as such, then the Court of Great Britton have to make Laws binding on the Independent states of America." Indeed, the same Return commented later, "to invest their Legeslature with power make Laws that are binding on Religious Society . . . is as much to say we will not have Christ to reign over us that the Laws of this Kingdom are not sufficient to govern us, that the prosperity of this Kingdom is note equally important with the Kingdoms of this world. . . . "[110]

A sixth group of critics argued that Article III's final guarantee of equality of all denominations simply contradicted the prior provisions on state tax support for some denominations. If "all religious sects or denominations peaceably demeaning themselves" are equal before the law, why are some supported by taxes and others not, and why are all required to register themselves, while others cannot. True religious liberty, critics argued, would leave the "several religious societies of the Commonwealth, whether corporate or incorporate" to their own peaceable devices. It would grant them "the right to elect their pastors of religious teachers, to contract with them for their support, to raise money for erecting and repairing houses for public worship, for the maintenance of religious instruction, and for the payment of necessary expenses."[111]

Support—John Adams had not drafted the controversial Article III—and, though he supported it in the convention, he offered little by way of apologia for it. A number of other theologians and jurists of the day, however, rose to the defense of Article III.

One group of proponents, comprised of congregationalist ministers, invoked traditional "theocratic" arguments for such an institutional establishment. One writer argued that since civil government is God's creation, it would "counter the divine command to provide for worship and the spiritual edification of the people but refuse to support religious institutions."[112] Others argued that outlawing the state collection of tithes would "deprive a respectable part of the people of the state of the privilege of discharging their duty to God in a way that they judge to be most agreeable to his will."[113] Others issued self-serving jeremiads, predicated on the covenantal language of the preamble, warning that "if the people and their representatives withhold their support of God's church, God will withhold His support of them, and raine down his woeful vengeance."[114] Such arguments had been constant and cogent in the more homogeneous and integrated civil and religious communities of seventeenth-century Puritan New England. In the more pluralistic and atomistic communities of the later-eighteenth century, they carried far less force.

A second group of proponents thought such an institutional establishment was an inevitable and innocuous act of a political majority seeking to promote the common good and the personal happiness of all subjects. Boston, which itself did not establish religious institutions, nonetheless supported Article III, arguing in its Return:

> Though we are not supporting the Kingdom of Christ, may we not be permitted to Assist civil society by an adoption, and by the teaching of the best act of Morals that were ever offered to the World? To object to these Morals, or even to the Piety and Religion we aim to inculcate, because they are drawn from the Gospel, must appear very singular to an Assembly generally professing themselves Christians. Suspend all provision for the inculcation of morality, religion, and Piety, and confusion and every evil work may be justly dreaded.[115]

A third group of proponents argued that tithing and other forms of state support for religious institutions would ultimately serve to keep the state small and efficient. Congregationalist preacher Joseph McKeen put this well:

> But in proportion as the principles, inculcated by the religion of Jesus Christ, prevail in the minds of a people, the number of crimes will be diminished, truth and justice will be maintained, kind and friendly offices will be multiplied, and happiness will be diffused through society. Were the benevolence of the gospel imbibed by all the members of the community, no human laws, nor officers of justice, would be necessary to compel them to do their duty, nor to restrain one from injuring another; and were their temper and conduct generally formed and regulated by it, civil rulers would need to exercise but little power to preserve tranquility in the state. The more, therefore, that the principles of piety, benevo-

lence, and virtues are diffused among a people, the milder may their government and laws be, and the more liberty are they capable of enjoying, because they govern themselves. But if there be little or no regard to religion or virtue among a people, they will not govern themselves, nor willingly submit to any laws, which lay restraint upon their passions; and consequently they must be wretched or be governed by force: they cannot bear freedom; they must be slaves.

For McKeen, therefore, the benefits of a "mild" institutional establishment of religion outweighed its risks—at least for the time being. "The wise institutions of our forefathers, the schools which they established for the education of youth, the provision which they made for the public worship of God, and a religious observance of the Christian Sabbath, have doubtless contributed very much to the tranquil state in which our country is at this day. Let us not discard these institutions, before we are certain that we have got something better to substitute in their room."[116]

These and other arguments were combined in Theophilus Parsons's lengthy defense of the utility and necessity of establishing religious institutions in Massachusetts. Parsons, already famous for penning the 1778 *Essex Result,* had also been a member of the seven-member ad hoc committee that had redrafted Article III during the heated convention debate in early November 1779. He was later appointed Chief Justice of the Massachusetts Supreme Juridical Court and had several occasions to enforce its provisions against detractors. In the case of *Barnes v. Falmouth* (1810), he offered "a diligent examination" of the "the motives which induced the people to introduce into the Constitution a religious establishment, the nature of the establishment introduced, and the rights and privileges it secured to the people, and to their teachers."[117]

Parsons first argued for the necessity and utility of maintaining religion in a civil society and government. In a nutshell, he argued that the happiness of citizens is the goal of government; morality and virtue are essential ingredients to the achievement of happiness; religion and faith are essential wellsprings of morality and virtue; and thus government must support religion and faith. "The object of a free civil government is the promotion and security of the happiness of the citizens," he wrote, invoking and discussing several provisions of the Constitution.

These effects cannot be produced but by the knowledge and practice of our moral duties, which comprehend all the social and civil obligations of man to man, and of the citizen to the state. If the civil magistrate in any state could procure by his regulations a uniform practice of these duties, the government of that state would be perfect. To obtain that perfection, it is not enough for the magistrate to define the rights of several citizens, as they are related to life, liberty, property, and reputation, and to punish those by whom they may be invaded. Wise laws, made to this end, and faithfully executed, may leave the people strangers to many of the enjoyments of civil and social life, without which their happiness will be extremely imperfect. Human laws cannot oblige to the performance of the duties of imperfect obligation; as the duties of charity and hospitality, benevolence and good neighborhood; as the duties of resulting from the relation of husband wife, parent and child; of man to man, as children of a common parent; and of real patriotism, by influencing every citizen to love his country, and to obey all of its laws. These are moral duties, flowing from the disposition of the heart, and not subject to the control of human legislation. Neither can the laws prevent, by temporal punishments, secret offences, committed without witness, to gratify malice, revenge, or any other passion by assailing the most inestimable rights of others. For human tribunals cannot proceed against any crimes, unless ascertained by evidence; and they are destitute of all power to prevent the commission of offences, unless by the feeble examples exhibited in the punishment of those who may be detected.

Civil government, therefore, availing itself only of its own power, is extremely defective; and unless it could derive assistance from some superior power, whose laws extend to the temper and disposition of the human heart, and before whom no offence is secret, wretched indeed would be the state of man under a civil constitution of any form. The most manifest truth has been felt by legislators in all ages; and as man is born, not only a social, but a religious being, so, in the pagan world, false and absurd systems of religion were adopted and patronized by the magistrate, to remedy the defects necessarily existing in a government merely civil.[118]

Having demonstrated the necessity and utility of religion generally for civil society and government, Parsons then turned to the reasons for state support of Christian institutions in particular—in effect, combining the arguments of Joseph McKeen and the Return of Boston.

[T]he people of Massachusetts, in the frame of their government, adopted and patronized a religion, which, by its benign and energetic influences, might cooperate with human institutions, to promote and secure the happiness of the citizens, so far as it might be consistent with the imperfections of man. In selecting a religion, the people were not exposed to the hazard of choosing a false and defective religious system. Christianity had long been promulgated, its pretensions and excellences well known, and its divine authority admitted. This religion was found to rest on the basis of immortal truth; to contain a system of morals adapted to man, in all possible ranks and conditions, situations and circumstances, by conforming to which he would be meliorated and improved in all the relations of human life; and to furnish the most efficacious sanctions, by bringing to light a future state of retribution. And this religion, as understood by Protestants, tending, by its effects, to make every man submitting to its influence, a better husband, parent, child, neighbor, citizen, and magistrate, was by the people established as a fundamental and essential part of their constitution.[119]

Parsons then moved to answer criticisms that the institutionalization of religion mandated by Article III was "inconsistent, intolerant, and impious."[120]

First, Parsons argued, "the manner in which this establishment was made, is liberal, and consistent with the rights of conscience on religious subjects. As religious opinions, and time and manner of expressing the homage due to the Governor of the universe, are points depending on the sincerity and belief of each individual, and do not concern the public interest, . . . the second article . . . guards these points from the interference of the civil magistrate . . . for every man, whether Protestant or Catholic, Jew, Mahometan, or Pagan."[121]

It is perfectly consistent for the state to maintain these guarantees of liberty of conscience for all and to "provide for the public teaching of the precepts of Protestant Christians to all the people" by collecting tithes to support their ministers and churches. To object that this is a violation of conscience, Parsons wrote, is "to mistake a man's conscience for his money" and to deny the state the power of collecting taxes from those whom it represents.

> But as every citizen derives the security of his property, and fruits of his industry, from the power of the state, so, as the price of this protection, he is bound to contribute, in common with his fellow-citizens, for such public uses, as the state shall direct. And if any individual can lawfully withhold his contribution, because he dislikes the appropriation, the authority of the state to levy taxes would be annihilated; and without money it would soon cease to have any authority. But all moneys raised and appropriated for public uses, by any corporation, pursuant to powers derived from the state, are raised and appropriated substantially by the authority of the state. And the people, in their constitution, instead of devolving the support of public teachers on the corporations, by whom they should be elected, might have directed their support to be defrayed out of the public treasury, to be reimbursed by the levying and collection of state taxes. And against this mode of support, the objection of an individual, disapproving of the object of the public taxes, would have the same weight it can have against the mode of public support through the medium of corporate taxation. In either case, it can have no weight to maintain a charge of persecution for conscience' sake. The great error lies in not distinguishing between liberty of conscience in religious opinions and worship, and the right of appropriating money by the state. The former is an unalienable right; the latter is surrendered to the state, as the price of protection.[122]

Second, Parsons argued, the notion that support for religious institutions was intolerant of the nonreligious fails to recognize the great public benefits that support of religious institutions brings them. "The object of public religious instruction is to teach, and to enforce by suitable arguments, that practice of a system of correct morals among the people, and form and cultivate reasonable and just habits and manners; by which every man's person and property are protected from outrage, and his personal and social enjoyments promoted and multiplied. From these effects every man enjoys the most important benefits; and whether he be, or be not, an auditor of any public teacher, he receives more solid and permanent advantages from the public instruction, than the administration of justice in courts of law can give him. The like objection may be made by any man to the support of public schools."[123]

Constitutional Solutions—Such arguments proved sufficient to defend Article III for more than half a century. This was the balance that Adams's dialectical model of religious liberty seemed to demand. All faiths were free, and it was up to individuals to devise their own religious institutions and practices in a manner they found convenient. One faith was fixed, and it was up to the state to devise its religious institutions and practices in a manner it found expedient. To leave private religious faiths uncontrolled would only encourage human depravity. To leave the public religious faith unsupported would only encourage social fragmentation. Hence the need to add to a ceremonial and a moral establishment a more robust institutional establishment of the public religion.

However convincing such arguments might have been in theory, they ultimately proved unworkable in practice. In the fifty-three years of its existence, Article III "was fruitful in lawsuits, bad feeling, and petty prosecution."[124] Both the casuistry and the clumsiness of the tithing and registration system were exposed in litigation. Resentment at Article III only increased as the religions of Massachusetts liberalized and pluralized—and the former congregational churches were splintered into an array of trinitarian and unitarian forms.[125] Eventually, detractors so outnumbered proponents that the Massachusetts Constitution was amended. In 1833, Amendment, Article XI outlawed the institutional establishment of the public religion, even while explicitly preserving the ceremonial and moral establishment:

> As the public worship of GOD and instructions in piety, religion and morality, promote the happiness and prosperity of a people and the security of a Republican Government;—Therefore, the several religious societies of the Commonwealth, whether corporate or incorporate, at any meeting legally warned and holden for that purpose, shall ever have the right to elect their pastors of religious teachers, to contract with them for their support, to raise money for erecting and repairing houses for public worship, for the maintenance of religious instruction, and for the payment of necessary expenses: And all persons belonging to any religious society shall be taken and held to be members, until they shall file with the Clerk of such Society, a written notice declaring the dissolution of their membership, and thenceforth shall not be liable for any grant or contract, which may be thereafter made, and denominations demeaning themselves peaceably and as good citizens of the Commonwealth shall be equally under the protection of the law; and no subordination of one sect or denomination to another shall every be established by law.

Subsequent amendments of 1855, 1917, and 1974 closed the door tightly against any form of state fiscal and material aid to religious institutions and endeavors—provisions that the Massachusetts courts have enforced with alacrity.[126]

CONCLUSIONS

In the preface to his *Defense of the Constitutions of Government in the United States of America* of 1788, John Adams wrote boldly: "The people in America have now the best opportunity and the greatest trust in their hands, that Providence ever committed to so small a number, since the transgression of the first pair; if they betray their trust, their guilt will merit even greater punishment than other nations have suffered, and in the indignation of Heaven." "The United States have exhibited, perhaps, the first example of governments erected on the simple principles of nature; and if men are now sufficiently enlightened to disabuse themselves of artifice, imposture, hypocrisy, and superstition, they will consider this event as a [new] era in history. Although the detail of the formation of the American governments is at present little known or regarded either in Europe or in America, it may hereafter become an object of curiosity" for it is "destined to spread over the northern part of that whole quarter of the globe." Indeed, "[t]he institutions now made in America will not wholly die out for thousands of years. It is of the last importance, then, that they should begin right. If they set out wrong, they will never be able to return, unless it be by accident to the right path."[127]

Two centuries later, such sentiments prove remarkably prescient. The American framers did begin on the right path of religious liberty, and today we enjoy a remarkable freedom of thought, conscience, and belief as a consequence. American models of religious liberty have had a profound influence around the globe, and their principles now figure prominently in a number of national constitutions and international human rights instruments.[128]

To be sure, as Adams predicated, there has always been "a glorious uncertainty" in the law of religious liberty, and a noble diversity of understandings of its details. This was as true in Adams's day as in our own. In Adams's day, there were competing models of religious liberty more overtly theological than his—whether Puritan, Anglican, Evangelical, or Catholic in inspiration. There were also competing models more overtly philosophical than his—whether Classical, Republican, Enlightenmentarian, or Whig in inclination. Today, these and other models of religious liberty have borne ample progeny, and the rivalries among them are fought out in the courts, legislatures, and academies throughout the land.

Prone as he was to a dialectical model of religious liberty and a federalist system of government, Adams would likely approve of our rigorous rivalries of principle—so long as all rivals remain committed to constitutional ideals of democracy, liberty, and rule of law. But Adams would also likely insist that we reconsider his most cardinal insights about the dialectical nature of religious freedom and religious establishment. Too little religious freedom, Adams insisted, is a recipe for hypocrisy and impiety. But too much religious freedom is an invitation to depravity and license. Too firm a religious establishment breeds coercion and corruption. But too little religious establishment allows secular prejudices to become constitutional prerogatives. Somewhere between these extremes, Adams believed, a society must find its balance.

The balance that John Adams struck in favor of a "mild and equitable establishment" of Protestantism can no longer serve a nation so fully given to religious pluralism. But the balance that the Supreme Court has struck in favor of a complete disestablishment of religion can also no longer serve a people so widely devoted to a public religion and a religious public. Somewhere between extremes, our society must now find a new constitutional balance—with Adams's efforts serving as a noble instruction.

NOTES

I would like to thank Henry Kimmel and Joel Nichols for their able and ample assistance in the preparation of this article. An abridged version of this article appears in *Journal of Church and State* 41 (1999): 213–252.

1. Thomas Jefferson, "Letter of November 21, 1808," in Saul K. Padover, ed., *The Complete Jefferson, Containing His Major Writings* (Freeport, N.Y.: Books for Libraries Press, 1943), p. 538; id., "Notes on the State of Virginia (1781–1785)," query 17 in ibid., pp. 673–676. See discussion in Sidney E. Mead, *The Lively Experiment: The Shaping of Christianity in America* (New York: Harper & Row, 1963), pp. 55–71.

2. Thomas Jefferson, "Autobiography" (1821), in *The Complete Jefferson*, pp. 1119–1194, at p. 1147.

3. See, e.g., Thomas Jefferson, Letter to Rev. Samuel Miller, January 23, 1808, in P. L. Ford, ed., *The Works of Thomas Jefferson* (New York: G. P. Putnam, 1904–1905), vol. 11, p. 7. See further discussion in the papers of Daniel Dreisbach and Thomas Buckley included herein, and Thomas E. Buckley, "The Political Theology of Thomas Jefferson," in Merrill D. Peterson and Robert C. Vaughan, eds., *The Virginia Statute for Religious Freedom: Its Evolution and Consequences in American History* (Cambridge: Cambridge University Press, 1988), pp. 75–108.

4. John Adams, "A Defense of the Constitutions of Government in the United States of America" (1788), preface, in J. F. Adams, ed., *The Works of John Adams,* 10 vols. (Boston: Little & Brown, 1850–1856), vol. 4, pp. 290–297; and id., "A Dissertation on the Canon and Feudal Law" (1774), in ibid., vol. 3, p. 451.

5. Letter to Dr. Price, April 8, 1785, in ibid., vol. 8, p. 232. Elsewhere, Adams wrote that in Massachusetts, "there is, it is true, a moral and political equality of rights and duties among all the individuals and as yet no appearance of artificial inequalities of conditions. . . . " Quoted in Frank Donovan, ed., *The John Adams Papers* (New York: Dodd, Mead & Company, 1965), p. 181. In a letter of October 2, 1818, to Adrian van der Kemp, Adams again praised "freedom of religion" so long as it was "consistent with morals and property." Quoted by John R. Howe, Jr., *The Changing Political Thought of John Adams* (Princeton: Princeton University Press, 1966), p. 227n.

6. Diary entry, October 14, 1774, in Adams, *Works,* vol. 2, p. 399 (referring to the congregational establishment of colonial Massachusetts, largely preserved in the 1780 Constitution).

7. On the relationship and influence of Jefferson and Adams, see Lester J. Cappon, ed., *The Adams-Jefferson Letters,* 2 vols. (Chapel Hill: University of North Carolina Press, 1959), and John Murray Allison, A*dams and Jefferson: The Story of a Friendship* (Norman: University of Oklahoma Press, 1966).

8. The phrase comes from Elisha Williams, *The Essential Rights and Liberties of Protestants: A Seasonable Plea for the Liberty of Conscience, and the Right of Private Judgment in Matters of Religion, Without any Controul from Human Authority* (Boston, 1744). John Adams also spoke of "our most essential rights and liberties." See "Instructions of the Town of Braintree to their Representative," in Adams, *Works,* vol. 3, p. 465.

9. Jefferson, Letter to Rev. Samuel Miller, in Jefferson, *Works,* vol. 11, pp. 7–9. He continued: "Fasting & prayer are religious exercises. The enjoining them is an act of discipline. Every religious society has a right to determine for itself the times for these exercises, & the objects proper for them, according to their own peculiar tenets. . . . "

10. Thomas Jefferson, "Freedom of Religion at the University of Virginia (October 7, 1822)," in *The Complete Jefferson,* p. 958. In ibid., p. 957, Jefferson called liberty of conscience and free exercise of religion "the most interesting and important to every human being."

11. "A Bill for Establishing Religious Freedom" (1779), in *The Complete Jefferson,* pp. 946–947.

12. See generally the papers of Buckley and Dreisbach herein and the masterful new study by Edwin S. Gaustad, *Sworn on the Altar of God: A Religious Biography of Thomas Jefferson* (Grand Rapids, Mich.: Wm. Eerdmans, 1996).

13. The phrase is from Benjamin Franklin, "Proposals Relating to the Education of Youth in Pensilvania" (1749), quoted and discussed in Martin E. Marty, "On a Medial Moraine: Religious Dimensions of American Constitutionalism," *Emory Law Journal* 39 (1990): 9, 16–17. The phrase became commonplace thereafter; in the nineteenth century, it was eventually transmuted into "civil religion." See Robert N. Bellah, *The Broken Covenant: American Civil Religion in Time of Trial* (New York: Harper and Row, 1975).

14. See, e.g., John Adams, Letter to Zabdiel Adams, June 21, 1776, in Adams, *Works,* vol. 4, p. 194: "The only foundation of a free constitution is pure virtue." John Adams, Letter to Benjamin Rush, February 2, 1807, in John A. Schutz and Douglass Adair, eds., *The Spur of Fame: Dialogues of John Adams and Benjamin Rush, 1805–1813* (San Marino, Calif.: The Huntington Library, 1966), pp. 75–77, at 76: "I say then that national morality never was and never can be preserved without the utmost purity and chastity in women; and without national morality a republican government cannot be maintained." Letter to Benjamin Rush, August 28, 1811, in ibid., pp. 191–195, at p. 192: "I agree with you in sentiment that religion and virtue are the only foundations not only of republicanism and of all free government but of social felicity under all governments and in all the combinations of civil society." In the same letter, Adams defended the "inculcation of 'national, social, domestic, and religious virtues,'" "fidelity to the marriage bed," "the sanctification of the Sabbath," prohibitions "against ardent spirits, the multiplication of taverns, retailers, dram shops, and tippling houses . . . idlers, thieves, sots, and consumptive patients made for the physicians in those infamous seminaries. . . . "

15. See, e.g. Letter to Benjamin Rush, February 2, 1807, pp. 75–76: "The Bible contains the most profound philosophy, the most perfect morality, and the most refined

policy that ever was conceived upon earth. It is the most republican book in the world, and therefore I will still revere it." See also Letter to Mrs. Adams, July 3, 1776, in Adams, *Works,* vol. 9, pp. 419–420, regarding the celebration of national symbols and events.

16. See esp. Massachusetts Constitution (1780), Article XVIII and notes thereon in Adams, *Works,* vol. 4, pp. 227–228.

17. Ibid., See also Letter to Benjamin Rush, June 12, 1812, in *Spur of Fame,* pp. 224–226, at 224 on Thanksgiving sermons.

18. Late in this life, Adams expressed regret about blasphemy laws. In a letter of January 23, 1825, to Jefferson, he wrote: "We think ourselves possessed, or, at least, we boast that we are so, of the liberty of conscience on all subjects, and of the right of free inquiry and private judgments in all cases, and yet how far are we from these exalted privileges in fact! There exists, I believe, throughout the whole Christian world, a law which makes it a blasphemy to deny or to doubt the divine inspiration of all the books of the Old and New Testament. . . . In America, it is not much better; even in our own Massachusetts, which I believe, upon the whole, is as temperate and moderate in religious zeal as most of the States, a law was made in the latter end of the last century, repealing the cruel punishments of the former laws, but substituting fine and imprisonment upon all blasphemers. . . . I think such laws a great embarrassment, great obstructions to the improvement of the human mind. . . . I wish they were repealed. The substance and essence of Christianity, as I understand it, is eternal and unchangeable, and will bear examination forever. . . . " Adams, *Works,* vol. 10, pp. 415–416.

19. See further Part III in this chapter. For Adams's earlier views on this, see esp. "A Dissertation on the Canon and Feudal Law" (1774), in ibid., vol. 3, pp. 448–464; and "Thoughts on Government Applicable to the Present State of the Colonies" (1776), in Adams, *Works,* vol. 4, pp. 193–209. For later formulations, see Howe, *Changing Political Thought of John Adams,* pp. 227ff.

20. See his "Dissertation on the Canon and Feudal Law," Adams, *Works,* vol. 3, pp. 452–456. Such views were commonplace in Massachusetts. See, e.g., Williams, *Essential Rights and Liberties,* pp. 7–8: "Every man has an equal right to follow the dictates of his own conscience in the affairs of religion. Every one is under an indispensable obligation to search the Scriptures for himself . . . and to make the best use of it he can for his own information in the will of God, the nature and duties of Christianity. As every Christian is so bound; so he has the inalienable right to judge of the sense and meaning of it, and to follow his judgment wherever it leads him; even an equal right with any rulers be they civil or ecclesiastical." See further examples in Ronald M. Peters, Jr., *The Massachusetts Constitution of 1780: A Social Compact* (Amherst: The University of Massachusetts Press, 1978), pp. 79–81.

21. John Adams, Letter to Thomas Jefferson, June 28, 1813, in *Adams-Jefferson Letters,* pp. 338–340, at pp. 339–340.

22. John Adams, Letter to Thomas Jefferson, June 25, 1813, in ibid., pp. 333–335, at p. 334. Jefferson had long maintained similar views. See, e.g., "Notes on the State of Virginia," query 17: "Difference of opinion is advantageous in religion." "The several sects perform the office of a *censor morum* over each other." *The Complete Jefferson,* pp. 675–676. James Madison wrote similarly that "the utmost freedom . . . arises from that multiplicity of sects which pervades America, . . . for where there is such a vari-

ety of sects, there cannot be a majority of any one sect to oppress and persecute the rest." Debates of June 12, 1788, in J. Elliot, ed., *The Debates in the Several State Conventions on the Adoption of the Federal Constitution* (1836), repr. ed., 5 vols. (Philadelphia: J. B. Lipponcott, 1941), vol. 3, p. 330.

Zabdiel Adams expressed comparable sentiments, which cousin John endorsed: "Modes and forms of religion; sentiments concerning doctrines, etc. people should be indulged in, without molestation. If coertion would bring mankind to a uniformity of sentiment, no advantage would result therefrom. It is on the contrary best to have different facts and denominations live in the same societies. They are a mutual check and spy upon each other, and become more attentive to their principles and practice. . . . [W]here Papists and Protestants live intermingled together, it serves to meliorate them both. . . . With madmen and enthusiasts there can be no agreement, except among people as distracted as themselves. But even such, where they put on a religious guise, and do not interrupt the peace of society, are not to be disturbed by the civil arm. . . . [Only] that part of religion which has an immediate aspect on the good of the community falls under the cognizance of the ruler." Zabdiel Adams, "An Election Sermon" (1782), in Charles S. Hynemann and Donald S. Lutz, *American Political Writing during the Founding Era,* 1760–1805, 2 vols. (Indianapolis: Liberty Press, 1983), vol. 1, pp. 539–564, at p. 556. On the close relationship between John Adams and Zabdiel, see references in Adams, *Works,* vol. 2, pp. 81, 83, 86, 86, 93, 105, 260; vol. 9, pp. 399–401.

23. For a good summary, see Jacob C. Meyer, *Church and State in Massachusetts from 1740–1833,* repr. ed. (New York: Russell & Russell, 1968), and the magisterial study of the religious liberty of dissenters in William G. McLoughlin, *New England Dissent 1630–1833,* 2 vols. (Cambridge: Harvard University Press, 1971).

24. For comparable provisions in the Constitutions of New Hampshire (1784), Connecticut (1818), and Maine (1820), see Chester J. Antieau et al., *Religion under the State Constitutions* (Brooklyn: Central Book Co., 1965), pp. 209–211, 181–182, 194–195.

25. Robert J. Taylor, *Construction of the Massachusetts Constitution* (Worcester, Mass.: American Antiquarian Society, 1980), p. 317. Among countless overviews, see esp. the classic of Samuel Eliot Morison, *A History of the Constitution of Massachusetts* (Boston: Wright & Potter, 1917). For principal primary texts, see Oscar and Mary Handlin, eds., *The Popular Sources of Political Authority: Documents on the Massachusetts Constitution of 1780* (Cambridge: Harvard University Press, 1966), and Robert J. Taylor, ed., *Massachusetts, Colony to Commonwealth: Documents on the Formation of Its Constitution* (Chapel Hill: University of North Carolina Press, 1961).

26. Reprinted in Handlin, *Popular Sources,* pp. 190–201.

27. "The Essex Result" (April 29, 1778), reprinted in ibid., pp. 324–365, at pp. 326, 330.

28. "Resolve on the Question of a Constitution, February 20, 1779," reprinted in ibid., pp. 383–384.

29. Reprinted in ibid., p. 423.

30. Reprinted in Taylor, ed., *Massachusetts, Colony to Commonwealth,* p. 118.

31. Reprinted in Handlin, *Popular Sources,* p. 419.

32. See Peters, *The Massachusetts Constitution,* pp. 24–30; Barry Shain, *The Myth of American Individualism: The Protestant Origins of American Political Thought* (Princeton: Princeton University Press, 1994), pp. 193–240.

33. Adams, *Works,* vol. 8, p. 55.

34. "Worcestriensis, Number IV (1776)," in Hynemann and Lutz, eds., *American Political Writing,* pp. 449–454, at p. 450 (emphases omitted)

35. Ibid., p. 452 (emphases and capitalization omitted).

36. Ibid., pp. 452–453 (emphases omitted). Samuel West, an influential Congregationalist preacher in Dartmouth, argued similarly:

> Our governors have a right to take every proper method to form the minds of their subjects so that they may become good members of society. . . . Hence the necessity of good laws to encourage every noble and virtuous sentiment, to suppress vice and immorality, to promote industry, to punish idleness, that parent of innumerable evils; to promote arts and sciences and to banish ignorance among mankind.
>
> And as nothing tends like religion and the fear of God to make men good members of the commonwealth, it is the duty of magistrates to become the patrons and promoters of religion and piety, and to make suitable laws for the maintaining [of] public worship, and decently supporting the teachers of religion. Such laws, I apprehend, are absolutely necessary for the well being of civil society. Such laws may be made, consistent with the liberties of conscience which every good member ought to be possessed of; for, as there are few, if any religious societies among us but what profess to believe and practice all the great duties of religion and morality that are necessary for the well being of society, and the safety of the state, let every one be allowed to attend worship in his own society, or in that way that he judges most agreable to the will of God, and let him be obliged to contribute his assistance to the supporting and defraying the necessary charges of his own meeting. In this case, no one can have any right to complain that he is deprived of liberty of conscience, seeing that he has a right to choose and freely attend that worship that appears to him to be most agreeable to the will of God; and it must be very unreasonable for him to object against being obliged to contribute his part towards the support of that worship which he has chosen.
>
> But for the civil authority to pretend to establish particular modes of faith and forms of worship, and to punish all that deviate from the standard which our superiors have set up, is attended with the most pernicious consequences to society. It cramps all free and rational inquiry, fills the world with hypocrites and superstitious bigots—nay, with infidels and skeptics it exposes men of religion and conscience to the rage and malice of fiery, blind zealots, and dissolves every tender tie of human nature; in short, it introduces confusion and every evil work.

Samuel West, "A Sermon Preached before the Honorable Council . . . of the Massachusetts-Bay in New England" (Boston: John Gill, 1776), reprinted in J. W. Thornton, *The Pulpit of the American Revolution* (Boston: Gould and Lincoln, 1860), pp. 259–322, at pp. 297–299.

37. Phillips Payson, "Election Sermon of 1778," reprinted in Hynemann and Lutz, eds., *American Political Writing,* pp. 523–538, and with minor differences in J. W. Thornton, *The Pulpit of the American Revolution* (Boston: Gould and Lincoln, 1860), pp. 323–353. I am using the first version.

38. Ibid., pp. 528–530. A bit later, Payson declared grandly: "The eyes of the whole world are upon us in these critical times, and, what is yet more, the eyes of Almighty God. . . . With diligence let us cultivate the spirit of liberty, of public virtue, of union and religion, and thus strengthen the hands of government and the great pillars of the state. Our own consciences will reproach us and the world condemn us if we do not properly obey, respect, and reverence the government of our choosing." Ibid., p. 538.

39. Isaac Backus, "Government and Liberty Described" (1778), reprinted in William G. McLoughlin, ed., *Isaac Backus on Church, State, and Calvinism: Pamphlets, 1754–1789* (Cambridge: Harvard University Press, 1968), pp. 345–369, at p. 351.

40. Ibid., p. 358. See also Isaac Backus, "Policy as Well as Honesty, Forbids the Use of Secular Force in Religious Affairs" (1779), reprinted in McLoughlin, ed., *Backus*, pp. 367–383: "The necessity of a well-regulated government in civil states is acknowledged by all, and the importance and benefit of true Christianity in order thereto is no less certain."

41. Ibid., pp. 373–374.

42. Ibid., p. 357.

43. Ibid. See further ibid., p. 361: "Many of the Baptists of this State have long been convinced, that a giving in the annual certificates required by the ruling party as the condition of our exemption from TAXES to their ministers contains an explicit acknowledgment of a power assumed by man which in reality belongs only to God. And in our *Appeal to the Public*, printed in Boston five years ago, we have given the particular reasons why we cannot in conscience perform that condition. Yet only because we have refused to wrong our consciences in that respect our people in various places have been taxed from year to year to [support] pedobaptist ministers."

44. Ibid., p. 375.

45. As reported by Isaac Backus, and quoted by McLoughlin, ed., *Backus on Church and State*, p. 12, and discussed in McLoughlin, *New England Dissent*, pp. 558–568. In his *Diary of 1774*, Adams records this quip as a reply not to Backus but to Israel Pemberton, a Pennsylvania Quaker: "I knew they might as well turn the heavenly bodies out of their annual and diurnal courses, as the people of Massachusetts at the present day from their meeting-house and Sunday laws." Adams, *Works*, vol. 2, p. 399.

46. See sources and discussion in James H. Hutson, *Religion and the Founding of the American Republic* (Washington: Library of Congress, 1998), pp. 59–74.

47. The delegates did not attend all sessions; the highest recorded vote on any issue was 247. Morison, "The Struggle," p. 356.

48. Peters, *The Massachusetts Constitution*, p. 24.

49. Ibid., pp. 23–31; McLoughlin, ed., *Backus*, p. 386.

50. See letter of June 7, 1780, to Edmund Jennings, quoted in Adams, *Works*, vol. 4, p. 216.

51. The draft is reprinted in Adams, *Works*, vol. 4, pp. 213–267.

52. Adams, *Works*, vol. 4, p. 221.

53. Chapter 1, section 3. See chapter 2, section 2 (requiring that the governor "shall be of the Christian religion"); section 3 (requiring that the lieutenant governor "shall be qualified, in point of religion"). See Adams, *Works*, vol. 4, pp. 241, 242, 245, 251.

54. See chapter 6, Article I, and *Journal*, pp. 97, 109–110 (summarizing debates on February 10, 14, and 15, 1780, about the same).

55. Chapter 6, Article I, with drafts in Adams, *Works*, vol. 4, pp. 260–266.

56. Amendment, Article VI (1821), required the following oath for all officers: "I A.B. do solemnly swear that I will bear true faith and allegiance to the Commonwealth of Massachusetts, and will support the Constitution thereof. So help me GOD." Quakers were again excused from the oath. Amendment, Article VII (1821), underscored this: "No oath, declaration or subscription, excepting the oath of the previous Article," was required of executive or legislative officers.

57. Taylor, *Construction,* p. 331.

58. Letter to William D. Williamson (February 25, 1812), quoted in Adams, *Works,* vol. 4, p. 222n.

59. Reprinted in ibid., vol. 4, pp. 221–222; a slightly reworded version appears in the *Journal,* appendix 2, at p. 193.

60. *Acts and Resolves, Public and Private, of the Province of Massachusetts Bay* . . . (Boston: Government Printer, 1869–1922), vol. 1, pp. 62–63.

61. See sources and discussion in my "Tax Exemption of Church Property: Historical Anomaly or Valid Constitutional Practice?" *Southern California Law Review* 64 (1991): 363–415, at 368–380.

62. Samuel Eliot Morison, "The Struggle over the Adoption of the Constitution of Massachusetts, 1780," *Massachusetts Historical Society Proceedings* 50 (1916–1917): 353–412, at 370.

63. See details in John D. Cushing, "Notes on Disestablishment in Massachusetts, 1780–1833," *William & Mary Quarterly,* 3d ser. 26 (1969): 169–190; McLoughlin, *New England Dissent,* pp. 547–565; Meyer, *Church and State in Massachusetts,* pp. 32–89.

64. *Journal,* pp. 38–40. Other members included Theophilus Parsons (later chief judge of the Massachusetts Supreme Juridical Court), Robert Treat Paine (judge of the same Court), Samuel Adams (future governor of Massachusetts), Caleb Strong (also future governor), Timothy Danielson (leading patriot from Western Massachusetts), and David Sanford (pastor of the Second Congregational Church in Medway).

65. Ibid., p. 43.

66. Ibid., p. 45.

67. Morison, "The Struggle," p. 371.

68. Ibid., p. 375.

69. *Journal,* appendix 3, at p. 218.

70. Arthur Lord, "Some Objections to the State Constitution, 1780," *Massachusetts Historical Society* 50 (1917): 54, at 55, indicates a state population of 378,000; the 15,090 who voted constitute 3.99% of that population. Morison, "The Struggle," p. 366, puts the population of Massachusetts proper at c. 307,000; the 15,090 who voted constitute 4.92% of that population.

71. Morison, "The Struggle," pp. 364–365.

72. Taylor, ed., *Documents,* p. 113. The Township Returns are included in Handlin, *Popular Sources,* pp. 475–932.

73. Taylor, ed., *Documents,* p. 113.

74. Reprinted in ibid., pp. 162–165, at p. 164.

75. For Adams's Puritan devotion, see esp. his "Dissertation on the Canon and the Feudal Law," in Adams, *Works,* vol. 3, pp. 451–456, and more generally Page Smith, *John Adams,* 2 vols. (Garden City: Doubleday, 1962); Catherine Drinker Bowen, *John Adams and the American Revolution* (Boston: Little, Brown, 1950), 26ff.

76. See diary entries, in ibid., vol. 2, pp. 364, 378, 380, 382, 392, 393, 395, 400, 401, and 404. See also Letter to Benjamin Rush, April 18, 1808, in *The Spur of Fame,* pp. 106–107: "Bigotry, superstition and enthusiasm on religious subjects I have long since set at defiance. I have attended public worship in all countries and with all sects and believe them all much better than no religion, though I have not thought myself obliged to believe all I heard." See further Letter to Benjamin Rush, August 28, 1811,

in ibid., pp. 191–195, at p. 193: "it is notorious enough that I have been a churchgoing animal for seventy-six years, i.e., from the cradle."

77. Letter to Benjamin Rush, January 21, 1810, in ibid., vol. 9, pp. 626, 627.

78. "Defense of the Constitutions," in Adams, *Works*, vol. 4, pp. 292–293, 297.

79. Letter to Josiah Quincy, February 9, 1811, Adams, *Works*, vol. 9, pp. 629–632, at p. 630.

80. Quoted by McLoughlin, *New England Dissent*, p. 560. See discussion in Edwin S. Gaustad, "Colonial Religion and Liberty of Conscience," in Peterson and Vaughan, eds., *The Virginia Statute*, pp. 23–42, at p. 39.

81. Adams, *Works*, vol. 8, p. 232.

82. Letter to Abigail Adams (1775), quoted and discussed in Edwin S. Gaustad, *A Religious History of America* (New York: Harper & Row, 1966), p. 127.

83. Letter to Benjamin Rush, August 28, 1811, in Adams, *Works*, vol. 9, pp. 635, 636.

84. Letter to Thomas Jefferson, April 19, 1817, in ibid., vol. 10, pp. 253 and 254.

85. Ibid., vol. 3, pp. 452–456.

86. Ibid. See also his long discussion of the rise of religious liberty among European Protestants, in the "Defense of the Constitutions," vol. 2.

87. Letter of May 16, 1780 to Isaac Smith, Sr., quoted by Taylor, *Construction*, pp. 333–334, n 32.

88. Amendment, Article CVI (1982) rendered "all men" as "all persons" and added: "Equality under the law shall not be denied or abridged because of . . . creed. . . . "

89. Peters, *Massachusetts Constitution*, pp. 51–52.

90. See sources and discussion in my *Religion and the American Constitutional Experiment* (Boulder, Colo.: Westview Press, 2000), chaps. 2, 3, and 5.

91. Adams, *Works*, vol. 8, p. 232.

92. This emphasis on human depravity, and the need for its restraint, is especially pronounced in Adams's earlier writings, notably his 1788 "Defense," vol. 1. Later in his life, Adams tempered this view somewhat. See, e.g., his Letter to Thomas Jefferson, April 19, 1817, in Adams, *Works*, vol. 10, pp. 253–255, at p. 254: "So far from believing in the total and universal depravity of human nature, I believe there is no individual totally depraved. The most abandoned scoundrel that ever existed, never yet wholly extinguished his conscience, and while conscience remains, there is some religion."

93. Simeon Howard, "A Sermon Preached before the Honorable Council . . . of Massachusetts-Bay" (Boston: John Bill, 1780), reprinted in Thornton, *The American Pulpit*, pp. 355–396, at pp. 362–363.

94. *Worcestriensis*, p. 452.

95. Ibid., p. 450.

96. See esp. Donald S. Lutz, *The Origins of American Constitutionalism* (Baton Rouge: Louisiana State University Press, 1988). See also my "How to Govern a City on a Hill: The Early Puritan Contribution to American Constitutionalism," *Emory Law Journal* 39 (1990): 41–64, and my "Blest Be the Ties That Bind: Covenant and Community in Puritan Thought," *Emory Law Journal* 36 (1987): 579–601.

97. See Payson, "Election Sermon," p. 529. This was also one reason that Adams wrote into his draft of Chapters 1 and 2 of the Frame of Government that every official must be "of the Christian religion."

98. W. Stoughton, "New Englands True Interest: Not to Lie" (1670), in Perry Miller and Thomas H. Johnson, eds., *The Puritans: A Sourcebook of Their Writings* (New York: Harper & Row, 1963), p. 243.

99. Quoted in Harold J. Berman, "Religious Foundations of Law in the West: An Historical Perspective," *Journal of Law and Religion* 1 (1983): 3–46, at 30. See also id., "Law and Belief in Three Revolutions," *Valparaiso Law Review* 18 (1984): 569, 595–97.

100. But cf. Amendments, Article XI (1833) and discussion later in this chapter.

101. See Robert A. Schapiro, "Identity and Interpretation in State Constitutional Law," *Virginia Law Review* 84 (1998): 389–457, for a penetrating discussion of state constitutional law as a source of state identity, and of conflicts between state and federal constitutional law. The most recent Supreme Court First Amendment case to outlaw a Massachusetts statute regarding religion is *Larkin v. Grendel's Den*, 459 U.S. 116 (1982) (outlawing a statute granting churches and schools the power to veto the issuance of liquor licenses to restaurants within 500 feet of them; such a statute, "provides a significant symbolic benefit to religion in the minds of some" and "enmeshes churches in the exercise of substantial governmental powers"). Generally, the Massachusetts courts have interpreted the religion clauses in conformity with the First Amendment interpretation of the Supreme Court. See, e.g., *Commonwealth v. Nissenbaum*, 404 Mass. 575 (1989) (the constitution does not protect religious use of illegal drugs), and cases discussed in the next note.

102. *Colo v. Treasurer and Receiver General*, 392 N.E. 2d 1195 (1979), consistent with *Marsh v. Chambers*, 463 U.S. 783 (1983); *Commonwealth v. Callahan*, 401 Mass. 627 (1988). See also the reflections of an associate justice of the Supreme Juridical Court of Massachusetts, Herbert P. Wilkins, "Judicial Treatment of the Massachusetts Declaration of Rights in Relation to Cognate Provisions of the United States Constitution," *Suffolk University Law Review* 14 (1980): 887–930, at 891–897 and 929–930.

103. Adams put it: "Happiness, whether in despotism or democracy, whether in slavery or liberty, can never be found without virtue. The best republics will be virtuous, and have been so; but we may hazard a conjecture, that the virtues have been the effect of the well-ordered constitution, rather than the cause. And, perhaps, it would be impossible to prove that a republic cannot exist even among highwaymen, by setting one rogue to watch another; and the knaves themselves may in time be made honest men by the struggle." Adams, *Works*, vol. 6, p. 219.

104. See, e.g., "The Returns of New Salem," in Handlin, *Popular Sources*, p. 482; "Town of Shutesbury," p. 597; "Town of Ashby," p. 633; "Town of Sherborn," p. 674; "Town of Westford," pp. 682–683; "Return of Buxton," p. 731; "Town of Petersham," p. 855; and "Return of Ashby," in Taylor, ed., *Documents*, pp. 151–152.

105. "Return of Dartmouth," in Handlin, *Popular Sources*, pp. 509–510.

106. See esp. Peters, *The Massachusetts Constitution*, pp. 33–35.

107. "Return of Westford," in Handlin, *Popular Sources*, pp. 681, 682.

108. "Return of Petersham," in ibid., p. 855.

109. *Continental Journal*, April 6, 1780, quoted in Peters, *The Massachusetts Constitution*, p. 82. See also "Return of the Town of Westford in Handlin," *Popular Sources*, pp. 682–683.

110. Quoted in Taylor, ed., *Documents*, pp. 151–152.

111. Ibid.

112. Boston Independent Chronicle, February 10, 1780, quoted by Charles H. Lippy, "The 1780 Massachusetts Constitution: Religious Establishment or Civil Religion?" *Journal of Church and State* 20 (1978): 533–549, at 539–540. See also Howard, *Election Sermon,* pp. 13–15.

113. Irenaeus, *Independent Ledger* (April 11, 1780), quoted in Morison, "The Struggle," p. 380.

114. Abel Holmes, *A Sermon Preached at Brattle Street Church in Boston* (Boston: Young & Minns, 1799), pp. 17–18.

115. Full text in Taylor, ed., *Documents,* pp. 148–150, with quote on p. 150.

116. Joseph McKeen, *A Sermon Preached on the Public Fast in the Commonwealth of Massachusetts* (Salem: Thomas C. Cushing, 1793), pp. 17–21.

117. *Barnes v. Falmouth,* 6 Mass. 401, 404 (1810) (Barnes, C. J.), reprinted with revisions as Theophilus Parsons, *Defence of the Third Article of the Massachusetts Declaration of Rights* (Worcester, 1820).

118. Ibid., pp. 404–405.

119. Ibid., p. 405.

120. Ibid., pp. 405, 408.

121. Ibid., pp. 405–406.

122. Ibid., pp. 407–408.

123. Ibid., pp. 408–409. See also the conclusion of Lippy, "The Massachusetts Constitution," pp. 534–535: Article III did not establish Puritan congregationalism but "providing public support for religious institutions was seen as a way to promote political stability and social cohesion by guaranteeing that individuals would receive instruction in moral principles, rooted in the common religious sensibilities of the people, which would make them good citizens. . . . "

124. Morison, *Constitutional History,* pp. 24–25.

125. See the careful sifting of this case law in McLoughlin, *New England Dissent,* pp. 636–659, 1084–1106, 1189–1284, with summaries in William G. McLoughlin, "The Balkcom Case (1782) and the Pietist Theory of Separation of Church and State," *William & Mary Quarterly,* 3d ser., 24 (1967): 267–283; Cushing, "Notes on Disestablishment in Massachusetts."

126. Amendment, Article 18 (1855) provides that tax "moneys shall never be appropriated to any religious sect for the maintenance exclusively of its own schools." This was superseded by Amendment, Article 46 (1917), which provides, in pertinent part, that "no law shall be passed prohibiting the free exercise of religion" and that no tax money was to be paid to religious groups or activities. Amendment, Article 46, in turn, was further amended by Amendment, Article 103 (1974): "No grant, appropriation, use of public money or property or loan of credit shall be made by the Commonwealth or any political subdivision thereof for the purpose of founding, maintaining, or aiding any . . . charitable or religious undertaking which is not publicly owned and under the exclusive control of [the Commonwealth]." For summary of the cases, see Wilkins, "Judicial Treatment," pp. 892–894.

127. Adams, *Works,* vol. 4, pp. 290, 292–293, 298.

128. See generally John Witte, Jr., and Johan D. van der Vyver, eds., *Religious Human Rights in Global Perspective,* 2 vols. (The Hague/London/Boston: Martinus Nijhoff, 1996).

2

The Use and Abuse of Jefferson's Statute: Separating Church and State in Nineteenth-Century Virginia

Thomas E. Buckley, S.J.

The Mathews County voters in Tidewater Virginia elected Humphrey Billups to the House of Delegates, the lower house of the state legislature, in 1826. A respected member of their community from a prominent family, Billups possessed a fine speaking voice, forensic skill, and strong determination; he would need them all.[1] Although no petitions from Mathews or elsewhere challenged his election, some legislators wanted him disqualified on the grounds that he was a minister of the gospel. Virginia's constitution of 1776 specifically excluded clergy from serving in the assembly; but ten years later the legislature had approved Thomas Jefferson's Statute for Religious Freedom. On the issue of Billups's eligibility for legislative service, the two documents appeared at odds.

The Virginia Statute is central to the story of religious freedom and the development of church–state separation in our republic. In its preamble, Jefferson proclaimed that "our civil rights have no dependence on our religious opinions" and that to exclude a citizen from public office "unless he profess or renounce this or that religious opinion," violated "natural right." The enacting clause concluded that no one should "suffer on account of his religious opinions or belief" and that religious opinion should not "diminish, en-

41

large, or affect their civil capacities." Finally, in a sweeping warning to future generations, the Statute concluded that any legislature that repealed or limited its guarantees violated "natural rights."[2]

What about Billups's rights and civil capacity? When the legislature debated his status, Billups admitted to being a Methodist deacon. Did that make him a minister or not? Speaking for the investigating committee, Henry Watkins summarized the evidence and presented its conclusions. Billups was authorized to preach. His church called him a deacon, not a minister, yet in terms of the constitution, preaching made him a minister and so disqualified him from membership in the House. But Watkins realized the conflict with the Statute, so he appealed over its text to its purpose. Interspersing quotations from Jefferson with the committee's perspective, he argued that while "our civil rights have no dependence on our religious opinions," yet "our ancestors . . . intended to keep separate Church and State."[3]

The constitutional prohibition against clerical legislators, he insisted, was precisely designed to achieve this objective. A historian happening on the scene might have fairly observed that church–state separation had not been the assembly's intent when its members wrote the constitution in 1776, but, rather, this was the interpretation that later Virginians gave Jefferson's Statute. Now, to achieve the Statute's purpose, Watkins proposed that the assembly violate its language. Thanks to Humphrey Billups and the Mathews County voters, the legislators in 1827 found themselves entangled in church–state controversy.

Surely, we can sympathize. Over the past half-century, issues of religious liberty and the respective claims of church and state have repeatedly divided our courts and our nation. The cases are familiar: prayer in public schools, Christmas crèches in public parks, public funding for parochial education—well over a hundred such cases have been litigated since the 1947 *Everson* decision, in which the Supreme Court extended the First Amendment's Establishment Clause to the states. The justices split 5–4 on the issue of that case, but they agreed in their interpretation of the historical background to the religion clauses of the First Amendment.

Speaking for the Court, Justice Hugo Black pointed out that the Virginia Statute had offered the most iron-clad guarantee of religious liberty in the new United States. The First Amendment, Black concluded, intended to provide "the same protection against governmental intrusion on religious liberty as the Virginia Statute." Writing for the minority, Justice Wiley Rutledge embraced Black's interpretive approach. "No provision of the Constitution," he asserted, "is more closely tied to or given content by its generating history than the religious clause of the First Amendment." Indeed, the Virginia Statute belongs, he wrote, to the "warp and woof of our constitutional tradition." From the Court's perspective in 1947, the First Amendment stipulated strict separation of church and state—a "wall of separation," as the justices quoted Jefferson.[4]

At the beginning of the nineteenth century, Virginians claimed that their Statute for Religious Freedom provided the bricks and mortar to build Jefferson's wall of strict separation. In this respect, the Virginia church–state relationship differed notably from those of other states, even as it anticipated the direction the Supreme Court would one day take the nation.[5] But simply invoking the First Amendment has not solved the church–state problematic in twentieth-century America. Nor did appeals to the Statute, first as state law and later as part of the state constitution, settle church–state controversies in the Old Dominion. In his recent prize-winning study, historian Joseph Ellis claimed that Jefferson's "most enduring legacy" was "religious freedom, defined as the complete separation of church and state."[6] Jefferson's legacy belongs first to Virginia. What did "strict" or "complete" separation mean to nineteenth-century Virginians?

This chapter will explore their lived experience of the Statute in the nineteenth century. The issues were multiple and immediate. Scarcely had the ink dried on the law in 1786 when some Virginians challenged the privileged position Episcopalians enjoyed. Shortly after the American Revolution, what had been the established Church of England reorganized itself into the Protestant Episcopal Church in Virginia. The state incorporated it as such and confirmed its title to the churches and church property. The erstwhile dissenters—mainly Presbyterians and Baptists—cried foul; and, after receiving repeated, insistent petitions, the legislature responded, first by repealing the incorporation act and then, as the eighteenth century ended, by voiding all previous laws dealing with religion except the Statute for Religious Freedom. That law became the standard for interpreting Virginia's bill of rights and constitution in terms of church–state relations. A few years later, in the most remarkable socioeconomic reversal in Revolutionary America, the legislature reneged on earlier guarantees and provided for the seizure and sale of the Episcopal Church's glebes, or farm lands. Churches, church plate, and burial grounds were left in Episcopalian hands, however. In a stunning burst of naive optimism, the lawmakers proclaimed that this law was designed "to reconcile all the good people of this commonwealth."[7] Chances of reconciliation were slender to nil. During the next century Virginians wrangled over numerous church–state issues in legislative petitions and newspapers, church meetings, assembly sessions, court cases, and four conventions called to rewrite the state constitution. Out of all the assorted controversies, this chapter will focus on three issues: clerical office-holding, the legal incorporation of churches and religious agencies, and the place of religion in public education. They illustrate the ways Virginians used and abused Jefferson's Statute, their evolving understandings of separation of church and state, and the cultural contexts that determined the settlements they reached.

CLERICAL POLITICIANS

We can begin by revisiting Humphrey Billups's efforts to gain an assembly seat. The legislative committee emphasized the constitutional argument against the Methodist deacon, but Henry Watkins detailed the potent dangers that ministers posed to government. Given the nature of their profession, clergymen would transform the assembly into a forum for theological debates. Once one religious group became dominant, it would impose its sectarian bias on the commonwealth and require the state to fund, in Jefferson's words, "the propagation of opinions in which we do not believe." Evoking vivid images of campground revivals, Watkins warned that charismatic preachers would create turmoil and chaos in the legislative chambers. While rabble-rousers usually belonged to the clergy's baser ranks, Watkins implied that such types were more likely to be elected. Perhaps that was a sly dig at Billups, who had shown himself quite capable of speaking in his own defense.

In an extended rebuttal, he argued that Methodist polity regarded him as simply a local preacher, not as a minister. He possessed no authority in the church and was not authorized to administer its ordinances. Impressive as some legislators found Billups's defense, they remained unconvinced. However Methodists might style him, they thought he fit the constitution's definition of a minister. Ignoring the language of the Statute for Religious Freedom, they disqualified him by a vote of 179 to 2.[8]

In excluding clergymen from the legislature, Virginia was not unusual. Most states did the same. Nor had Jefferson disagreed. Though to his regret he had not had a hand in writing Virginia's 1776 constitution, his draft for a new one in 1783 also excluded clergy. When James Madison challenged him for denying a "civil right" on the basis of "religious profession," Jefferson argued that given their geographical distribution, influential positions, and persuasive skills, ministers would quickly dominate the assembly.[9] He later reversed his position, but his fellow Virginians did not follow suit.[10]

Two years after Billups's exclusion, Mathews County's voters again elected him to the House of Delegates. Before the legislature met, however, the issue of clerical politicians came under full dress review at Virginia's constitutional convention of 1829–1830. The distinguished gathering included former Presidents Madison and Monroe, and Chief Justice John Marshall. From the outset the convention unanimously favored incorporating Jefferson's Statute into the new constitution. But with that motion, several speakers urged the convention to eliminate the disqualification of clergymen. Echoing Madison's judgment voiced half a century earlier, they asserted that such discrimination violated the Statute. But opponents of change appealed to the practice in other states, the wisdom of Virginia's "old constitution," and, most frequently, the radical disjunction between a clerical calling and the worldly concerns of a secular vocation. Repeatedly invoking the gospel text "My kingdom is not of this world," they claimed that ministers were unfit for politics. The last speaker, John Randolph of Roanoke, an evangelical himself, embellished the argument when in apocalyptic terms he warned that "the admission of gentlemen of the cloth" meant "*ipso facto* the union of Church and State." Religious opinions were not at stake, but the mutual incompatibility of professions. Again, the culture spoke. Clerics, like women, were unsuited for the rough and tumble of the legislative halls. It would stain and defile them. "No countries," Randolph concluded, quoting an unnamed authority, "are so ill-governed as those which were ruled by the counsels of women, except such as have been governed by the counsels of priests."[11]

The new constitution included the enacting clause of Jefferson's Statute followed by a prohibition against religious tests. But the section concluded with the explicit statement that "the foregoing clauses shall not be so construed, as to permit any Minister of the Gospel, or Priest of any denomination, to be eligible to either House of the General Assembly." Only fourteen members voted to strike that restriction. Among them were Alexander Campbell, the only minister elected to the convention, and, predictably, James Madison.[12]

While the convention met at the spanking-new Presbyterian Church in Richmond, the legislature assembled a few blocks away at the capitol, with Humphrey Billups on the doorstep. Though the Methodist deacon vigorously asserted that he had quit preaching entirely, the lawmakers remained unpersuaded. In early January 1830, they once more ousted the would-be politician by a vote of 159 to 3.[13]

Clerical exclusion would remain for another forty years. Virginians would separate church and state in their own way, within their own historically conditioned cultural context, rather than depending upon Jeffersonian principles of civil or natural rights.[14] After the Civil War, when the Reconstruction Convention dropped the disqualification of ministers from the constitution of 1868, the language of Jefferson's Statute did not persuade them, but they felt the need to elect legislators who would elevate the moral tone of politics. Having excluded entire categories of white males from political life on grounds of Confederate service, the radicals who controlled the convention may have hoped that some ministers, perhaps high-minded Yankee missionaries, would make able Republican candidates. Context was important then also.[15]

DENYING CORPORATE STATUS

Context also proved critical to the other church–state issue the convention debated in 1829: the incorporation of seminaries and other church-sponsored agencies. Recall that the state legislature had first repealed the incorporation of the Protestant Episcopal Church in 1787 and later proclaimed Jefferson's Statute the sole norm for interpreting Virginia's church–state polity. The prologue to that declaration stated that laws incorporating churches violated the constitution and Jefferson's Statute and tended "to the reestablishment of a National Church."[16] Over the next years, the assembly routinely rejected applications for incorporation from a variety of local churches. A major battle erupted, however, when the Presbyterians led by John Holt Rice, a minister and publisher, petitioned in 1815 for a charter for their seminary. The legislature balked, arguing that such legal support violated the separation required by the Statute for Religious Freedom. Rice and other Presbyterian leaders protested vigorously, but to no avail. They had run into a stone wall marked *"an establishment of religion."*[17]

The Methodists encountered the same intransigence a few years later when they wanted to establish a school for potential ministers. In 1825 trustees appointed by the Virginia Conference of Methodists launched a subscription drive to build Randolph-Macon College with both ministerial education and religious training for laymen in mind.[18] Their petition for incorporation in 1829 touched off an angry debate in the assembly. One delegate attacked the charter bill as a "snake in the grass," whose real purpose was to establish a seminary. Various trustees who were also members of the legislature rejected that intent, but the assembly would have refused to charter Randolph-Macon if its backers had not attached to the incorporation act a rider that the college could never appoint a professor of theology.[19]

The assembly had not debated the Randolph-Macon bill in a vacuum. The nearby constitutional convention had only recently put the finishing touches on the church–state provisions. After disqualifying clergy from legislative service, the convention considered religious incorporation laws. William Brodnax, a long-time civil servant and pious Episcopalian, proposed that the constitution include an explicit statement of legislative freedom to incorporate seminaries and church agencies and organizations with the proviso that the assembly might always revoke and alter any charter so granted. The debate became testy when Alexander Campbell, the future founder of Bethany College, argued against theological education for ministers and warned that such incorporation acts might include provisions requiring public "support of religion." An irritated Brodnax noted sarcastically that schools might at least teach the clergy "good morals and good manners." The *"Right* Reverend" Campbell, he protested, had read something unintended and "expressly prohibited" into his amendment. But the convention rejected it nonetheless.[20]

When, almost a month later, the members finalized their work, the new constitution expressly forbade preferential treatment or special favors for one denomination over another. It also reconfirmed church support as absolutely voluntary. Later that day, Campbell offered an extraordinary amendment: "That no incorporation, for any ecclesiastical or religious purpose, shall ever be granted, or have validity" in Virginia. John Marshall and others objected that such an extreme measure discriminated against religion and denied churches any security in their property. They thought Campbell, in his fear of rich, established churches, misread the American scene and ignored legislative antipathy toward a concentration of church wealth. Philip Norbonne Nicholas, who had served as state attorney general for two decades, expressed the views of the majority. While the commonwealth needed both religion and virtue, the state should treat all denominations equally, protect their free exercise of religion, and "let them alone." In typical Virginia fashion, Nicholas thought the present system worked just fine. When Brodnax moved to reintroduce his incorporation proposal, the weary convention quickly tabled the whole subject, 77 to 19.[21]

Although by silence the constitution left the door open for religious incorporations, the next generation of legislators refused to grant charters to churches, church agencies, and seminaries on the grounds of church–state entanglement. The state court of appeals bolstered this perspective, asserting that such acts would violate Jefferson's Statute, now embedded in Virginia's constitution.[22] This denial of corporate status, unparalleled elsewhere in the United States, left churches and religious groups in legal tangles, without secure titles to their property or the capacity to conduct ordinary secular business. Years earlier John Holt Rice accurately identified the situation: the state treated the church "as a nonentity."[23] But instead of removing the state from religious affairs, this mode of separation kept the churches securely under the civil government's thumb. Rather than religious freedom, it represented a throw-back to colonial times when lay vestries and assemblies controlled the established church in Virginia and strictly regulated dissenters. Now this policy inflicted real hardship, as, for example, when churches and church-sponsored agencies and charities could not receive bequests, because they lacked standing in law.[24]

Legal disabilities, however, did not impede the growing sacralization of Virginia's landscape. Individuals calling themselves trustees continually purchased land or received conveyances for the rapidly growing denominations. When at last in 1842 the assembly finally passed a bill permitting trustees to hold legal title to churches, graveyards, and parsonages, some lawmakers may have intended it as a brake on church expansion and land holdings. The law limited the amount of property a church might own to two acres in town or thirty in the countryside; it said nothing about receiving bequests or engaging in property transactions.[25] Three years later, after protracted debate, the assembly rejected a general incorporation law for churches and church agencies. In 1851 a new constitution explicitly prohibited incorporating "any church or religious denomination" but authorized the legislature to "secure the title to church property to an extent to be limited by law."[26] Instead of separating church and state in any modern American sense, these restrictions on religious groups continually entangled the legislature and the courts in the churches' temporal affairs and provided numerous occasions for legislation and litigation.[27]

The state's court of appeals, in several major church–state cases, explained the legislative and constitutional intent. A determination to control and limit the churches in their acquisition of land and money, not a desire for separation or disengagement, drove government policy. "Wealth is power," wrote Justice George Tucker in 1832. Tucker, Madison, and others in Virginia's ruling class were determined that churches would never amass the wealth and power enjoyed by religious establishments in Britain or pre-Revolutionary France.[28] Significantly, they found allies among some clergymen.

Gradually, however, momentum for change developed. In the 1850s the assembly began to reverse field by incorporating seminaries. Then, in the decades after the Civil War, various church agencies, charities, and benevolent societies sought and received charters. Virginia courts approved these acts.[29] Finally, some members of the constitutional convention of 1901–1902 proposed to drop the prohibition against incorporating churches and to treat religious corporations like any other. Why grant charters to church organizations and refuse them to churches? asked William Gordon Robertson, a prominent lawyer, who pointed out that clergy from various denominations had requested the change. But a Baptist minister, Wayland Dunaway, led the opposition in the convention. His chief ally, Richard McIlwaine, a Presbyterian clergyman and the only other clerical member of the convention, later credited Dunaway with defeating the change.[30]

Proponents argued that forty-three of the forty-six states allowed church incorporation without ill effect to religion or the state, but the ministers thundered back with appeals from scripture. Cries of "My kingdom is not of this world" echoed through the hall. After repeated biblical citations, one wag asked, "Is not the church frequently described in the Scriptures as the bride. Now, the question is, What will the bridegroom do when he comes and finds the bride incorporated?" Advocates for change argued that nonincorporation discriminated against the churches. They characterized Dunaway and his supporters as captives of imaginary fears of a nonexistent "religious octopus" and "chained to a past that is dead and gone."[31]

The past won. The mystique of old Virginia, which Raymond Pulley correctly identified as emblematic of the progressive era in the Old Dominion, held true for church and state as well.[32] In true Jeffersonian fashion, Virginians understood the Statute to guarantee absolute freedom for individual conscience and its fullest expression consonant with public peace. But the document said nothing explicit about the legal rights of communities of believers gathered in churches, meetinghouses, or synagogues. The individual was free; the collectivity was less so. Although membership rolls burgeoned, organized religious bodies enjoyed few corporate rights and faced significant disadvantages. Despite their professed devotion to separation, Virginians did not achieve anything like our present church–state arrangements. Instead, somewhat after the fashion of nineteenth-century anticlerical European states, they sought to dominate and regulate the churches. Fear controlled this policy, particularly in the antebellum era. Fear of undue clerical influence in politics. Fear of excessive ecclesiastical wealth. Fear that one denomination might gain an advantage over the others. And a goodly number of evangelicals, laity and clergy, embraced those fears and supported these policies.

NONSECTARIAN RELIGIOUS EDUCATION

But neither clerical exclusion from the assembly nor the refusal to incorporate churches meant that nineteenth-century Virginians were irreligious. Quite the reverse. Examples abound, but the protracted discussion of education illustrates what church–state separation meant within an evangelical culture.[33] As with Americans today, so also for nineteenth-century Virginians, education represented a core value, the transmission of culture from one generation to the next. As the century unfolded, the Old Dominion increasingly demonstrated a profound commitment to evangelical Protestant Christianity. Legal and constitutional development adjusted and kept pace with that transformation.

The early quarrels over theological education provide a point of entry into the situation. Even before his religious liberty statute became law, Jefferson signaled his own perspective. While Virginia's governor in the last years of the Revolution, he served on the Board of Visitors at William and Mary College. In that capacity, Jefferson helped erase theology from the curriculum. It had no place in his scheme of useful knowledge, so the college eliminated the chair in theology and the Episcopalians lost their training ground for ministers.[34]

We have already noted the problems the assembly presented to Presbyterian John Holt Rice's seminary plans. The Episcopalians tried a different tack. After the War of 1812 and under the dynamic leadership of Bishop Richard Channing Moore, they persuaded the trustees of William and Mary to institute a chair that included, in the bishop's words, "the history and doctrines of Christianity."[35] Meanwhile Episcopalian leaders worked out a novel arrangement with the college trustees. The church would establish a seminary in Williamsburg with a professor of theology. Seminary students, though not enrolled at William and Mary, would be able to attend college lectures *gratis* and use the school's library. Because Virginia refused to incorporate a seminary, the college trustees would manage the seminary's funds.[36] Soon after the newspapers announced these plans, irate articles in the press complained that the proposed relationship between college and seminary violated Jefferson's Statute. Despite Moore's pledge that Episcopalians welcomed all Christians to their school and his suggestion that other denominations might open seminaries of their own in Williamsburg if they wished, his scheme collapsed.[37]

If Brother Rice and Bishop Moore felt frustrated and constrained in their educational designs, so also did ex-President Jefferson. During this same period, he became locked in ferocious controversies over the curriculum and faculty at his proposed University of Virginia. Revivals, camp meetings, preachers, and churches were busily transforming the religious atmosphere of the Old Dominion. In an 1818 report designed to win legislative support, Jefferson felt obliged to justify the exclusion of a "Professor of Divinity" from the faculty of his proposed university. In the first place, he explained, Virginia's constitution placed "all sects . . . on a[n] equal footing, with the jealousy of the different sects in guarding that equality from encroachment and surprise." Second, the General Assembly's views on religious liberty mandated the separation of church and state. How should that be implemented in education?

By implicitly defining theology as sectarian, Jefferson eliminated it from consideration; but he did not exclude religion and morality. In his curriculum design, a "professor of ethics" would treat "the proofs of the being of a God, the creator, preserver, and supreme ruler of the universe, the author of all the relations of morality," with their "laws and obligation." Instruction in those "moral obligations . . . in which all sects agree," together with a study of Hebrew, Greek, and Latin, would provide a basic education "common to all sects" and acceptable to the state's constitution.[38] Where is the wall? Sectarian theology is ruled out, to be sure. But Jefferson is essentially arguing that nonsectarian religious education and moral formation taught under the aegis of moral philosophy did not violate separation of church and state. Some might argue, of course, that he was only proposing his own brand of sectarianism, a vague Unitarianism. Nevertheless, the legislature accepted his interpretation.

A few months after submitting this report, a satisfied Jefferson rejoiced as the assembly approved his university and selected him as its first rector. That position, however, did not give undisputed sway. When he selected Thomas Cooper as his school's first professor, Jefferson found himself challenged by John Holt Rice and other Presbyterian clergy.[39] Rice appealed to the public through the pages of his magazine, and Jefferson lost. Writing to Cooper in 1822, the sage of Monticello lashed out at the Presbyterians, comparing them to Jesuits in their efforts to control education. But only compromise would save his cherished plans. In a desperate effort to defuse the idea that his university would be hostile to Christianity, Jefferson piggybacked on Bishop Moore's proposal for William and Mary. He suggested that various denominations install professors of divinity in separate quarters on the Charlottesville campus to enable students to combine university training with sectarian theological education. Though the churches never seized that opportunity, Jefferson's proposal loosened up building funds in the state's assembly and his "academical village" opened for business in March 1825.[40]

The university would be not irreligious but nonsectarian; and the assembly sought to guarantee that same character to other colleges, even those under denominational auspices. The debate over the Randolph-Macon charter revealed an extraordinary hostility toward "sectarian prejudices" that perdured through the antebellum period. So, for example, the 1839 incorporation act for Methodist Emory and Henry College attempted to ensure that the school would remain nonsectarian. The charter forbade any church from establishing a "theological school or professorship" or having its members constitute a majority of the trustees. Nor could church affiliation be a basis for any position in the college. The next year, charters for the Baptists' Richmond College and Bethany College, founded by Alexander Campbell for the Disciples of Christ, lacked some of these specifics but both included the ban on a professor of theology, a prohibition that continued in other college charters almost to the Civil War.[41]

The absence of a chair in theology, however, did not render collegiate education irreligious.[42] The schools emphasized moral philosophy, taught the Bible, and expected regular attendance at chapel services. College presidents such as Stephen Olin at Randolph Macon and Henry Ruffner at Washington (later Washington and Lee) insisted on the intrinsic connection between religion and morality. Olin pledged to preach "the cross" and teach "the doctrines and sanctions of Christianity." Presbyterian Ruffner, at his inauguration in 1837, argued that philosophy without religion was insufficient. "I shall deem it my indispensable duty," he said, "to teach the Christian religion, to all who will be committed to my charge." But both presidents made clear that the flavor would be nonsectarian. Because Washington College drew students from every denomination, Ruffner pledged that chapel services and classroom instruction would not engage "those theological questions, which unhappily divide our religious community." No denominational peculiarities, he assured the world at large, marred the curriculum, neither "scholastic theology" nor "sectarian bigotry."[43]

But nonsectarian did not mean nondenominational. Methodists, Presbyterians, Baptists, and Disciples of Christ operated their own colleges and Episcopal Bishop Moore worked successfully to keep William and Mary "subservient to the cause of religion in general, and to the good of the Church of Christ"; that is, Episcopalian. His choice for college president and professor of moral philosophy was Adam Empie, an Episcopal minister who conducted services in the school chapel and served as rector of Bruton Parish.[44] At state institutions various denominations contented for supremacy. Presbyterians worried that Colonel Francis Smith, the first superintendent of the

Virginia Military Institute and a "thoroughly stitched Episcopalean," was turning the college into a center for his denomination by bringing in an Episcopalian chaplain, sponsoring services from the Book of Common Prayer, and selecting students mainly from Episcopalian families.[45] In the early years of the University of Virginia some of its trustees and friends anguished over its irreligious character and wondered how that might be rectified without violating Jefferson's Statute. When Episcopal Bishop William Meade preached at faculty request in 1829, he suggested nothing less than the transformation of the curriculum with a new emphasis on Christianity, scripture, and a biblically based morality. His talk provoked strong negative reactions.[46]

By the early 1840s, however, ministers from various denominations rotated services in the Rotunda and the campus Bible society included a majority of students and faculty. Students, faculty, and administrators also voluntarily contributed to pay the salary of a university chaplain. Presbyterian minister William H. McGuffey, editor of the famous series of readers, arrived in 1845 to fill the chair in moral philosophy and, on the side, instructed prospective ministers in theology. For the next several decades, the distinguished professor of law and evangelical Episcopalian, John B. Minor, taught Sunday Bible classes that he clearly expected all his law students to attend; Presbyterian chaplain William Henry Ruffner treated the university to a lecture series, subsequently published, on the "Evidences of Christianity"; and several warm revivals passed through Charlottesville, leaving behind multiple conversions, a missionary society, and the Y.M.C.A. By the eve of the Civil War, as the administration selected a site on which to build a chapel, Mr. Jefferson's university had clearly adopted a nonsectarian evangelical Protestant character.[47]

Below the collegiate level, numerous private schools and academies dotted the landscape for those families who could afford them; but despite elaborate plans and valiant efforts, no state system of publicly funded education existed until after the war. The legislature, by setting aside various sources of public revenue, had established the Literary Fund in 1810 to provide basic schooling for poor children; but the system did not function effectively, in part because it stigmatized the poor and lacked sufficient money. Meanwhile, private academies and denominational colleges also tapped into the Literary Fund to support their strained budgets.[48] Both in private schools, which educated the majority of those white children who achieved literacy, and in county free schools established for poor whites, nonsectarian religious instruction with the Bible as a principal text formed an academic staple. When a few counties in the 1840s opted to establish free schools at their own expense, the legislature insisted that teaching be without denominational bias and texts contain nothing immoral, irreligious, or sectarian in nature.[49]

A major educational convention in northwest Virginia in 1841 urged the churches to support the schoolhouse and distinguished between "a union of church and state" and "the diffusion of Christianity," which would benefit everyone. Addressing the convention, Alexander Campbell expressed a typical antebellum perspective when he asserted that, despite "sectarian differences," Virginians shared "a *common* christianity—that there are certain great fundamental matters—indeed, every thing elementary, is what is properly called piety and morality, in which all good men of all denominations are agreed; and that these great common principles and views form a common ground on which all christian people can unite, harmonize and co-operate in one great system of moral and Christian education."[50] In terms of education, separation of church and state meant nonsectarian Protestant Christianity. That suited the antebellum culture; and no one apparently objected.

Following the Civil War, religion in public education became more controversial. To implement the public school system mandated by the reconstruction constitution of 1868, the General Assembly elected William Henry Ruffner as state superintendent of public instruction. Ruffner had campaigned vigorously for the position and even considered resigning from the ministry lest his preacher status cost him the job. He accurately believed himself eminently qualified. The work would absorb his talents and energies for the next decade.[51]

Negotiating the shoals of religious controversy became his immediate concern. The school legislation in 1870 established a fixed curriculum. On the question of religious instruction, the law said nothing. A recently formed private organization, the Educational Association of Virginia, concerned that public education would be godless, demanded Bible reading as essential for moral development and basic Christian knowledge. Some Presbyterians had supported denominational schools even before the war, and now the Episcopal diocese of Virginia urged parishes to establish their own schools along the lines of the Catholic parochial system.[52] From the outset, Ruffner countered the objection that public schools would be irreligious by arguing that they would reflect the "moral influence" of the neighborhoods in which they were located; but when a local superintendent took it upon himself to ban Bible reading in the schools under his care, Ruffner made his position even more explicit.[53]

First in a published letter in 1871 and later in other newspaper articles and writings, Virginia's foremost educator enunciated a policy he called the "Virginia doctrine," claiming that Jefferson had initiated it in his reports on the University of Virginia. While state schools must not teach or sponsor sectarian doctrines or worship, or prefer one denomination over another, authorities could permit religious activities including Bible reading and instruction, that were compatible with the local community's desires and sensibilities. In sum, it amounted to local option. Conscience rights must be respected and no one be forced to attend either religious services or classes.[54]

A few years later, responding first to Robert Lewis Dabney, the prominent Presbyterian minister and professor at Hampden Sidney, and then to

Bennett Puryear, a Baptist minister and professor at Richmond College, Ruffner amplified his views. Both ministers attacked public education on the grounds that schools funded by the state could not teach religious truth and must consequently become seedbeds of atheism. Ruminating on his own Presbyterian upbringing, Ruffner wondered whether private schools taught religious truth, either. Christian parents, homes, Sunday schools, and churches performed that task, he asserted. But Ruffner hearkened back to Jefferson's plans for moral philosophy at the university. The schools taught "Christian ethics," without teaching sectarianism, Ruffner asserted. The "State may formally teach the recognized morality of the country, and the will of God as the standard and ultimate authority of all morality." Moreover, Virginia law did not forbid religious teaching nor did Virginia law need to mandate it. "Christianity," he argued, "*will go in of itself.*" All public school authorities need do is "regulate voluntary religious observances" and protect minority rights. As for religious education: "schools maintained by free, popular governments of necessity express and conserve the religion of the people."[55]

As state superintendent for over a decade, Ruffner established the standard. In effect, the law's silence left the issue up to local school authorities; and, overwhelmingly, Virginia public schools embraced Bible reading together with other nondenominational Christian activities, such as hymn singing and the recitation of the Lord's Prayer. "The religion of the people," as Ruffner styled it, dominated public education on every level until the Supreme Court intervened in the 1960s.[56] In proposing his chair in moral philosophy and voluntary religious services on the campus of the university, Jefferson had opened the door for possibilities far beyond his own vision. He had wanted to encompass all sects. Virginians agreed. But the exploding evangelical context transformed his educational program of rationalistic religion and moral formation into an expression of the Bible-based Protestant culture that the vast majority of Virginians embraced. This became the staple of the public school system.

CONCLUSION: REDEFINING SEPARATION

In effect, the Old Dominion redefined separation and moved Jefferson's wall out into the midst of Roger Williams's garden. In virtually every area touching church–state life and practice, nineteenth-century Virginians experienced a culturally contextualized separation. Evangelicals controlled the religious dimension of political culture from the time the Statute for Religious Freedom was passed. In demanding repeal of the Episcopal Church's charter and the seizure of the church's lands, Baptists led the fight. In the assemblies and constitutional conventions that restricted clergy from political office for the first two-thirds of the century, evangelicals supplied the votes. In the continuing debates over religious incorporation laws, the clergy opposed one another and repeatedly defeated the movement toward incorporation. It was a minister, William Henry Ruffner, who defined separation in public education. Fidelity to the Statute for Religious Freedom meant not the absence of religious education and worship in the public schools, but freedom from coercion and compulsion. In fairness to Ruffner, he had no other choice if he wanted a public school system. Evangelical Protestants to the core, Virginians would have rejected any other arrangement. As might be expected, the churches provided public support for community-based nonsectarian expressions of religious belief. But surprisingly, some clergy favored regulating, and even restricting, the institutions of believing communities. Motives for this latter position were undoubtedly mixed, but Jefferson was not alone in recognizing the realities of sectarian jealousy and fear.

Throughout the nineteenth century, Virginians claimed that they had separated church and state, but their lived expression of that principle was far different from our own. Their experience underlines the truth of Justice Felix Frankfurter's observation in the *McCullom* case: "the mere formulation of a relevant Constitutional principle is the beginning of the solution of a problem, not its answer. . . . because the meaning of a spacious conception like that of the separation of Church from State is unfolded as appeal is made to the principle from case to case."[57]

The meaning of the Virginia Statute, of separation of church and state, not only unfolded in Virginia, it changed. Its application, like that of the First Amendment, has been and always will be culturally contextualized. Even the strictest separationists, from Thomas Jefferson to Wayland Dunaway, refused to follow rigid principles to their logical, absolute conclusion when they perceived that higher concerns and values were at stake. Jefferson, after all, would have his university, even if it meant clergymen hovering on the edges. At the convention of 1901, Baptist Dunaway, almost single-handedly, turned back the momentum toward church incorporation and spoke long and eloquently against any public support for sectarian institutions. But when the question of taxing churches and parsonages came to the floor, he backpeddled vigorously. The welfare of the commonwealth, he argued, depended upon religion; so the government should recognize it and support it.[58] Most Virginians then, and most Americans today, would agree. Religious freedom we count among our most prized legacies from the founding era. Like the founders, we also recognize the important benefits the religious faith of our people confers on our republic, paradoxically because state and church are separated. Where to place Jefferson's wall, or draw Madison's line, is always the tricky part.[59] One need not be an evangelical to know, that in matters of church and state the devil is in the details.

NOTES

1. His father, Richard Billups (1753–1822), was a merchant and ship builder, who served multiple terms in the House of Delegates and was a major figure in the Methodist church. His brother William Armisted Billups became an important Methodist minister. See Katie-Prince W. Esker, *Billups and Allied Families* (Baltimore, Gateway Press, 1984), pp. 8, 16, 17; Peter Wrike, "Billups of Mathews County, Virginia," *Virginia Tidewater Genealogy* 13 (1982): 61; Mathews County Personal Property Tax Records, 1825–1830 (microfilm), the Library of Virginia, Richmond, Virginia [hereinafter Vi].

2. The text of the statute is in Julian P. Boyd, ed., *The Papers of Thomas Jefferson* (27 vols. to date, Princeton, N.J., Princeton University Press 1950–),Vol. 2, pp. 545–553. For its passage, see Thomas E. Buckley, S.J., *Church and State in Revolutionary Virginia, 1776–1787* (Charlottesville, Va., University of Virginia Press, 1977); and Rhys Isaac, *The Transformation of Virginia, 1740–1790* (Chapel Hill, N.C.,University of North Carolina Press, 1982), pp. 273–295.

3. *Journal of the House of Delegates of Virginia* [hereinafter cited as *JHDV*] (2 February 1827): 132.

4. *Everson v. Board of Education*, 330 U.S. at pp. 13, 18, 33, and 39. The Court had cited the statute earlier in an 1878 Free Exercise case involving plural marriage in Utah Territory. Chief Justice Morrison Waite emphasized Virginia's experience in passing the statute and Madison's and Jefferson's views as normative for interpreting the First Amendment (*Reynolds v. United States*, 98 U.S. at p. 164).

5. See, for example, John Webb Pratt, *Religion, Politics, and Diversity: The Church–State Theme in New York History* (Ithaca, N.Y., Cornell University Press, 1967), pp. 108–116.

6. Joseph J. Ellis, *American Sphinx: The Character of Thomas Jefferson* (New York, Alfred A. Knopf, 1997), p. 296.

7. Samuel Shepherd, ed., *The Statutes at Large of Virginia, 1792–1806: Being a Continuation of Hening* (Richmond, 1835–1836), Vol. 2, p. 314. This contest is recounted in Thomas E. Buckley, S.J., "Evangelicals Triumphant: The Baptists' Assault on the Virginia Glebes, 1786–1801," *William and Mary Quarterly* [hereinafter *WMQ*], 3rd ser., 45 (1988): 33–69.

8. *JHDV* (2 February 1827) 132 (quotations), 133; *The Virginian* [Lynchburg], 9 February 1827, 5. Billups was not the first minister to be excluded. John Corbley, a Baptist minister, had been ruled ineligible in 1777 (*JHDV* [1 November 1777]: 9; Otto Lorenz, "The Virginia Clergy and the American Revolution, 1774–1799," Ph.D. diss., University of Kansas, 1970, p. 274); Edward Folkes, who had been exempted as a minister from militia duty, withdrew his candidacy in 1816 after discovering his ineligibility ("To the Freeholders of Charles-City," *Richmond Enquirer*, 6 April 1816).

9. Boyd, ed., *Papers of Jefferson*, Vol. 1, p. 382; Vol. 6, pp. 297, 311; Vol. 8, p. 470. For the practice in Virginia and elsewhere, see E. G. Swem, "The Disqualification of Ministers in State Constitutions," *WMQ*, 1st ser., 26 (1917): 69–78; Frederick S. LeClercq, "Disqualification of Clergy for Civil Office," *Memphis State University Law*

Review 7 (1977): 555–614; and William M. Hogue, "The Civil Disability of Ministers of Religion in State Constitutions," *Journal of Church and State* 36 (1994): 329–355.

10. Paul Leicester Ford, ed., *The Writings of Thomas Jefferson*, 10 vols. (New York, G. P. Putnam's Sons, 1892–1899), Vol. 9, p. 143.

11. *Proceedings and Debates of the Virginia State Convention of 1829–30* (Richmond, S. Shepherd, 1830), pp. 457–459. Hugh Blair Grigsby observed that Virginia held "a strong distrust of theologians" (*The Virginia Convention of 1829–30* [Da Capo Press reprint; New York, 1971], p. 68); Randolph had faced clerical opposition in his own political campaigns (William Cabell Bruce, *John Randolph of Roanoke, 1773–1833* [New York, G. P. Putnam, 1922], Vol. 1, p. 594).

12. *Journal, Acts and Proceedings, of a General Convention of the Commonwealth of Virginia, Assembled in Richmond, . . .* (Richmond, 1829), p. 130. For Campbell's campaign, see Robert Richardson, *Memoirs of Alexander Campbell . . . ,* 2 vols. (Philadelphia, J. P. Lippincott, 1870), Vol. 2, pp. 304–310. Grigsby criticized him in his history of the convention (*Convention of 1829–30*, pp. 68–69) and even more so in private correspondence (Hugh Blair Grigsby to John N. Tazewell, 31 October 1829, Tazewell Family Papers, 1756–1931, Box 12, Vi). Of the fourteen members who voted to eliminate the clerical restriction, twelve belonged to the reform element at the convention. See Robert P. Sutton, "The Virginia Constitutional Convention of 1829–30· A Profile Analysis of Late Jeffersonian Virginia," Ph.D. diss., University of Virginia, 1967, pp. 265–290.

The convention may have added the prohibition against religious tests in reaction to a proposed amendment that "all persons who disbelieved in God or a future state of rewards and punishments" would be "incapable of being received as witnesses in any Court of law in the Commonwealth" (*Proceedings and Debates . . . 1829 30*, p. 457). For this controversy in New York, see Pratt, *The Church–State Theme in New York*, pp. 121ff.

13. *JHDV,* (8 January 1830): 70–72. Billups later moved to Henrico County. See Humphrey Billups to William A. Billups, 8 April 1846, William A[rmistead] Billups Letters, 1846–1851, ViHi.

14. For Virginia's assault on Jeffersonian principles shortly after his death, see Sutton, "Virginia Constitutional Convention," pp. 180–182.

15. See speech of John C. Underwood in W[illiam] H. Samuel, *The Debates and Proceedings of the Constitutional Convention of the State of Virginia, Assembled at the City of Richmond, Tuesday, December 3, 1867* (Richmond, Office of the New Nation 1868), pp. 458–460; *Journal of the Virginia Constitutional Convention of 1867–1868.* The Supreme Court voided the disqualification of clergy in *McDaniel v. Paty,* 435 U.S. (1978), p. 618.

16. Shepherd, ed., *Statutes at Large*, Vol. 2, p. 149.

17. John H. Rice to William Wirt, 31 January 1816, John Holt Rice Papers, Union Theological Seminary Library, Richmond (photocopy of originals in the Maryland Historical Society, Baltimore). The seminary continued to exist, but the Presbyterian General Assembly, which was incorporated in Pennsylvania, appointed trustees to manage its funds (Records, 23 October 1826, 30 April 1827, Hanover Presbytery, Union

Theological Seminary, pp. 241–246, 293; *Minutes of the General Assembly of the Presbyterian Church in the United States of America with an Appendix, A.D. 1826* [Philadelphia, State Clerk of the Assembly; 1826], pp. 30–31; *Minutes of the General Assembly, 1827* [Philadelphia, State Clerk of the Assembly; 1827], pp. 126–127).

18. "Address, to the Members and Friends of the Methodist Episcopal Church," 13 January 1825; "A Circular Address of the Trustees of Randolph Macon College, to the public generally, and to the Ministers and members of the Methodist Episcopal Church in particular," John Early Papers, McGraw-Page Library, Randolph-Macon College. William Warren Sweet, *Virginia Methodism: A History* (Richmond, Whittet and Shepperson, 1955), pp. 305–335.

19. *Richmond Enquirer*, 30 January 1830, 23.

20. *Proceedings and Debates . . . 1829–30*, pp. 459, 460; H. F. Turner, "General William Henery (sic) Brodnax," *The John P. Branch Historical Papers of Randolph-Macon College* 3 (1909): 15.

21. *Proceedings and Debates . . . 1829-30*, pp. 706–709; *Journal . . . of a General Convention*, pp. 130, 133–135.

22. *Selden v. Overseers of the Poor of Loudoun*, 11 Leigh (1840) p. 132. For a vigorous dissent against the decision upheld by the appeals court, see "A Layman" in *Selden and Others v. the Overseers of the Poor of Loudoun County, and Others* (Richmond? Va., 1825?) in Church pamphlets, VIII, ViHi. Pauline Maier traces the early history of the corporation in the United States in "The Revolutionary Origins of the American Corporation," *WMQ*, 3rd ser., 50 (1993): 51–84.

23. John Holt Rice, "The Mutual Relations of Church and State," Rice Papers. For a recent legal comment on the incorporation situation, see A. E. Dick Howard, *Commentaries on the Constitution of Virginia* (Charlottesville, Va., University Press of Virginia, 1979), Vol. 1, p. 546.

24. For a typical complaint, see Bishop William Meade's report to the Episcopal Convention of 1850 (T. Grayson Dashiell, *A Digest of the Proceedings of the Conventions and Councils in the Diocese of Virginia* [Richmond, Wm. Ellis Jones, 1883], p. 209).

25. *Acts of the General Assembly of Virginia, Passed at the Session of 1841–42* (Richmond, 1842), chap. 102, p. 60. The recorded indentures for the gifts or purchase of church property evidence the growth of the churches, especially the Baptists and Methodists. For a typical pattern, see the following Albemarle County Deed Books. Book 12: 1794, pp. 10–11; Book 15: 1 July 1805, p. 172; Book 16: 12 March 1808, p. 375; Book 25: 23 July 1825, pp. 280–81; Book 26: 2 January 1826, 1 June 1827, pp. 45–46, 381; Book 27: 4 July 1828, 31 July 1829, pp. 192–93, 331–332; Book 29: 5 November 1831, pp. 394–395; Book 30: 22 March, 8 November 1832, 10 January 1833, pp. 73–75, 196–197, 429–430; Book 31: 15 February, 2 December 1833, 2 June, 22 October 1834, pp. 203, 216, 398–400, 491–492; Book 32: 10 October 1834, 25 February 1835, pp. 8–9, 529–531; Book 33: 7 December 1835, 28 April 1836, pp. 83–86, 383–386; Book 34: 19 December 1836, pp. 53–55; Book 35: 15 November 1837, pp. 369-370; Book 36: 1 January 1838, pp. 24–25; Book 38: 17 March, 30 April, 6 July 1840, 25 May 1841, pp. 115–116, 119–120, 361–363, 493–494; Book 39: 12 January 1842, 28 December 1841, 13 January, 17 February 1842, pp. 152–153, 158–159,

173–174, 363–364 (microfilm), Vi. Some of these holdings amounted to more property than the 1842 law would permit.

26. *The Constitution of the Commonwealth of Virginia, Adopted . . . 1851* (Richmond, 1851), p. 22. For the debates over religious incorporation in the 1840s, see Thomas E. Buckley, S.J., "After Disestablishment: Thomas Jefferson's Wall of Separation in Antebellum Virginia," *Journal of Southern History* 61 (1995): 445–480.

27. In 1852 the assembly passed a new law authorizing circuit courts to sell church lands (*Acts of Assembly, 1851–52,* chap. 99, p. 60). But that was not a self-denying ordinance to the legislature, which continued to decide church property issues. See *Acts of the Assembly, 1853–54,* chap. 205, pp. 130–131. For the legal arrangements on the eve of the Civil War, see *The Code of Virginia,* 2d ed. (Richmond, 1860), chap. 77: "Of Church Property and Benevolent Associations," pp. 410–413.

28. *Gallego's Executors v. Attorney General,* 3 Leigh (1832), p. 451 (quote on p. 477). For the same perspective, see, for example, *Seaburn's ex'or v. Seaburn,* 16 Grattan (1859), pp. 430, 432; and *Kelly v. Love's adm'rs,* 20 Grattan (1870), p. 131. For Madison's aversion to religious incorporation, see Elizabeth Fleet, ed., "Madison's 'Detached Memoranda,'" *WMQ,* 3rd ser., 3 (1946): 556–557; and Madison to Jasper Adams, Gaillard Hunt, ed., *The Writings of James Madison,* 9 vols. (New York, G. P. Putnam, 1900–1910), Vol. 9, p. 487.

29. *Trustees v. Guthrie,* 86 Va. (1889), p. 125. For the incorporation of the Episcopalian and Presbyterian seminaries, see *Acts of Assembly, 1853–54,* chap. 107, pp. 65–66; and *Acts of Assembly, 1855–56,* chap. 277, pp. 190–191.

30. *Proceedings and Debates of the Constitutional Convention, 1901–1902* (Richmond, 1906), Vol. 1, pp. 744–759; Richard McIlwaine, *Memories of Three Score Years and Ten* (New York, The Neale Publishing Co., 1908), p. 365. See also Ralph Clipman McDanel, *The Virginia Constitutional Convention of 1901–1902. Johns Hopkins U. Studies in History and Political Science,* ser. 46, no. 3 (Baltimore, Johns Hopkins University Press, 1928), p. 95. For clerical opposition to the general incorporation bill proposed in the 1840s, see Buckley, "After Disestablishment," pp. 457–464.

31. *Proceedings . . . of the Convention, 1901–02,* Vol. 1, pp. 776, 781.

32. Raymond H. Pulley, *Old Virginia Restored: An Interpretation of the Progressive Impulse, 1870–1930* (Charlottesville, Va., University Press of Virginia, 1968).

33. Sadie Bell collected a massive amount of material for her important, though dated, study, *The Church, the State, and Education in Virginia* (Philadelphia, The Science Press Printing Company, 1930).

34. Smith to Jefferson, Boyd, ed., *Papers of Jefferson,* Vol. 2, p. 247; Ford, ed., *Works of Jefferson,* Vol. 1, p. 78; Madison to Ezra Stiles, in *The Literary Diary of Ezra Stiles,* ed. by F. B. Dexter (New York, 1901), Vol. 2, p. 447. For Jefferson's plan for a remodeled William and Mary, see Boyd, ed., *Papers of Jefferson,* Vol. 2, pp. 535–543 and Robert M. Healey, *Jefferson on Religion in Public Education* (New Haven, Yale University Press, 1962), pp. 210–213. According to the most recent school history, the divinity position was restored in 1790 (Susan H. Godson, and others, *The College of William and Mary: A History* [Williamsburg, Va., King and Queen Press, 1993], Vol. 1, pp. 173, 196), but it does not appear to have been activated.

35. Richard Channing Moore to John Hartwell Cocke, 15 July 1819, Cocke Papers, #1480, Alderman Library, University of Virginia, Charlottesville, Va. (hereinafter UVa). Godson, *College of William and Mary*, Vol. 1, pp. 212–213. According to the college president a few years later, the chair was actually titled "History and Humanity" (*Richmond Enquirer*, 5 February 1825).

36. Broadside: "To the Members and Friends of the Protestant Episcopal Church in the Diocese of Virginia," 1821, ViHi; "Literary and Religious Intelligence," *Richmond Enquirer*, 1 June 1821.

37. *Richmond Enquirer*, 14 August 1821. For more of this controversy, see ibid., 27, 31 July, 1821; 7, 17, 21 August 1821; 5 February 1825. Also see Philip Barraud to St. George Tucker, 1 August 1821, Tucker-Coleman Papers, William and Mary College Library, Williamsburg, Va.; Joseph C. Cabell to John H. Cocke, 21 November 1821, Cabell Family Papers, #38–111, Box 14, UVa.; Richard Channing Moore to William Meade, 19 January 1822, 23 August 1823, William Meade Papers, 1822–1862, LC; Richard Channing Moore to [John Stark] Ravenscroft, 1 August 1823, Letterbook D, 5 November 1823, Letterbook E, Richard Channing Moore Letterbooks [xerox of originals in private hands], Virginia Theological Library, Alexandria, Va. Two years later Keith withdrew from William and Mary and with several other clergymen founded the Episcopal seminary at Alexandria (William A. R. Goodwin, *History of the Theological Seminary in Virginia and Its Historical Background* [New York, E. S. Gorham 1923], Vol. 1, pp. 147–149).

38. *JHDV*, 8 December 1818, p. 14. Jefferson probably offered this explanation because a year earlier, the legislature had rejected an amendment to the university bill that would have forbidden "the establishment of any professorship of Theology or Divinity in any of the Academies, or Colleges," supported by the state, "or in the University of Virginia" (*JHDV* [18 February 1817]: 214).

39. John Holt Rice to John Hartwell Cocke, 6 January 1820, Cocke Papers, #640, UVa.

40. Jefferson to Cooper, 2 November 1822, in Ford, ed., *Works of Jefferson*, Vol. 12, p. 271; Thomas Jefferson, "Report . . . to the President and Directors of the Literary Fund," 7 October 1822, *JHDV*, Session of 1822, Appendix 4; Joseph C. Cabell to Thomas Jefferson, 3 February 1823, Nathaniel F. Cabell, ed., *Early History of the University of Virginia as Contained in the Letters of Thomas Jefferson and Joseph C. Cabell* (Richmond, J. W. Randolph, 1856), p. 273; Healey, *Jefferson on Religion in Public Education*, pp. 215–224, 231–240; David E. Swift, "Thomas Jefferson, John Holt Rice and Education in Virginia, 1815–1825, *Journal of Presbyterian History* 49 (1971): 32–58; George M. Marsden, *The Soul of the American University: From Protestant Establishment to Established Nonbelief* (New York and Oxford, Oxford University Press, 1994), pp. 68–78. He had also encountered opposition to building the Rotunda which some thought extravagant. Hence, he noted that religious services would be held there (Joseph C. Cabell to Thomas Jefferson, 6 March 1822, Cabell, ed., *Early History of the University*, p. 248; Jefferson, *Report*, 7 October 1822, p. 3).

41. *Acts of the Assembly, 1839*, chap. 184, p. 136. *Acts of Assembly, 1839–40*, chaps. 115, and 116, pp. 94, 97. Richmond College began as a Baptist seminary. See W. Harrison Daniel, "To Erect a Seminary of Learning," *The Virginia Baptist Register* 5 (1966):

195–210; "The Virginia Baptist Seminary, 1832–1842," Parts 1 and 2, *The Virginia Baptist Register* 9 (1970): 387–406, and 10 (1971): 472–480. For other examples, see the charters of Roanoke College (*Acts of Assembly, 1852–53*, chap. 344, p. 239) and Marshall College (*Acts of Assembly, 1857–58*, chap. 35, p. 213). Nathan Hatch suggests that Campbell's opposition to a "clerical monopoly over learning" led to this ban; but the assembly no doubt required the clause in Bethany's charter as it did in every other Virginia college in this period (Nathan O. Hatch, *The Democratization of American Christianity* [New Haven and London, Yale University Press, 1989], p. 163). Charles Ambler proposed that while the Bethany charter "did not authorize the teaching of theology, it did not forbid it." The college had required courses in "sacred history" and Bible, which were taught by Campbell, and students were expected to attend religious services (Charles H. Ambler, *A History of Education in West Virginia from Early Colonial Times to 1949* [Huntington, West Va., Standard Print and Publishing Co., 1951], p. 119).

42. Some church leaders even accepted Jefferson's position, because it kept ministerial formation under the secure control of church authority (see Landon C. Garland to John Early, 16 December 1839, McGraw-Page Library, Randolph-Macon College).

43. "Inaugural Address, Delivered by the Rev. Stephen Olin," *Southern Literary Messenger* 1 (1834): 16; Henry Ruffner, *Inaugural Address by Henry Ruffner, President of Washington College, Va. Delivered on the Twenty-Second of February 1837* (Lexington, 1837), pp. 9–10. For Olin's explicit religious agenda at Randolph-Macon, see *The Life and Letters of Stephen Olin* 2 vols. (New York, Harper & Brothers, 1853), Vol. 1, pp. 180–187. An educational reformer, Ruffner drew up an elaborate reform for common schools. (Henry Ruffner, "Proposed Plan for the Organization and Support Common Schools in Virginia, . . ." *JHDV*, 1841–1842, Doc. no. 35). See also W. Harrison Daniel, "The Genesis of Richmond College, 1843–1860," *The Virginia Magazine of History and Biography* 83 (1975): 131–149.

44. Petition of Robert Anderson, Williamsburg City, 8 December 1831, Legislative Petitions, Vi. See also Richard Channing Moore to William Meade, 24 August 1826; Moore to Adam Empie, 26 August, 22 September 1827, Letter Book H, Moore Letterbooks; and George Junkin to Francis McFarland, 11 January 1848, Manuscript Collection #100, Washington and Lee University Library, Lexington, Va.

45. A[lfred] Leyburn to James McDowell, 31 January 1843, James McDowell Papers, Southern Historical Collection, University of North Carolina.

46. See, for example, William Meade to John H. Cocke, 29 May 1827, John Faulcon to John H. Cocke, 16 August 1828, Cocke Papers; Nicholas Trist to James Madison, 6 May 1827, Nicholas Philip Trist Papers, 1791–1836, ViHi; William Meade, *Old Churches, Ministers, and Families of Virginia* (Philadelphia, J. B. Lippencott, 1891), Vol. 2, pp. 54-56.

47. William S. White to James McDowell, 3 March 1841, James McDowell Papers, Southern Historical Collection. "The University of Virginia," *Southern Literary Messenger* 8 (1842): 50–54; Robert R. Howison, *A History of Virginia, from its Discovery and Settlement by Europeans to the Present Time* 2 vols. (Philadelphia, Carey & Hart, 1846–1848), Vol. 2, p. 426; Bell, *The Church, the State, and Education*, pp. 384–390. For McGuffey's impact on American education, see John Westerhoff, *McGuffey and*

His Readers: Piety, Morality, and Education in Nineteenth-Century America
(Nashville, Tenn., Abingdon, 1978).

48. President and Director of the Literary Fund to Joseph C. Cabell, 29 June 1811, Cabell Family Papers, Box 8; Cornelius J. Heatwole, *A History of Education in Virginia* (New York, Macmillan, 1916), pp. 100–136. The county commissioners' annual reports detailing the problems may be found in *JHDV*, 1820–1860, Doc. No. 4, Section L.

49. "Books in Use at the Common Schools in 1840," *JHDV*, 1841–1842, Doc. No. 4, p. 40; for typical laws requiring that tax-supported schools have only nonsectarian religious teaching, see *Acts of Assembly, 1846–47*, chaps. 32 and 33, pp. 29–37; and *Acts of Assembly, 1847–48*, chaps. 98 and 101, pp. 64–70, 71–77.

50. "Address of the Educational Convention, Held at Charksburg, Sept. 8, 1841," *JHDV*, 1841–1872, Doc. No. 7, p. 18; Alexander Campbell, "An Address . . . on the Subject of Primary or Common Schools, September 8, 1841," ibid., p. 36. For the significance of such meetings, see A. J. Morrison, *The Beginnings of Public Education in Virginia, 1776–1860: Study of Secondary Schools in Relation to the State Literary Fund* (Richmond, Superintendent of Public Printing, 1917), pp. 13–14.

51. William Henry Ruffner to William Brown, 22 December 1869, *The Central Presbyterian*, Correspondence, 1868–1873, Brock Collection, Box 181; P[eter] T. Penick to W[illiam] Brown, 11 November 1875, *The Central Presbyterian*, Correspondence, 1874–1878, Brock Collection, Box 182, Henry E. Huntington Library, San Marino, Calif.; Walter J. Fraser, Jr., "William Henry Ruffner and the Establishment of Virginia's Public School System, 1870–1874," *Virginia Magazine of History and Biography* 79 (1971): pp. 259–279. Frazer does not mention the church–state issue.

52. *Reports and Other Papers Delivered Before the Educational Association of Virginia, . . . 1867* (n.p., n.d), pp. 11, 13, 15. Though Presbyterians argued bitterly about establishing parochial schools, the Winchester Presbytery had favored it, and ten schools were established in Virginia by 1870 (Lewis Joseph Sherrill, *Presbyterian Parochial Schools, 1846–1870* [New Haven and London, Yale University Press, 1932], 82). For Episcopalian activity and concern that Episcopalian children were attending Catholic schools, see Dashill, *Digest of Proceedings*, pp. 129, 304–309, 311, 327–328.

53. *Report of the Superintendent of Public Instruction*, 28 March 1870, Document No. VI, in Circulars, Vi. For more of the Bible controversy, see B[enjamin] M. Smith, "Merits and Defects of Common School Education in the United States," *Educational Journal of Virginia* 1 (1870): pp. 318–329.

54. William Henry Ruffner, "Religious Worship in the Public Schools," *Educational Journal of Virginia* 2 (1871): 197; and "Religion in the Public Schools," ibid., 5 (1874): 258–262.

55. William Henry Ruffner, *The Public Free School System*, pp. 31, 32. For the newspaper exchange between Dabney and Ruffner on which this publication was based, see *Richmond Enquirer*, 5, 6, 8, 12, 13, 20, 22, 26 April; 6, 10, 17, 24, 28 May; 2 June 1876. Puryear's articles first appeared in the *Southern Planter and Farmer*. See B[ennett] Puryear, *The Public School in Its Relations to the Negro. By Civis. Republished by Request. From the Southern Planter and Farmer* (Richmond, Clemmitt and Jones, 1877), pp. 30–32. For an exchange between Puryear and Ruffner, see *Richmond Enquirer*, 21, 29 July 1876.

56. For a summary judgment, see the editorial in the *Virginia School Journal* 8 (1899): 4. For a Jewish perspective that the schools must become totally secular and so open to all children, see Edward N. Calisch, "The Democracy in the Public Schools," *Virginia School Journal* 6 (May 1897): 152–153. For Bible reading and general Christian education in public school textbooks, see Alvin W. Johnson and Frank H. Yost, *Separation of Church and State in the United States* (revised ed., Minneapolis, University of Minnesota Press, 1948), pp. 33–73; Westerhoff, *McGuffey and His Readers;* and Ruth Miller Elson, *Guardians of Tradition: American Schoolbooks of the Nineteenth Century* (Lincoln, Nebr., University of Nebraska Press, 1964).

57. *McCollum v. Board of Education*, 333 U.S. (1948), p. 203.

58. *Proceedings and Debates . . . 1901–1902*, Vol. 2, pp. 2687–2692.

59. Madison acknowledged the difficulty of drawing "the line of separation, between the rights of Religion and the Civil authority" but, like Jefferson, the operative word here and throughout his writing was *Separation* (Madison to Jasper Adams, September 1833, in Daniel L. Dreisbach, ed., *Religion and Politics in the Early Republic: Jasper Adams and the Church-State Debate* (Lexington, Ky., University Press of Kentucky, 1996), p. 120.

3

Thomas Jefferson, a Mammoth Cheese, and the "Wall of Separation Between Church and State"

Daniel L. Dreisbach

On New Year's Day, 1802, President Thomas Jefferson received a gift of mythic proportions. Amid great fanfare, a "mammoth" Cheshire cheese was delivered to the White House by the itinerant Baptist preacher and political gadfly Elder John Leland (1754–1841). It measured more than four feet in diameter, thirteen feet in circumference, and seventeen inches in height; once cured, it weighed 1,235 pounds. According to eyewitnesses, its crust was painted red and emblazoned with Jefferson's favorite motto: "Rebellion to tyrants is obedience to God."[1]

The cheese was made under Leland's direction by the staunchly Republican and predominantly Baptist citizens of Cheshire, a small farming community in the Berkshire Hills of western Massachusetts. The idea for making a giant cheese to celebrate Jefferson's electoral victory was announced from the pulpit by Leland and enthusiastically endorsed by his congregation. The cheese-makers were both a religious and a political minority subject to legal discrimination in a Commonwealth dominated by a Congregationalist-Federalist establishment.

Much preparation and material was required for such a monumental project. Organizers had to calculate the quantity of available milk and instruct housewives on how to prepare and season the curds. No ordinary cheese press could accommodate a cheese of such gargantuan dimensions, so a modified "cyder" press with a reinforced hoop was constructed. On the morning of July 20, 1801, the devout Baptist families of Cheshire, in their finest Sunday frocks, turned out with pails and tubs of curds for a day of thanksgiving, hymn-singing, and cheese pressing at the centrally located farm of Elisha Brown, Jr. The cheese was distilled from the single day's milk production of nine hundred or more "Republican" cows. (Since this was a gift for Mr. Jefferson, the new Republican president, the milk of "Federalist" cows was scrupulously excluded. Many months later when the cheese began to rot, Leland purportedly explained the decay by saying that undoubtedly the curds of one or two Federalist cows found their way into the cheese.)[2]

The month-long procession bearing the giant cheese to Washington attracted enormous public attention. Large crowds turned out all along the route to witness the spectacle. The cheese was transported down the eastern seaboard by sloop and sleigh, arriving in the Federal City on the evening of December 29 in a "waggon drawn by six horses."[3] (By the time it reached Baltimore, one wag reported, the cheese, now nearly six months removed from the cows, was strong enough to walk the remaining distance to Washington.)[4] The "Mammoth Priest," as Leland was dubbed by the press, recounted that "all the way there and on my return" to Massachusetts he frequently paused to preach to "large congregations" of curious onlookers.[5] The trek to Washington was covered extensively by the popular press, and, as newspapers of the day often had partisan Federalist or Republican affiliation, the mammoth cheese was either ridiculed or praised, respectively.[6]

In one of the most curious spectacles witnessed in the nation's capital, the cheese was personally received by Jefferson on New Year's morning. The Washington press corps reported that the cheese was conveyed down Pennsylvania Avenue on a dray drawn by two horses. The president, dressed in his customary black suit, stood in the White House doorway, arms outstretched, eagerly awaiting the cheese's arrival. The gift was received with an exchange of cordial expressions of mutual admiration and gratitude and exuberant cheese-tasting.[7] The cheese-makers heralded their creation as "the greatest cheese in America, for the greatest man in America." In an address accompanying the cheese, a committee of Cheshire citizens wrote: "It is not the last stone in the Bastile [sic], nor is it of any great consequence as an article of worth, but as a free-will offering, we hope it will be [favorably] received." It was offered, said the Cheshire citizens, "as a pepper-corn of the esteem which we bear to our chief magistrate," as a "mite into the scale of democracy."[8] (A peppercorn is something trivial offered in return for a favor.) The cheese symbolized political support among New England's religious dissenters for Jeffersonian Republicanism, the new administration, and the president's celebrated defense of religious liberty. This most unusual gift, Jefferson informed his son-in-law, Thomas Mann Randolph, Jr., is "an ebullition of the passion of republicanism in a state where it has been under heavy persecution."[9]

The president and the eccentric parson had crossed paths before. Leland was a self-educated preacher-farmer.[10] He was an ardent individualist and democrat who throughout his adult life admired Jefferson's devotion to democratic principles and the rights of conscience. Although a native New Englander, Leland spent nearly fifteen years as an itinerant preacher in central Virginia, where he emerged a leader among the Commonwealth's Baptists. He was instrumental in allying the Baptists with Jefferson and Madison in the bitter Virginia struggle to disestablish the Episcopal Church and secure freedom for religious dissenters. In 1791, Leland returned to New England where he fought arduously and successfully for disestablishment and religious liberty in Connecticut and Massachusetts.[11] According to L. H. Butterfield, Leland "was as courageous and resourceful a champion of the rights of conscience as America has produced."[12] The parson was effusive in his praise of the president. Upon news of Jefferson's election, Leland enthused: "This exertion of the American genius, has brought forth the *Man of the People,* the defender of the rights of man and the rights of conscience, to fill the chair of state. . . . What may we not expect, under the auspices of heaven, while JEFFERSON presides, with *Madison* in state by his side[?] Now the greatest orbit in America is occupied by the brightest orb. . . ."[13]

On the same New Year's Day that Jefferson welcomed Leland to the White House, he penned a letter to the Baptist Association of Danbury, Connecticut. This letter, in our time, has become the *locus classicus* of the notion that the First Amendment separated religion and the civil state, thereby mandating a strictly secular polity. In response to an address of the Danbury Baptists, Jefferson used the celebrated "wall of separation" metaphor to describe the constitutionally prescribed relationship between church and state:

> Believing with you that religion is a matter which lies solely between Man & his God, that he owes account to none other for his faith or his worship, that the legitimate powers of government reach actions only, & not opinions, I contemplate with sovereign reverence that act of the whole American people which declared that *their* legislature should "make no law respecting an establishment of religion, or prohibiting the free exercise thereof," thus building a wall of separation between Church & State.[14]

The missive, Jefferson said, provided an occasion to articulate his views on church–state relations and, in particular, to explain to critics his reasons for refusing to issue presidential proclamations of days for national fasting and thanksgiving.[15]

Occasionally, a metaphor is thought to encapsulate so thoroughly an idea or concept that it passes into the vocabulary as the standard expression of that idea. Such is the case with the graphic phrase "wall of separation between Church & State," which in the twentieth century has profoundly influenced discourse and policy on church–state relations. Jefferson's "wall" is accepted by many Americans as a pithy description of the constitutionally prescribed church–state arrangement. More important, the judiciary has found the metaphor irresistible, adopting it not only as an organizing theme of church–state analysis but also as authoritative gloss on the First Amendment religion provisions.[16]

The communications of the Cheshire and Danbury Baptists, two loyal Republican communities, coincidentally commanded the president's attention on the same day. The "monster" cheese, as Jefferson reportedly called it,[17] symbolized the same issues and themes addressed by the Danbury Baptists. The Cheshire cheese mongers and the Danbury Baptists alike viewed themselves as persecuted and marginalized religious and political minorities in New England states firmly controlled by a Congregationalist-Federalist establishment. Both Baptist communities celebrated Jefferson's election as the harbinger of a new dawn of religious liberty. Jefferson, in return, expressed solidarity with the persecuted New England Baptists in their aspirations for political and religious liberty.

From the summer of 1801 to the spring of 1802, the mammoth cheese received extensive coverage in the popular press. Even before it was fully cured, the cheese had been woven into New England folktales and legends. By late January 1802, copies of the Danbury Baptists' address and Jefferson's reply were appearing in New England Republican journals.[18] At the time, parallels were noted between the Cheshire and Danbury Baptists' expressions to the president and the concurrence of their concerns. Newspapers reported on the mammoth cheese and "wall of separation" in the same column.[19]

Accounts vary as to what eventually happened to the legendary cheese. Remnants remained in the executive mansion for at least a year, and perhaps for another two years or more, where it was prominently displayed and served at important Republican party functions. According to one graphic account, the decaying, maggot-infested remains were unceremoniously dumped into the Potomac River.[20]

The mammoth cheese was for a brief season at once the most celebrated and most lampooned object in America, but in the course of time it faded from public memory as an emblem of the religious dissenters' aspirations for liberty of conscience. Jefferson's "wall," by contrast, represented an idea quietly "sow[n] among the people" that in two centuries, to continue Jefferson's own gardening metaphor, has "germinate[d] and become rooted among their political tenets."[21] Today, the "wall" is a defining image of the constitutional relationship between religion and public life.

Few letters in American history have had such a profound impact on public discourse as Jefferson's Danbury letter, yet surprisingly little has been written about the context in which it was written. Although it is one of Jefferson's most celebrated pronouncements, it is also among his most misunderstood. This chapter describes the circumstances that prompted Jefferson's correspondence with the Connecticut Baptists, reflects on his deliberations in framing the letter, and investigates the origins, use, interpretation, and continuing influence of the "wall of separation" metaphor. Section I examines the correspondence between the Danbury Baptists and President Jefferson. Section II offers an interpretation of Jefferson's metaphor consistent with the text of the

Danbury letter and the context in which it was written. Although Jefferson is often credited with coining the metaphor, section III discusses uses of the metaphor prior to Jefferson's. Attention is focused on references to the "wall of separation" by Roger Williams, the colonial champion of religious liberty, and by James Burgh, an eighteenth-century British political writer widely read in revolutionary America. Section IV briefly tracks the entrance of the metaphor into popular and legal discourse, and surveys judicial comment on the U.S. Supreme Court's reliance on the "wall" as the theme of many church–state pronouncements. Section V, the conclusion, identifies alternatives to and refinements of the "wall" and reflects on the continuing appeal of Jefferson's metaphor to participants in church–state debate.

I. JEFFERSON AND THE DANBURY BAPTISTS

Jefferson was inaugurated the third president of the United States on March 4, 1801, following one of the most bitterly contested presidential elections in American history. Jefferson's religion, or the alleged lack thereof, emerged a critical issue in the campaign.[22] His implacable Federalist opponents vilified him as an unreformed Jacobin, libertine, and atheist. The campaign was so vitriolic that, when news of Jefferson's election swept across the country, housewives in Federalist New England were seen burying the family Bible in their gardens or hiding them in wells because they fully expected the Holy Scriptures to be confiscated and burned by the new administration in Washington.[23]

One pocket of support for Jeffersonian politics in the otherwise rabidly Federalist New England was among the Baptists. The Danbury Baptists wrote to Jefferson on October 7, 1801, congratulating him on his "appointment to the chief Magistracy in the United States."[24] It was not uncommon for civic and religious associations to write messages of courtesy and appreciation to newly elected presidents. Organized in 1790, the Danbury Baptist Association was an alliance of "twenty-six churches, most of them in the Connecticut Valley, stretching from Suffield to Middletown and including several as far west as Amenia, New York." By the turn of the century, "[t]hese twenty-six churches had a total of 1484 members but this number could be multiplied by five to include all the nominal adherents of these churches."[25] The Connecticut Baptists were a religious minority in a state where Congregationalism was the established church. They supported Jefferson politically because of his unflagging commitment to religious liberty.[26] The Danbury Baptists were thus among the minority of Republican partisans in a bastion of ardent Federalist sentiment.[27] In short, like the Cheshire cheese-makers, they were outsiders—a beleaguered religious and political minority in a state where a Congregationalist-Federalist axis dominated political life.

In their letter, the Danbury Baptists celebrated Jefferson's election, affirmed their devotion to religious liberty, and chastised those who had criticized the president "as an enemy of religion & good order" because he refused as civil magistrate to craft "Laws to govern the Kingdom of Christ." The Baptists wrote:

Our Sentiments are uniformly on the side of Religious Liberty—That Religion is at all times and places a Matter between God and Individuals—That no man ought to suffer in Name, person or effects on account of his religious Opinions—That the legitimate Power of civil Government extends no further than to punish the man who *works ill to his neighbour.* But Sir, our constitution of government is not specific. Our antient charter, together with the Laws made coincident therewith, were adopted as the Basis of our government, At the time of our revolution; and such had been our Laws & usages, & such still are; that Religion is consider'd as the first object of Legislation; & therefore what religious privileges we enjoy (as a minor part of the State) we enjoy as favors granted, and not as inalienable rights: and these favors we receive at the expence of such degrading acknowledgements, as are inconsistent with the rights of fre[e]men. It is not to be wondered at therefore; if those, who seek after *power* & *gain* under the pretence of *government* & *Religion* should reproach their fellow men—should reproach their chief Magistrate, as an enemy of religion Law & good order because he will not, dares not assume the prerogative of Jehovah and make Laws to govern the Kingdom of Christ.

Sir, we are sensible that the President of the united States, is not the national Legislator, & also sensible that the national government cannot destroy the Laws of each State; but our hopes are strong that the sentiments of our beloved President, which have had such genial Effect already, like the radiant beams of the Sun, will shine & prevail through all these States and all the world till Hierarchy and tyranny be destroyed from the Earth. Sir, when we reflect on your past services, and see a glow of philanthropy and good will shining forth in a course of more than thirty years we have reason to believe that America's God has raised you up to fill the chair of State out of that good will which he bears to the Millions which you preside over. May God strengthen you for the arduous task which providence & the voice of the people have cal'd you to sustain and support you in your Administration against all the predetermin'd opposition of those who wish to rise to wealth & importance on the poverty and subjection of the people.[28]

The issue of foremost importance to the Baptists was whether "religious privileges" (and the rights of conscience) are rightly regarded as "inalienable rights" or merely as "favors granted" and subject to withdrawal by the civil state. The Baptists, of course, believed that religious liberty was an inalienable right, and they were deeply troubled that the religious privileges of dissenters in Connecticut were treated as favors that could be granted or denied at the whim of political authorities. They described religion as an essentially private matter between an individual and his God. No citizen, they reasoned, ought to suffer civil disability on account of his religious opinions. The legitimate powers of civil government reach actions, but not opinions. These were principles Jefferson embraced, and he reaffirmed them in his reply to the Baptists.

Letters of courtesy, like the one sent by the Danbury Baptists, were not particularly welcomed by the president but neither were they to be lightly dismissed with merely a cordial response in kind. Rather, Jefferson thought such correspondence furnished an occasion for "sowing useful truths & principles among the people, which might germinate and become rooted among their political tenets."[29] Jefferson drafted a response to the Danbury Baptists, which he circulated for comment from two key members of his cabinet. The surviving manuscripts reveal that Jefferson's reply to the Connecticut Baptists was written with meticulous care and planned effect. The fact that a rough draft of the letter, with scribbled amendments and a margin note explaining one major change, was retained in Jefferson's papers along with a copy of the final version indicates the significance the president attached to this statement.

Although the Danbury Baptists did not request a religious proclamation,[30] Jefferson thought their letter provided an opportunity to explain why he declined to follow the tradition of Presidents George Washington and John Adams in designating days for public fasting and thanksgiving.[31] Jefferson had been criticized for departing from the practice of his presidential predecessors and virtually all state chief executives who routinely designated days for prayer, fasting, and thanksgiving.[32] The president used his response to the Baptists, wrote Constance B. Schulz, to communicate his true convictions on matters of faith and morality to loyal "Republicans in New England, who might be sensitive to or confused by" the Federalist press's unrelenting attacks on Jefferson's alleged immorality and irreligion.[33] Edward S. Corwin speculated that Jefferson's Federalist tormentors were the intended audience. The missive, Corwin quipped, "was not improbably motivated by an impish desire to heave a brick at the Congregationalist-Federalist hierarchy of Connecticut, whose leading members had denounced him two years before as an 'infidel' and 'atheist.'"[34]

Drawing on the recently revealed text of a preliminary draft of the Danbury letter,[35] James H. Hutson similarly argued that the Danbury letter served both to soothe Jefferson's allies and frustrate his enemies. It was a political statement written to reassure Jefferson's Baptist constituents in New England of his continuing commitment to their religious rights and to strike back at the Federalist-Congregationalist establishment in Connecticut for shamelessly vilifying him as an "infidel" and "atheist" in the rancorous presidential campaign of 1800.[36] More specifically, Jefferson used the Danbury letter to explain his refusal to "proclaim fastings & thanksgivings,"[37] and thus diffuse a thorny political controversy his opponents had used to bait him in a continuing campaign to smear Jefferson as an enemy of religion. Indeed, the propriety of executive thanksgiving and fast-day proclamations was a highly politicized issue in both the Adams and Jefferson administrations, exploited by partisans on all sides to demonize political opponents.[38] Before posting his considered response, Jefferson solicited the political advice and comment of "his chief consultants on New England," Attorney General Levi Lincoln, a Massachusetts Republican, and Postmaster General Gideon Granger, a Connecticut Republican.[39] Jefferson's own notes reveal that political considerations guided his revision of the letter. He explained, for example, that a sentence in a preliminary draft was omitted from the final version "on the suggestion that it might give uneasiness to some of our republican friends."[40] Only days after it was written, the letter was reprinted in partisan Republican newspapers, where it served its maximum political purpose.[41] (This suggests that Jefferson was writing for an audience beyond the Danbury Baptists—namely, the New England Federalists.) Jefferson candidly acknowledged in his letter to Lincoln an objective to use statements, such as his reply to the Baptists, to inform the people's "political tenets."[42] For these and other reasons, Hutson concluded that the president "regarded his reply to the Danbury Baptists as a political letter, not as a dispassionate theoretical pronouncement on the relations between government and religion." In short, "it was meant to be a political manifesto, nothing more."[43]

In any case, Jefferson was acutely aware of the political implications of his pronouncement on a delicate church–state issue. Therefore, he solicited the political advice of New England representatives in his cabinet. In a brief note to Levi Lincoln, Jefferson remarked that "the Baptist address . . . furnishes an occasion too, which I have long wished to find, of saying why I do not proclaim fastings & thanksgivings, as my predecessors did. [T]he address to be sure does not point at this, and it's [sic] introduction is awkward. [B]ut I foresee no opportunity of doing it more pertinently. I know," the president candidly acknowledged, "[my response] will give great offence to the New England clergy: but the advocate for religious freedom is to expect neither peace nor forgiveness from them. [W]ill you be so good," he asked Lincoln, "as to examine the answer and suggest any alterations which might prevent an ill effect, or promote a good one, among *the people?* [Y]ou understand the temper of those in the North, and can weaken it therefore to their stomachs: it is at present seasoned to the Southern taste only."[44]

Jefferson confided in Lincoln his hope that the letter would contain "useful truths & principles" that "might germinate and become rooted among [the people's] political tenets."[45] Significantly, while Jefferson believed his separationist construction of the First Amendment revealed "useful truths & principles," he implicitly conceded that it was not yet a political tenet accepted by the people. The admission that "his position did not reflect then-prevailing public attitudes," observed one scholar, makes it difficult to maintain that the general separationist themes of the Danbury letter (or at least their most radical, sweeping implications) were widely and popularly accepted in the founding era as the proper construction of the constitutional principles governing church–state relations.[46]

In compliance with the president's request, Lincoln perused the letter and promptly returned his comments. The attorney general counseled caution and tact in the manner of Jefferson's expression. Not only the Federalists-Congregationalists, but also the Republicans in New England, he warned, might be offended by Jefferson's departure from the ancient and venerable "habit of observing fasts and thanksgivings in performance of proclamations from their respective Executives. . . . I think the religious sentiment expressed in your proposed answer of importance to be communicated, but that it would be best to have it so guarded, as to be incapable of having it construed into an implied censure of the usages of any of the States."[47] Lincoln's advice apparently prompted Jefferson to delete the following sentence from his preliminary draft: "Congress thus inhibited from acts respecting religion, and the Executive authorised only to execute their acts, I have refrained from prescribing even occasional performances of devotion, prescribed indeed legally where an Executive is the legal head of a national church, but subject here, as religious exercises only to the voluntary regulations and discipline of each respective sect."[48] (The excised language included the only oblique reference to executive proclamations of religious devotion, which Jefferson told Lincoln was an issue he wanted to address in the letter.)

Gideon Granger, whom Jefferson "entrusted with important party responsibilities in Connecticut," registered less political concern than Lincoln with the response to the Danbury Baptists.[49] Indeed, he opined that the president had expressed truths embraced by the "great Majority" of New Englanders, including nearly half the citizens of Connecticut. Therefore, he recommended that nothing be changed, even though Jefferson's response might "occasion a temporary Spasm among the Established Religionists."[50]

Jefferson considered the comments of Lincoln and Granger and within hours composed the final draft of a letter sent to the Danbury Baptists. The president wrote:

> To messrs. Nehemiah Dodge, Ephraim Robbins, & Stephen S. Nelson, a committee of the Danbury Baptist association in the state of Connecticut.
>
> Gentlemen
>
> The affectionate sentiments of esteem and approbation which you are so good as to express towards me, on behalf of the Danbury Baptist association, give me the highest satisfaction. [M]y duties dictate a faithful & zealous pursuit of the interests of my constituents, & in proportion as they are persuaded of my fidelity to those duties, the discharge of them becomes more and more pleasing.

Believing with you that religion is a matter which lies solely between Man &
his God,[51] that he owes account to none other for his faith or his worship, that
the legitimate[52] powers of government reach actions only, & not opinions, I contemplate with sovereign reverence that act of the whole American people which
declared that *their* legislature should "make no law respecting an establishment
of religion, or prohibiting the free exercise thereof,"[53] thus building a wall of separation[54] between Church & State.[55] [A]dhering to this expression of the supreme
will of the nation in behalf of the rights of conscience, I shall see with sincere satisfaction the progress of those sentiments which tend to restore to man all his natural rights, convinced he has no natural right in opposition to his social duties.[56]

I reciprocate your kind prayers for the protection & blessing of the common
father and creator of man, and tender you for yourselves & your religious association,[57] assurances of my high respect & esteem.

Th: Jefferson
Jan. 1. 1802.[58]

Memorable phrases and key principles in Jefferson's reply correspond to
language in the Danbury Baptists' address. Both letters, for example, asserted in similar language that religion is an essentially private "matter which
lies solely between Man & his God." Both maintained that "the legitimate
powers of government reach actions only, & not opinions."[59] The Baptists
drew on sentiments Jefferson had championed in the celebrated Virginia
Statute for Establishing Religious Freedom and in other public pronouncements on the rights of conscience. Jefferson, no doubt, was genuinely offended by discrimination against religious minorities in Connecticut, and he
expressed the desire that the rights of conscience protected from infringement by the federal government would be enjoyed by citizens in the respective states. Following his metaphoric construction of the First Amendment, Jefferson wrote: "adhering to this expression of the supreme will of the
nation in behalf of the rights of conscience, I shall see with sincere satisfaction the progress of those sentiments which tend to restore to man all his natural rights, convinced he has no natural right in opposition to his social duties." Jefferson's remarks parallel the desire expressed by the Danbury
Baptists in their address: "our hopes are strong that the sentiments of our
beloved President, which have had such genial Effect already, like the radiant beams of the Sun, will shine & prevail through all these States and all the
world till Hierarchy and tyranny be destroyed from the Earth." Both Jefferson and the Baptists understood that, as a matter of federalism, the nation's
chief executive could not disturb church–state relationships and policies
governing religious liberty in the respective states. In their letter, the Baptists
observed: "Sir, we are sensible that the President of the united States, is not
the national Legislator, & also sensible that the national government cannot
destroy the Laws of each State."

The "wall," strictly speaking, was a metaphoric construction of the First Amendment, which governed relations between religion and the *national* government. Therefore, this "wall" did not specifically address relations between religion and *state* authorities. It is not self-evident that Jefferson thought the metaphor, more generally, described his views on the constitutional and prudential relationship between religion and *all* civil government.[60]

It is also striking, as historian Jon Butler observed, that Jefferson "subtly shifted the First Amendment's meaning in the most complex ways" when he described an ideal "wall of separation between Church & State." His use of "the term *church* inevitably narrowed the meaning of an amendment concerned instead with religion and government." The word *church* rather than *religion* in Jefferson's restatement of the First Amendment emphasized that the constitutional separation was between ecclesiastical *institutions* and the civil state. His choice of language, no doubt, appealed to pious, evangelical Protestant dissenters who disapproved of established churches but believed religion played an indispensable role in public life.[61]

How much significance did Jefferson attach to the "wall of separation" metaphor? Did he regard it as the defining motif of his church-state views? The "wall" was neither Jefferson's first nor his last word on the constitutional and prudential relationship between church and state. So far as the extant evidence indicates, he never again used the "wall" metaphor. In short, there is little evidence that Jefferson thought the "wall" expressed a universal principle or encapsulated the most salient aspects of his church–state views.

What was Jefferson's understanding of the "wall" metaphor as it was used in the Danbury letter? This is the historical question to which attention is now turned.

II. JEFFERSON'S UNDERSTANDING OF THE "WALL OF SEPARATION"

The "wall" Jefferson erected in his letter to the Danbury Baptists served primarily to separate state and nation in matters pertaining to religion rather than to separate ecclesiastical and all governmental authorities. The principal importance of his "wall," like the First Amendment it metaphorically represents, is its clear delineation of the legitimate jurisdictions of federal and state governments on religious matters. In short, the "wall" constructed by Jefferson separated the federal regime, on one side, and ecclesiastical institutions and state governments, on the other. This jurisdictional interpretation of the metaphor is rooted in the text, structure, and historic, pre-Fourteenth Amendment understanding of the Bill of Rights, in general, and the First Amendment, in particular. This view is buttressed by the text of the Danbury letter (including evidence gleaned from a preliminary draft), as well as by

Jefferson's explanation of the letter and his stance on specific church–state issues apparently addressed in his correspondence with the Baptists.

Jefferson and Thanksgiving Day Proclamations

While, as president, Jefferson refused to designate a day for public fasting, thanksgiving, and prayer, his general views on the propriety of such proclamations by civil magistrates is not entirely free of ambiguity. His refusal to issue religious proclamations, despite some political costs, is often portrayed as an example of his principled commitment to church–state separation. Jefferson's stance on religious proclamations merits further scrutiny.

In his correspondence with Levi Lincoln, Jefferson said the Danbury letter "furnishes an occasion too, which I have long wished to find, of saying why I do not proclaim fastings & thanksgivings, as my predecessors did."[62] Jefferson, perhaps, wanted to address this topic since religious proclamations had emerged a sensitive political issue in the days leading to the election of 1800. President John Adams's recommendation for a national "day of solemn humiliation, fasting, and prayer," issued in March 1799,[63] was used by his political adversaries to depict him as a tool of conservative religionists intent on establishing a national church. "A general suspicion prevailed," Adams recounted more than a decade later, "that the Presbyterian Church [which was presumed to be behind the proclamation] was ambitious and aimed at an establishment as a national church." While disclaiming any involvement in such a scheme, Adams ruefully reported that he "was represented as a Presbyterian [which he was not] and at the head of this political and ecclesiastical project. The secret whisper ran though all the sects, 'Let us have Jefferson, Madison, Burr, anybody, whether they be philosophers, Deists, or even atheists, rather than a Presbyterian President.'"[64] This reservoir of opposition to "national fasts and thanksgivings," according to Adams, cost him the election in 1800. Jefferson was the political beneficiary, if not the instigator, of this sentiment and, no doubt, was eager to go on the record denouncing presidential religious proclamations. This episode challenges the often-repeated claim that Jefferson steadfastly refused to issue religious proclamations despite political costs, thereby emphasizing that his position was principled. Clearly, political benefits, as well as costs, accompanied action on either side of this controversial issue.

In the Danbury letter, Jefferson concluded that the First Amendment prohibited the president of the United States from issuing religious proclamations. Yet, as president, he employed rhetoric in official utterances that, in terms of religious content, was virtually indistinguishable from the traditional thanksgiving day proclamations issued by his presidential predecessors and state chief executives.[65] In his first annual message, for example, he wrote: "While we devoutly return thanks to the beneficent Being who has been pleased to breathe into them the spirit of conciliation and forgiveness, we are bound with peculiar gratitude to be thankful to him that our own peace has been preserved through so perilous a season, and ourselves permitted quietly to cultivate the earth and to practice and improve those arts which tend to increase our comforts."[66] His second annual message to Congress opened with the following thanksgiving: "When we assemble together, fellow citizens, to consider the state of our beloved country, our just attentions are first drawn to those pleasing circumstances which mark the goodness of that Being from whose favor they flow, and the large measure of thankfulness we owe for his bounty."[67] His public papers are replete with similar expressions of thanksgiving and devotion. More important to the present discussion, Jefferson had a hand in crafting proclamations for religious observances when he was an elected official in his native Commonwealth. A careful scrutiny of Jefferson's public record on this issue buttresses a jurisdictional interpretation of the "wall" erected in the Danbury letter.

In marked contrast to the separationist message of the Danbury letter, Jefferson demonstrated a willingness to issue religious proclamations in colonial and state government settings. For example, as a member of the House of Burgesses, on May 24, 1774, he participated in drafting and enacting a resolution designating a "Day of Fasting, Humiliation, and Prayer."[68] Jefferson recounted in his *Autobiography:*

> We were under conviction of the necessity of arousing our people from the lethargy into which they had fallen, as to passing events [the Boston port bill]; and thought that the appointment of a day of general fasting and prayer would be most likely to call up and alarm their attention. . . . [W]e cooked up a resolution . . . for appointing the 1st day of June, on which the portbill was to commence, for a day of fasting, humiliation, and prayer, to implore Heaven to avert from us the evils of civil war, to inspire us with firmness in support of our rights, and to turn the hearts of the King and Parliament to moderation and justice.[69]

Jefferson seemed pleased with this accommodation between religion and the state in May 1774 through a "cooked up" religious proclamation issued to excite a public reaction against England.[70] In 1779, when Jefferson was governor of Virginia, he issued a proclamation appointing "a day of publick and solemn thanksgiving and prayer to Almighty God."[71] (This proclamation was issued after Jefferson had penned his famous "Bill for Establishing Religious Freedom.") Also, in the late 1770s, as chair of the Virginia Committee of Revisors, Jefferson was chief architect of a revised code that included a measure entitled "A Bill for Appointing Days of Public Fasting and Thanksgiving."[72] This legislation apparently was framed by Jefferson and introduced in the Virginia legislature by James Madison on October 31, 1785.[73] The bill authorized "the Governor, or Chief Magistrate [of the Commonwealth], with the advice of the Council," to designate days for thanksgiving and fasting and to notify the public by proclamation. Far from simply granting the governor power to appoint "days of public fasting and humiliation, or thanksgiving," the bill included the following punitive provision: "Every minister of the gospel shall on each day so to be appointed, attend and perform divine service and preach a sermon, or discourse, suited to the occasion, in his church, on pain of forfeiting fifty pounds for every failure, not having a reasonable excuse."[74] Although the measure was never enacted, it was sponsored by Madison, and a surviving manuscript copy of the bill bears a notation in the "clerk's hand," indicating that it was "endorsed" by Jefferson.[75] The final disposition of this legislation is unimportant to the present discussion. The relevant consideration here is that Jefferson and Madison jointly sponsored a bill that authorized Virginia's chief executive to designate days in the public calendar for fasting and thanksgiving.

A Jurisdictional Interpretation of the "Wall"

How is Jefferson's record on religious proclamations in Virginia reconciled with the position taken in the Danbury letter? A careful review of Jefferson's actions throughout his public career suggests that he believed, as a matter of federalism, the national government had no jurisdiction in religious matters, whereas state governments were authorized to accommodate and even prescribe religious exercises. Therefore, Jefferson saw no inconsistency in authoring a religious proclamation as a state official and refusing to release a similar proclamation as the federal chief executive. The "wall" metaphor was not offered as a general pronouncement on the prudential relationship between religion and all civil government; rather, it was, more specifically, a statement delineating the legitimate constitutional jurisdictions of the federal and state governments on matters pertaining to religion. Jefferson's "wall," strictly speaking, was a gloss on the First Amendment, and it arguably had less to do with the separation between church and all civil government than with the separation between the federal and state governments. As a figurative device to illuminate the First Amendment, the "wall" is limited to the scope of the First Amendment. One way to interpret the metaphor is to ascertain Jefferson's understanding of the First Amendment.

The U.S. Constitution provided for a national government of limited, strictly delegated, and enumerated powers. Those matters not explicitly entrusted to the federal government were assumed to be reserved by the individual or the states (so far as they legitimately resided in any governmental authority). "American federalism as formulated in the Constitution," Mark DeWolfe Howe noted, "made national disability the rule and national power the exception."[76] Since the new federal government had delegated powers only, and affirmative power in the religious sphere had not been so delegated, it was acknowledged that authority over religious matters was not extended to the federal regime, and the states were free to maintain their own church–state arrangements and policies. Moreover, by imposing its restrictions specifically on "Congress," the First Amendment affirmed, by implication, that the states retained authority to determine church–state policies within their respective jurisdictions.[77] Neither the Article VI, clause 3 ban on religious tests for federal officeholders nor the First Amendment religion provisions were "laid upon the individual states. . . . Broad as were the principles upon which the national government was based, the matter of church establishment or dis-establishment, of taxation compulsory or voluntary contribution, of test acts, oaths and religious qualifications for office, was left entirely to the discretion of the sovereign states."[78] Indeed, some states retained religious establishments well into the nineteenth century. Each state was free to define the content and scope of civil and religious liberties and structure church–state arrangements pursuant to its own constitution, declaration of rights, and statutes.[79] In short, ratification of the U.S. Constitution in 1788 and the Bill of Rights in 1791 had no immediate legal effect on church–state arrangements in the states and altered nothing in matters regarding federal involvement with religion. They merely made explicit the jurisdictional policies that were already implicit in the constitutional order.

The federal Bill of Rights, which includes the First Amendment, served a dual purpose: to assure the citizenry that the federal government would not encroach upon the civil and religious liberties of individuals, and to guarantee the states that the federal government would not usurp the states' jurisdiction over civil and religious liberties.[80] The Bill of Rights embodied a principle of federalism; it was essentially a states' rights document. "Indeed, the federalism of the Bill of Rights was widely regarded in 1791 as far more important than the protection it afforded to the individual. Odd as it may seem today, the First Amendment was not only a guarantee to the individual that Congress could not establish a national religion, but also a guarantee to the states that they were free to determine the meaning of religious establishment within their jurisdictions, and to newly establish, maintain, or disestablish religion as they saw fit."[81] This accords with Edward S. Corwin's observation that "the principal importance of the [First] Amendment lay in the separation which it effected between the respective jurisdictions of State and nation regarding religion, rather than in its bearing on the question of the Separation of Church and State."[82]

This was the prevailing interpretation of the Bill of Rights and the First Amendment shared by Jefferson and his contemporaries. Chief Justice John Marshall, writing for a united Court in *Barron v. Baltimore* (1833), declared that the liberties guaranteed in the Bill of Rights "contain no expression indicating an intention to apply them to the state governments."[83] Specifically addressing religious liberty in the Constitution, the Supreme Court ruled unanimously in *Permoli v. Municipality* (1845) that "[t]he Constitution makes no provision for protecting the citizens of the respective States in their religious liberties; this is left to the state constitutions and laws: nor is there any inhibition imposed by the Constitution of the United States in this respect on the states."[84] Justice Joseph Story concurred in his authoritative *Commentaries on the Constitution of the United States* (1833). The purpose of the First Amendment, he wrote, was "to exclude from the national government all power to act upon the subject [of religion]."[85] He further opined that "the whole power over the subject of religion is left exclusively to the state governments, to be acted upon according to their own sense of justice, and the state constitutions. . . ."[86]

Jefferson embraced this jurisdictional view, which was virtually unchallenged in the founding era. In an 1808 letter to the Reverend Samuel Miller, written, like the Danbury Baptist letter, to explain Jefferson's refusal to issue thanksgiving day proclamations, Jefferson wrote: "I consider the government of the United States as interdicted by the Constitution from intermeddling with religious institutions, their doctrines, discipline, or exercises. This results not only from the provision that no law shall be made respecting the establishment or free exercise of religion [First Amendment], but from that also which reserves to the States the powers not delegated to the United States [Tenth Amendment]. Certainly, no power to prescribe any religious exercise, or to assume authority in religious discipline, has been delegated to the General [i.e., federal] Government. It must then rest with the States, as far as it can be in any human authority."[87] (Note how Jefferson tied together the First and Tenth Amendments to explain his reasons, rooted in federalism, for refusing to appoint a day for religious observance.) Jefferson thought other important First Amendment rights were similarly subject to state jurisdiction. For example, notwithstanding his commitment to a free press, he acknowledged in an 1804 letter to Abigail Adams that, as a matter of federalism, regulation of the press was a matter of state sovereignty: "While we deny that Congress have a right to control the freedom of the press, we have ever asserted the right of the States, and their exclusive right, to do so."[88]

Addressing the issue of thanksgiving day proclamations in his letter to Samuel Miller, Jefferson specifically relied upon the Tenth Amendment principles of federalism and strictly delegated powers. He took the position that since no authority to appoint days for religious observance was delegated to the federal government (including the nation's chief executive), one must assume, pursuant to the Tenth Amendment and the principle of limited federal powers, that power in religious matters was "reserved to the States respectively, or to the people."[89] Jefferson, in short, acknowledged state sovereignty, rather than federal supremacy, in matters of religious liberty and establishment. He did not think the principle of federalism was inconsistent or at odds with the goals of separationism inasmuch as both were concerned with checking the power of civil government, thereby protecting the rights of conscience.[90] The states, Jefferson believed, provided a valuable check on the abuse of these rights by the federal regime.[91] The separation of powers and checks and balances, which were indispensable features of American federalism, provided vital protections for liberty that in Jefferson's view were arguably more important than a bill of rights. Although Jefferson, no doubt, desired each state through its respective constitutions and laws to protect the natural rights of citizens, it is unlikely that he thought the First Amendment with its "wall of separation" was the appropriate device to achieve this goal. The use of a First Amendment wall to protect dissenters' religious rights in the states would have dangerously undermined that other great protector of civil and religious liberty—federalism.

Additional confirmation that the "wall of separation" was erected between religion (i.e., the church) and the federal regime is found in Jefferson's second inaugural address delivered in March 1805:[92]

> In matters of religion, I have considered that its free exercise is placed by the constitution independent of the powers of the general [i.e., federal] government. I have therefore undertaken, on no occasion, to prescribe the religious exercises suited to it; but have left them, as the constitution found them, under the direction and discipline of State or Church authorities acknowledged by the several religious societies.[93]

The second inaugural address and the letter to Samuel Miller addressed concerns identical to those raised in the Danbury letter. One could argue that, in a sense, these subsequent statements were Jefferson's own commentary on the "wall of separation."

Strictly speaking, Jefferson's "wall" was a metaphoric construction of the First Amendment, which governed relations between religion and the *national* government. His "wall," therefore, did not and *could not* specifically address relations between religion and *state* authorities. It is not self-evident that Jefferson thought the metaphor, more generally, usefully represented a universal, prudential doctrine of church–state relations governing the interaction between religion and *all* civil government—local, state, and federal.[94] Jefferson's "wall" expressly described the First Amendment and, thus, is appropriately construed in the context of the federalist design for the Bill of Rights.[95]

Jefferson qualified his separationist stance with another separation of powers argument. A constitutional question addressed in the Danbury letter was whether the First Amendment restricted only the *Congress* in matters respecting an establishment of religion, or whether its prohibitions extended to the coequal branches of the federal government (and the entire federal government), thereby denying the executive branch the prerogative to issue religious proclamations.[96] "I contemplate with sovereign reverence," Jefferson wrote, "*that act of the whole American people* [i.e., the people's ratification of the First Amendment] which declared that *their legislature* [i.e., the federal Congress] should 'make no law respecting an establishment of religion, or prohibiting the free exercise thereof [First Amendment religion clauses],' thus building a wall of separation between Church & State" (emphasis added). Since the powers of the executive are derivative of the creative powers of the legislature, Jefferson concluded that he, as president, could not assume power over matters (such as religion) denied Congress. This separation of powers argument was made forcefully in a sentence Jefferson included in the initial draft, but deleted from the final version, of the Danbury letter: "Congress thus inhibited from acts respecting religion, and the Executive authorised only to execute their acts, I have refrained from prescribing even occasional performances of devotion."[97] The text suggests, and Jefferson's actions as president confirm, that he concluded that the *federal* chief executive was as restrained in making religious proclamations as he believed the U.S. Congress to be pursuant to the First Amendment. This argument relating to the three branches of the federal government coincided with the federalism argument. The powers explicitly denied Congress were, in short, the powers denied all branches and agencies of the federal government. Therefore, the president, like Congress, must refrain from prescribing "performances of devotion."

Jefferson took seriously the jurisdictional prohibition on federal involvement with religion, and in this respect he was more separationist than virtually all of his contemporaries. He went further than most national public figures of his day in limiting the federal government's acknowledgment of, or interaction with, religion. Many of Jefferson's contemporaries, by contrast, did not believe thanksgiving proclamations by the national executive constituted a direct exercise of power over the subject of religion; thus, they did not view the practice as a violation of federalism or the nonestablishment provision.[98] By taking the position that thanksgiving day proclamations by the federal chief executive offended the First Amendment, he adopted a more extreme view than the First Congress and his two presidential predecessors. Indeed, Jefferson's views on this matter were outside the mainstream. The strictures of the First and Tenth Amendments notwithstanding, the First Congress, which framed the First Amendment, called on President George Washington to appoint "a day of public thanksgiving and prayer,"[99] and appointed legislative chaplains paid from the public treasury.[100] Both Presidents Washington and Adams designated days in the public calendar for religious observance.[101] By staking out a radical separationist position (in both the church–state and federalism senses) *at the federal level,* Jefferson was sowing principles that, as he implicitly conceded in his letter to Lincoln, were not yet political tenets widely and popularly accepted by the people.[102]

A First Amendment "Wall"

The Danbury letter touched on a variety of issues worthy of analysis, one of which was the principle of church–state separation. A comprehensive examination of Jefferson's church–state views is beyond the scope of this chapter. The purpose and function of the "wall" he erected, however, are under review. The "wall of separation" unquestionably was a figurative device used to describe the First Amendment, which explicitly prohibited Congress from making laws "respecting an establishment of religion, or prohibiting the free exercise thereof." Prior to incorporation by way of the Fourteenth Amendment,[103] the First Amendment imposed its restrictions only on Congress and, by extension, Jefferson concluded, the entire federal regime. In short, the "wall" Jefferson erected in the Danbury letter was between the federal government, on one side, and church authorities and state governments, on the other. Pursuant to the First and Tenth Amendments and the purely executive nature of his office, President Jefferson concluded that while state governments had the authority to act on matters pertaining to religion, such power was denied the entire federal government, including the national chief executive. Accordingly, Jefferson saw no contradiction in authoring a religious proclamation to be issued by *state* authorities and refusing to issue a similar proclamation as the *federal* chief executive.

Jefferson clearly disapproved of discrimination against the Baptists in Connecticut. In his address, he looked forward to the "progress of those sentiments which tend to restore to man all his natural rights. . . ." It is unlikely, however, that Jefferson thought the First Amendment "wall," which he described in the Danbury letter, was the device to achieve the "progress of those sentiments" at the state level.[104] The argument that a "wall" erected by the First Amendment was an instrument for church–state separation in the respective sovereign states would have been contrary to the fundamental principle of federalism; the unchallenged jurisdictional understanding of the federal Bill of Rights; and Jefferson's commitment to a limited federal government, the sovereignty of the states, and a separation of powers between the state and national governments that served to protect the liberties of the people.[105] It is plausible, even likely, that Jefferson desired each state through its respective constitutions and laws to erect its own wall of separation between ecclesiastical and state authorities, but these state walls would not be the same First Amendment "wall" described in the Danbury letter. There is every reason to believe that he would have wanted the states to follow the model implemented in Virginia with passage in 1786 of his celebrated "Statute for Establishing Religious Freedom." In his 1808 letter to the Reverend Miller, Jefferson once again ardently defended the rights of conscience with arguments applicable, it would seem, to both state and federal magistrates;[106] but, as in the Danbury letter, while he specifically denied that the federal government had the "power to prescribe any religious exercise," he acknowledged that such power "rest[s] with the States, as far as it can be in any human authority." Notwithstanding the useful purposes Jefferson thought were served by the First Amendment "wall," he understood that its strictures were not imposed on state governments or the voluntary religious societies.

Jefferson's "wall," like the First Amendment, affirmed the policy of federalism. This policy emphasized that all governmental authority over religious matters was allocated to the states. The metaphor's principal function was to delineate the legitimate jurisdictions of state and nation on religious issues, and it was largely devoid of substantive content independent of its federalism. Insofar as Jefferson's "wall," like the First Amendment, was primarily jurisdictional in nature, it offered little in the way of a substantive right or universal principle of religious liberty.[107] This controverts the conventional notion that Jefferson's metaphor encapsulated a general constitutional, prudential, and libertarian doctrine of church–state relationships and religious liberty. Indeed, a jurisdictional understanding of the "wall" raises serious questions regarding the way the metaphor is typically used by courts and commentators and recommends an honest reappraisal of the propriety of its conventional use in discourse on church and state. There is no evidence that Jefferson considered the metaphor the quintessential symbolic expression of his church–state views. There is little evidence to indicate that Jefferson thought the metaphor encapsulated a *universal* principle of religious liberty or the prudential relationships between religion and *all* civil government (local, state, and federal). There is much evidence, as set forth above, that the "wall" has been used in ways—rhetorically and substantively—that its architect almost certainly would not have recognized and, perhaps, would have repudiated.

III. EARLY USES OF THE "WALL" METAPHOR

Although Jefferson is often credited with coining the "wall of separation" metaphor, he was not the first to use it in discourse on church–state relations. Indeed, the separation of ecclesiastical and civil authorities was a familiar theme of the age. It is not certain, however, that Jefferson was familiar with earlier references to the metaphor (indeed, there is evidence that in at least one case he did not know of the metaphor's use).

A century and a half before Jefferson penned the Danbury letter, the colonial champion of religious liberty, Roger Williams (1603?–1683), erected a "wall of separation" to serve an arguably different purpose than Jefferson's "wall." Williams's earlier, lesser-known, and essentially theological expression was used in stark contrast to Jefferson's later and primarily political version.[108] Williams's construction of the "wall" is found in a 1644 tract entitled

"Mr. Cotton's Letter Lately Printed, Examined and Answered." The Separatist Williams, who agitated for a complete separation of the civil state from the true church as a necessary presupposition for liberty of conscience, clashed with the preeminent Massachusetts clergyman John Cotton. A conservative Puritan divine, Cotton promoted the idea that there was one objective, revealed truth of God articulated to a Christian society by the visible, organized church and defended by a civil state (ordained by God) and by godly civil magistrates.[109] In a response to Cotton, Williams set forth the necessity for a "hedge or wall of separation":

> [T]he faithful labors of many witnesses of Jesus Christ, extant to the world, abundantly proving that the church of the Jews under the Old Testament in the type and the church of the Christians under the New Testament in the antitype were both separate from the world; and that when they have opened a gap in the hedge or wall of separation between the garden of the church and the wilderness of the world, God hath ever broke down the wall itself, removed the candlestick, and made His garden a wilderness, as at this day. And that therefore if He will ever please to restore His garden and paradise again, it must of necessity be walled in peculiarly unto Himself from the world; and that all that shall be saved out of the world are to be transplanted out of the wilderness of the world, and added unto His church or garden.[110]

Williams's evangelical view held that a "wall of separation" was peculiarly appropriate to safeguard the "most sweet and fragrant *Garden* of the *Church*"[111] (and religious truth) from the rough and corrupting hand of the world.[112] "When the imagination of Roger Williams built the wall of separation," according to legal historian Mark DeWolfe Howe, "it was not because he was fearful that without such a barrier the arm of the church would extend its reach. It was, rather, the dread of the worldly corruptions which might consume the churches if sturdy fences against the wilderness were not maintained."[113] In contrast, the Enlightenment perspective attributed to Jefferson viewed the First Amendment "wall of separation" as a device to safeguard the secular polity "against ecclesiastical depredations and excursions" or to protect civil society from sectarian strife.[114] Howe concluded that "if the First Amendment codified a figure of speech[,] it embraced the believing affirmations of Roger Williams and his heirs no less firmly than it did the questioning doubts of Thomas Jefferson and the Enlightenment."[115] Howe lamented that in the modern mind the Enlightenment construction of the "wall" had eclipsed Williams's religious motives.

Critics have charged that Howe's interpretation of Williams's "wall" is simplistic, if not erroneous. For example, both David Little and William Lee Miller contended that Williams believed that both the civil state and the church have their proper, divinely ordained functions and that, contrary to Howe's suggestion, Williams was as critical of the pretensions of ecclesiastical authority to encroach upon the legitimate activities of the civil state as he was of the tendency of civil authorities to regulate the church.[116] Similarly disputing Howe's characterization of Williams's "wall," Timothy L. Hall observed that "Williams viewed it as a sign of disrespect of the secular city when the Church usurped the authority God had granted to the civil magistrate. He thus complained that the clergy, relying on state support, had made the civil magistrates 'but *steps* and *stirrops* to ascend and mount up into their *rich* and *honourable Seats* and *Saddles*.'"[117]

Several commentators have speculated that in his message to the Danbury Baptists, Jefferson deliberately borrowed a figure of speech used by Roger Williams, a colonial Baptist leader whose legacy was revered in Baptist circles. Howe opined that Jefferson's imagery "could easily, perhaps even properly, be read as an ingratiating effort to echo a Baptist orthodoxy."[118] While Jefferson almost certainly knew of Roger Williams, there is little, if any, evidence that Jefferson was familiar with Williams's use of the "wall" metaphor. In his religious biography of Jefferson, Edwin S. Gaustad reported that "[n]o evidence survives of Jefferson's or Madison's having read Roger Williams."[119] Williams's works, which for the most part were published in England, were not generally accessible or widely read in America until they were republished in the mid-nineteenth century.[120] Other commentators have argued more broadly that Williams's views had a negligible impact on the development of religious liberty in the founding era. "As for any direct influence of his thought on the ultimate achievement of religious liberty in America," Perry Miller bluntly concluded, "he had none."[121]

A more plausible source for Jefferson's "wall" metaphor is the work of the dissenting Scottish schoolmaster James Burgh (1714–1775). Although largely unknown to modern audiences, this radical Whig Commonwealthman was "one of Britain's foremost spokesmen for political reform," whose writings influenced political thought in revolutionary America.[122] Jefferson read and admired the Scotsman's work and quite likely encountered Burgh's use of the "wall of separation" metaphor in his extensive readings.

The Real Whigs or Commonwealthmen, with whom Burgh is often associated,

> espoused the right of resistance, separation of powers, freedom of thought, religious toleration, the secularization of education, and the extension of the rights of Englishmen to all mankind, including the less privileged sections of British society. . . . [T]hey advocated reforms including the extension of the franchise, reapportionment of legislative representation, annual parliaments, rotation in office, and the exclusion of placemen and pensioners from the House of Commons.[123]

Burgh and his fellow reformers shared a faith in "science, education, and the application of the principles of correct reason to the problems of the day. Earnestly dedicated to doing right, they believed in the power of moderate common sense and knowledge to improve the lot of their fellow men."[124]

In keeping with the Commonwealthman tradition, Burgh promoted reforms in various areas of mid-eighteenth-century English life, including parliamentary government, the standing army, public education, rhetoric and grammar, public morals and manners, poor relief, and religious toleration. He not only promoted his own reforms, but also drew on and popularized the ideas of others. His three-volume *magnum opus, Political Disquisitions* (1774–1775), was a veritable sourcebook of reform ideas.[125]

Burgh was a man of faith, as well as a man of reason. Indeed, he was preoccupied with religion, which was the wellspring of his politics and his moral code.[126] In this respect, he was not alone among the Commonwealthmen, who were "dominated and controlled" by religion. As Colin Bonwick observed: "Religious belief . . . suffused their entire understanding of political morality and behavior and nourished their conceptualization of social and governmental processes."[127]

Burgh brought to his writings a dissenter's zeal for religious toleration and a distrust of established churches. Indeed, his antipathy to ecclesiastical establishments was a logical extension of his staunch defense of religious toleration.[128] Burgh thought religion was a matter between God and one's conscience; and he contended that two citizens with different religious views are "both equally fit for being employed, in the service of our country."[129] He alerted his audience to the potential corrupting influences of established churches. Danger existed, he warned, in "a church's getting too much power into her hands, and turning religion into a mere state-engine."[130] Therefore, in his work *Crito* (1766, 1767), Burgh proposed building "an impenetrable wall of *separation* between things *sacred* and *civil*."[131] He dismissed the conventional argument that the public administration of the church was necessary to preserve religion's salutary influence in society.

> I will fairly tell you what will be the consequences of your setting up such a mixed-mungrel-spiritual-temporal-secular-ecclesiastical establishment. You will make the dispensers of religion *despicable* and *odious* to all men of sense, and will destroy the *spirituality,* in which consists the whole *value,* of religion. . . .
>
> Shew yourselves superior to all these follies and knaveries. Put into the hands of the *people* the clerical emoluments; and let them give them to whom they will; *choosing* their public teachers, and maintaining them decently, but *moderately,* as becomes their *spiritual* character. We have in our times a proof, from the conduct of some among us, in respect of the appointment of their public administrators of religion, that such a scheme will answer all the necessary purposes, and prevent infinite corruption;—*ecclesiastical* corruption; the most odious of all corruption.
>
> Build an impenetrable wall of *separation* between things *sacred* and *civil.* Do not send a *graceless* officer, reeking from the arms of his *trull,* to the performance of a *holy* rite of *religion,* as a test for his holding the command of a regiment. To *profane,* in such a manner, a religion, which you pretend to *reverence;* is an impiety sufficient to bring down upon your heads, the roof of the sacred building you thus defile.[132]

Burgh concluded that entanglements between religion and the civil state led to the very corruption that establishmentarians argued was countered by an ecclesiastical establishment.

Jefferson admired and recommended Burgh's writings. In 1790, he advised Thomas Mann Randolph, his future son-in-law, that a young man preparing for a legal career should read, among other works, Smith's *Wealth of Nations,* Montesquieu's *Spirit of Laws* (with reservations), Locke's "little book on Government," the *Federalist,* Burgh's *Political Disquisitions,* and Hume's *Political Essays.*[133] In 1803, while president, he even "urged" one of Burgh's books on Congress.[134] Given his enthusiasm for Burgh's work, it is plausible that Jefferson's construction of the First Amendment was influenced by Burgh's recommendation for "an impenetrable wall of separation." Jefferson was not the only American in the founding era who admired Burgh's writings.[135] The Philadelphia publisher of *Political Disquisitions* (who "published [the treatise in America] on a subscription basis within sixteen months of the English" edition)[136] listed over one hundred prominent American "encouragers" or subscribers, including George Washington, Thomas Jefferson, Samuel Chase, John Dickinson, John Hancock, Robert Morris, Benjamin Rush, Roger Sherman, and James Wilson.[137] Oscar and Mary Handlin, the first twentieth-century authors to "rediscover" Burgh, opined that the Scotsman "was as close to American thought as any European of his time."[138]

For various reasons, Burgh's considerable influence on the founding generation has been relegated to a historical footnote. If, in fact, Jefferson appropriated Burgh's figure of speech in the Danbury letter, the Scotsman's most enduring impact on American political thought may well be the "wall" metaphor.[139] Interestingly, Burgh dedicated the second volume of *Crito* "To The Good People of BRITAIN of THE TWENTIETH CENTURY," because he expected "twentieth-century gentlemen and ladies to be of a more composed way of thinking than my contemporaries."[140] It was only in the last half of the twentieth century, since *Everson v. Board of Education* (1947), that the "wall" metaphor emerged as a popular symbol of church–state relations in the United States. Burgh was perhaps correct to believe that only a "twentieth-century" audience would be receptive to his ideas. In the Danbury letter, Jefferson, like Burgh, seems to have looked forward to a day when there would be wide acceptance of his understanding of the rights of conscience.[141]

IV. "USEFUL TRUTHS AND PRINCIPLES . . . GERMINATE AND BECOME ROOTED" IN THE AMERICAN MIND

Jefferson's letter to the Danbury Baptists was printed almost immediately, which must have pleased the president, who hoped the "useful truths & principles" sown in the letter "might germinate and become rooted among [the people's] political tenets." In the course of time, the celebrated "wall" metaphor profoundly influenced, if not defined, public debate on the constitutionally prescribed relationship between church and state in the United States. By late January 1802, a number of partisan journals in New England had published the full text of both the Baptists' address and Jefferson's response.[142] Following the letter's initial printing, it would be some time before it was republished in a forum accessible to a wide audience. The letter was not included in the first collection of Jefferson's papers, printed in 1829.[143] Another two decades passed before the letter was published in a new collection of Jefferson's writings. In 1853 Henry A. Washington was commissioned by the U.S. government to compile a comprehensive edition of Jefferson's works.[144] Washington's nine-volume collection included both Jefferson's letter to Levi Lincoln and the final response to the Danbury Baptists.

It is difficult to track the entrance of the "wall" metaphor into popular and scholarly discourse and its emergence as a basic theme of church–state discussion. There are occasional references to the "wall" metaphor and the Danbury letter in late-nineteenth-century church–state commentaries. For example, the respected nineteenth-century jurist and U.S. attorney general, Jeremiah S. Black, spoke of a "wall" in an 1856 lecture on religious liberty in the United States:

> The manifest object of the men who framed the institutions of this country, was to have a *State without religion,* and a *Church without politics*—that is to say, they meant that one should never be used as an engine for any purpose of the other, and that no man's rights in one should be tested by his opinions about the other. As the Church takes no note of men's political differences, so the State looks with equal eye on all the modes of religious faith. The Church may give her preferment to a Tory, and the State may be served by a heretic. Our fathers seem to have been perfectly sincere in their belief that the members of the Church would be more patriotic, and the citizens of the State more religious, by keeping their respective functions entirely separate. For that reason they built up a wall of complete and perfect partition between the two.[145]

Church historian Philip Schaff excerpted the Danbury letter in his influential paper, *Church and State in the United States* (1888).[146]

The phrase "wall of separation" entered the lexicon of American constitutional law in 1878. In *Reynolds v. United States,* the U.S. Supreme Court opined that the Danbury letter "may be accepted almost as an authoritative declaration of the scope and effect of the [first] amendment thus secured."[147] Nearly seven decades later, in the landmark case of *Everson v. Board of Education* (1947), the Supreme Court returned to the metaphor: "In the words of Jefferson, the [First Amendment] clause against establishment of religion by law was intended to erect 'a wall of separation between church and State.'

. . . That wall," the justices concluded in a sweeping separationist declaration, "must be kept high and impregnable. We could not approve the slightest breach."[148]

Judicial uses of the metaphor have not been without criticism and controversy. A year after *Everson,* Justice Stanley F. Reed denounced the Court's reliance on the metaphor. "A rule of law," he protested, "should not be drawn from a figure of speech."[149] Over a decade later in the first school-prayer case, Justice Potter Stewart similarly cautioned his judicial brethren. The Court's task in resolving complex constitutional controversies, he opined, "is not responsibly aided by the uncritical invocation of metaphors like the 'wall of separation,' a phrase nowhere to be found in the Constitution."[150] Justice Robert H. Jackson quipped that, absent sure "legal guidance" in this matter, the justices "are likely to make the legal 'wall of separation between church and state' as winding as the famous serpentine wall designed by Mr. Jefferson for the University he founded."[151] Justice Thurgood Marshall warned that "[t]he metaphor of a 'wall' or impassable barrier between Church and State, taken too literally, may mislead constitutional analysis."[152] A few months later, Chief Justice Warren E. Burger seemingly disavowed the metaphor: "Judicial caveats against entanglement must recognize that the line of separation, far from being a 'wall,' is a blurred, indistinct, and variable barrier depending on all the circumstances of a particular relationship."[153] Chief Justice William H. Rehnquist, perhaps the most vociferous critic of the "wall," concluded:

> It is impossible to build sound constitutional doctrine upon a mistaken understanding of constitutional history, but unfortunately the Establishment Clause has been expressly freighted with Jefferson's misleading metaphor for nearly 40 years. Thomas Jefferson was of course in France at the time the constitutional Amendments known as the Bill of Rights were passed by Congress and ratified by the States. His letter to the Danbury Baptist Association was a short note of courtesy, written 14 years after the Amendments were passed by Congress. He would seem to any detached observer as a less than ideal source of contemporary history as to the meaning of the Religion Clauses of the First Amendment.
>
> . . . There is simply no historical foundation for the proposition that the Framers [of the First Amendment] intended to build the "wall of separation" that was constitutionalized in *Everson.*
>
> Notwithstanding the absence of a historical basis for this theory of rigid separation, the wall idea might well have served as a useful albeit misguided analytical concept, had it led this Court to unified and principled results in Establishment Clause cases. The opposite, unfortunately, has been true; in the 38 years since *Everson* our Establishment Clause cases have been neither principled nor unified. Our recent opinions, many of them hopelessly divided pluralities, have with embarrassing candor conceded that the "wall of separation" is merely a "blurred, indistinct, and variable barrier," which "is not wholly accurate" and can only be "dimly perceived." *Lemon v. Kurtzman,* 403 U.S. 602, 614

(1971); *Tilton v. Richardson,* 403 U.S. 672, 677–678 (1971); *Wolman v. Walter,* 433 U.S. 229, 236 (1977); *Lynch v. Donnelly,* 465 U.S. 668, 673 (1984).

Whether due to its lack of historical support or its practical unworkability, the *Everson* "wall" has proved all but useless as a guide to sound constitutional adjudication. . . . [N]o amount of repetition of historical errors in judicial opinions can make the errors true. The "wall of separation between church and State" is a metaphor based on bad history, a metaphor which has proved useless as a guide to judging. It should be frankly and explicitly abandoned.[154]

"It is one of the misfortunes of the law," Justice Oliver Wendell Holmes observed, "that ideas become encysted in phrases, and thereafter for a long time cease to provoke further analysis."[155] Figures of speech designed to simplify and liberate thought end often by trivializing or enslaving it. Therefore, as Justice Benjamin Cardozo counseled, "[m]etaphors in law are to be narrowly watched."[156] Critics of judicial reliance on the "wall" metaphor say this is advice courts would do well to heed.

V. CONCLUSION: THE MENDING WALL?

Jefferson was not alone among his contemporaries in championing metaphoric barriers for protecting civil and religious liberties. For example, in a May 1789 letter to the United Baptist Churches in Virginia, written only months before Congress drafted the First Amendment, President George Washington wrote that if the Constitution "might possibly endanger the religious rights of any ecclesiastical Society" or the federal "Government might ever be so administered as to render the liberty of conscience insecure," then he would labor zealously "to establish effectual barriers against the horrors of spiritual tyranny, and every species of religious persecution."[157] In his celebrated "Memorial and Remonstrance Against Religious Assessments," James Madison argued that "[t]he preservation of a free Government requires not merely, that the metes and bounds which separate each department of power be invariably maintained; but more especially that neither of them be suffered to overleap the great Barrier which defends the rights of the people."[158]

In an 1833 letter to the Reverend Jasper Adams, a South Carolina educator and moral philosopher, Madison crafted a subtle metaphor that acknowledged the complex and shifting intersection of church and state: "I must admit, moreover, that it may not be easy, in every possible case, to trace the *line of separation,* between the rights of Religion & the Civil authority, with such distinctness, as to avoid collisions & doubts on unessential points."[159] Proponents of Madison's "line of separation" argue that it describes more precisely actual church–state relationships in the United States than Jefferson's "wall." A wall conjures up the image of "two distinct and settled institutions in the society once and for all time separated by a clearly defined and impregnable barrier."[160] Walls also tend to set "two sides at odds with one another, as antagonists."[161] Madison's "line" is fluid, adaptable to changing relationships, and, unlike Jefferson's "wall," can be overstepped.[162]

Critics of the "wall" argue that it has done what walls frequently do—it has obstructed the view. The Supreme Court's use of the metaphor has polarized students of church–state relations and, in application, has frequently excluded religious citizens from public life and discourse.[163] Jefferson's figurative language, detractors continue, has not produced the solutions that its apparent clarity and directness led the wall-builders to expect. It has obfuscated our understanding of constitutional principles.[164] Indeed, it has unnecessarily infused the church–state debate in modern America with inflexibility and fostered distortions and confusion. The "wall" metaphor, some critics complain, mischaracterizes the First Amendment. Paul G. Kauper argued that "the Court's adoption of Jefferson's statement about the establishment of a wall suggests that separation of church and state is the ultimate principle in the first amendment. This view is subject to the criticism so aptly made by Professor [Wilber] Katz that religious freedom is the ultimate value captured in the twin religion clause and that separation is a supplemental principle which is useful in so far as it serves to protect and advance religious freedom."[165] Further, the First Amendment prohibition on religious establishment was a clear restraint on the power of civil government to give legal preference to any single sect or combination of sects or to invade the religious domain. A "wall," however, is a bilateral barrier that also prevents religion from influencing the conduct of civil government and public life. This inhibition on religion, critics say, exceeds the limitations imposed by the Constitution. Therefore, the critics reflect with the poet Robert Frost who observed in his eloquent poem "Mending Wall": "Something there is that doesn't love a wall / That wants it down."[166]

The "wall," proponents counter, has profitably illuminated our understanding of the constitutional arrangement for church–state relations. In *Larkin v. Grendel's Den* (1982), Chief Justice Warren E. Burger, who had earlier expressed misgivings about Jefferson's imagery,[167] praised the metaphor: "Jefferson's idea of a 'wall' . . . was a useful figurative illustration to emphasize the concept of separateness. . . . [T]he concept of a 'wall' of separation is a useful signpost."[168] A commitment to church–state separation, proponents argue, does not necessarily signal indifference, much less hostility, toward religion. Indeed, defenders of strict separation often argue that true religion flourishes when left to the voluntary support of adherents without assistance from or entanglements with civil government. Religious liberty cannot survive as long as civil government enforces belief in religious dogma or is entangled with ecclesiastical institutions. Therefore, defenders say a "wall of separation" is a useful construct for avoiding destructive sectarian conflict and governmental interference with religion and for promoting the voluntary support of religion in an environment in which freedom of religion can flourish. As Justice Wiley B. Rutledge remarked in *Everson:* "we have staked the very existence of our country on the faith that complete separation between the state and religion is best for the state and best for religion."[169] Constitutional historian Leonard W. Levy effusively praised the metaphor: "Despite its detractors and despite its leaks, cracks, and its archways, the wall ranks as one of the mightiest monuments of constitutional government in this nation."[170] Also quoting Frost, the defender of the "wall," regarding Jefferson as a paternal figure, "will not go behind his father's saying, / And he likes having thought of it so well / He says again, 'Good fences make good neighbours.'"[171]

As Jefferson desired, the seeds of "useful truths & principles" sown in the Danbury letter have "germinate[d] and become rooted" in the American public mind. His celebrated metaphor has entered the lexicon of popular, scholarly, and legal discourse on the prudential and constitutional relationship between religion and civil government. The "wall" was built in the midst of controversy and has continued to generate querulous debate. For as long as Americans care deeply about religion and politics, it will, no doubt, continue to provoke controversy, as its proponents and opponents debate whether it informs or distorts constitutional doctrines regarding the nonestablishment and free exercise of religion. The "wall" stands as one of Jefferson's most poignant and enduring contributions to the vocabulary of American politics and jurisprudence. As architect of the "wall of separation," it could be said, in the words of John Adams's memorable deathbed declaration, that "Thomas Jefferson still survives."[172]

NOTES

An earlier version of this chapter appeared in *Journal of Church and State* 39 (Summer 1997): 455–501, and is reprinted by permission.

1. For a discussion of Jefferson's affinity for this motto, see *The Papers of Thomas Jefferson,* ed. Julian P. Boyd, 27 vols. to date (Princeton, N.J.: Princeton University Press, 1950–), vol. 1, pp. 494–497, 677–679 [hereinafter *Papers of Jefferson*]; Dumas Malone, *Jefferson and His Time,* vol. 1, *Jefferson the Virginian* (Boston: Little, Brown and Co., 1948), pp. 242–243.

2. For the fullest account of the making of the cheese, see C. A. Browne, "Elder John Leland and the Mammoth Cheshire Cheese," *Agricultural History* XVIII (1944): 145–153. For contemporaneous accounts, see *Impartial Observer* (Providence, R.I.), 8 August 1801, as quoted in L. H. Butterfield, "Elder John Leland, Jeffersonian Itinerant," *Proceedings of the American Antiquarian Society* LXII (1952): 219–220; *Constitutional Telegraphe* (Boston), 12 August 1801, p. 3; *Courier of New Hampshire* (Concord), 27 August 1801, p. 3; *Washington Federalist,* 31 August 1801, p. 1.

3. *National Intelligencer, and Washington Advertiser,* 30 December 1801, p. 3; *Washington Federalist,* 31 August 1801, p. 2 (arriving "in a waggon drawn by 5 horses").

4. Browne, "Elder John Leland and the Mammoth Cheshire Cheese," p. 149.

5. "Events in the Life of John Leland: Written by Himself," in *The Writings of the Late Elder John Leland,* ed. L. F. Green (New York: G. W. Wood, 1845), p. 32.

6. The word *mammoth,* by some accounts, was first used in America to describe the Cheshire cheese. Borrowed from the Russian name for an extinct Siberian elephant, the word was gaining currency contemporaneously in connection with Charles Willson Peale's excavation of a North American mastodon fossil in the Hudson Valley. Butterfield, "Elder John Leland, Jeffersonian Itinerant," pp. 220–222; Charles Coleman Sellers, *Charles Willson Peale* (Philadelphia: American Philosophical Society, 1947), vol. 2, pp. 142–144.

7. See *Washington Federalist,* 2 January 1802, p. 3; *Washington Federalist,* 5 January 1802, p. 2; *National Intelligencer, and Washington Advertiser,* 20 January 1802, p. 1; *Baltimore Federalist Gazette,* 6 January 1802, p. 2; *Boston Gazette,* 18 January 1802, p. 2; *Columbian Centinel, Massachusetts Federalist,* 30 January 1802, p. 1; *Commercial Advertiser* (New York), 9 January 1802, p. 3; *Connecticut Courant,* 18 January 1802, p. 4; *New York Evening Post,* 7 January 1802, p. 3.

8. Address of the inhabitants of the town of Cheshire, Berkshire County, Massachusetts, to Thomas Jefferson, reprinted in *American Citizen and General Advertiser* (New York), 18 January 1802, p. 2; *American Mercury* (Hartford, Conn.), 28 January 1802, p. 3; *Centinel of Freedom* (Newark, N.J.), 19 January 1802, p. 3; *Columbian Centinel, Massachusetts Federalist,* 30 January 1802, p. 1; *Commercial Advertiser* (New York), 15 January 1802, p. 3; *Constitutional Telegraphe* (Boston), 23 January 1802, p. 2; *Gazette of the United States* (Philadelphia), 20 January 1802, pp. 2–3; *Mercantile Advertiser* (New York), 16 January 1802, p. 3; *National Intelligencer, and Washington Advertiser,* 20 January 1802, p. 2; *New Hampshire Gazette* (Portsmouth), 2 February 1802, p. 2; *New York Evening Post,* 16 January 1802, pp. 2–3; *Providence Gazette,* 23 January 1802, pp. 2–3; *The Republican; or, Anti-Democrat* (Baltimore), 13 January 1802, p. 3 (Baptist address only); *Rhode Island Republican* (Newport), 23 January 1802, p. 3; *Salem Gazette,* 16 February 1802, p. 1; *Salem Register,* 25 January 1802, pp. 2–3; *The Spectator* (New York), 16 January 1802, p. 2; *The Sun* (Pittsfield, Mass.), 8 February 1802, p. 1; *The Times, and District of Columbia Daily Advertiser* (Alexandria, Va.), 28 January 1802, p. 2; Browne, "Elder John Leland and the Mammoth Cheshire Cheese," p. 150. Jefferson's response to the Cheshire citizens is reprinted in most of these journals.

9. Letter from Thomas Jefferson to Thomas Mann Randolph, 1 January 1802, as quoted in Dumas Malone, *Jefferson and His Time,* vol. 4, *Jefferson the President: First Term, 1801–1805* (Boston: Little, Brown and Co., 1970), p. 108.

10. Bernard Mayo, "A Peppercorn for Mr. Jefferson," *Virginia Quarterly Review* 19 (1943): 222.

11. See generally *The Writings of the Late Elder John Leland* (New York: G. W. Wood, 1845); Butterfield, "Elder John Leland, Jeffersonian Itinerant," pp. 155–242; J. T. Smith, "Life and Times of the Rev. John Leland," *Baptist Quarterly* 5 (1871): 230–256.

12. Butterfield, "Elder John Leland, Jeffersonian Itinerant," p. 157.

13. John Leland, "A Blow at the Root: Being a Fashionable Fast-Day Sermon (1801)," in *The Writings of the Late Elder John Leland,* p. 255.

14. Letter from Thomas Jefferson to Messrs. Nehemiah Dodge, Ephraim Robbins, and Stephen S. Nelson, a committee of the Danbury Baptist association in the state of

Connecticut, 1 January 1802, Presidential Papers Microfilm, Thomas Jefferson Papers (Manuscript Division, Library of Congress), Series 1, Reel 25, November 15, 1801–March 31, 1802.

15. Letter from Thomas Jefferson to Levi Lincoln, 1 January 1802, Presidential Papers Microfilm, Thomas Jefferson Papers (Manuscript Division, Library of Congress), Series 1, Reel 25, November 15, 1801–March 31, 1802.

16. The "wall" metaphor was the central theme of the U.S. Supreme Court's landmark ruling in *Everson v. Board of Education:* "In the words of Jefferson, the [First Amendment] clause against establishment of religion by law was intended to erect 'a wall of separation between church and State'. . . . That wall must be kept high and impregnable. We could not approve the slightest breach." *Everson,* 330 U.S. 1, 16, 18 (1947). In *McCollum v. Board of Education* (1948), Justice Hugo L. Black revealed the extent to which the Court had constitutionalized the "wall" metaphor: "The majority in the *Everson* case, and the minority as shown by quotations from the dissenting views . . ., agreed that the First Amendment's language, properly interpreted, had erected a wall of separation between Church and State." *McCollum,* 333 U.S. 203, 211 (1948). Harold D. Hammett remarked: "The metaphor of the 'wall of separation' between church and state has become an enduring element of First Amendment analysis. Resurrected from Jefferson by the Supreme Court in 1878, since 1947 the vision of the wall seems to have molded almost all attempts to analyze the First Amendment's control over the Government's relationship to religion. Indeed, Court opinions, and scholarly analyses of those opinions, have relied on it so much that the 'wall of separation' has become more than a mere symbol or a basis for analysis; it is a rule of law." Hammett, "The Homogenized Wall," *American Bar Association Journal* 53 (October 1967): 929 (footnotes omitted).

17. Jefferson, as quoted in Browne, "Elder John Leland and the Mammoth Cheshire Cheese," p. 150.

18. See, for example, *American Citizen and General Advertiser* (New York), 18 January 1802, p. 2; *American Mercury* (Hartford, Conn.), 28 January 1802, p. 3; *The Centinel of Freedom* (Newark, N.J.), 16 February 1802, pp. 2–3 (Baptist address), 23 February 1802, p. 3 (Jefferson's reply); *Constitutional Telegraphe* (Boston), 27 January 1802, p. 2; *Independent Chronicle* (Boston), 25 January 1802, pp. 2–3; *New Hampshire Gazette* (Portsmouth), 9 February 1802, p. 2; *Rhode-Island Republican* (Newport), 30 January 1802, p. 2; *Salem Register,* 28 January 1802, p. 1; *The Sun* (Pittsfield, Mass.), 15 February 1802, p. 4.

19. See, for example, *American Citizen and General Advertiser* (New York), 18 January 1802, p. 2; *American Mercury* (Hartford, Conn.), 28 January 1802, p. 3; *Independent Chronicle* (Boston), 25 January 1802, pp. 2–3

20. See Harriet Taylor Upton, *Our Early Presidents, Their Wives and Children* (Boston: D. Lothrop Co., 1890), p. 166 ("In 1805 a portion of the 'mammoth cheese' was still in existence, and was served at a Levee, along with cake and a great urn of hot punch."); Butterfield, "Elder John Leland, Jeffersonian Itinerant," pp. 228–229.

21. Letter from Thomas Jefferson to Levi Lincoln, 1 January 1802.

22. See Nobel E. Cunningham, Jr., "Election of 1800," in *History of American Presidential Elections: 1789–1968,* ed. Arthur M. Schlesinger, Jr. (New York: Chelsea House, 1985 [1971]), vol. 1, pp. 101–156; Norman DeJong, with Jack Van Der Slik, "The Presidential Election of 1800: Thomas Jefferson's Second Revolution?" in *Sepa-*

ration of Church and State: The Myth Revisited (Jordan Station, Ontario, Canada: Paideia Press, 1985), pp. 147–168; Charles O. Lerche, Jr., "Jefferson and the Election of 1800: A Case Study in the Political Smear," William and Mary Quarterly, 3d ser., 5 (1948): 467–491; Fred C. Luebke, "The Origins of Thomas Jefferson's Anti-Clericalism," Church History 32 (1963): 344–356; Mark A. Noll, "The Campaign of 1800: Fire Without Light," in One Nation Under God?: Christian Faith and Political Action in America (San Francisco: Harper and Row, 1988), pp. 75–89; Charles F. O'Brien, "The Religious Issue in the Presidential Campaign of 1800," Essex Institute Historical Collections 107, no. 1 (1971): 82–93; Constance B. Schulz, "'Of Bigotry in Politics and Religion': Jefferson's Religion, the Federalist Press, and the Syllabus," Virginia Magazine of History and Biography 91 (1983): 73–91.

23. Dumas Malone, Jefferson and His Time, vol. 3, Jefferson and the Ordeal of Liberty (Boston: Little, Brown and Co., 1962), p. 481; David Saville Muzzey, Thomas Jefferson (New York: Charles Scribner's Sons, 1918), pp. 207–208; Albert Jay Nock, Jefferson (New York: Harcourt, Brace and Co., 1926), p. 238; James Parton, Life of Thomas Jefferson (Boston: James R. Osgood and Co., 1874), p. 574; Henry S. Randall, The Life of Thomas Jefferson, 3 vols. (New York, 1857), vol. 1, p. 495; vol. 2, pp. 567–568.

24. Letter from a committee of the Danbury Baptist association to Thomas Jefferson, 7 October 1801, Presidential Papers Microfilm, Thomas Jefferson Papers (Manuscript Division, Library of Congress), Series 1, Reel 24, June 26, 1801–November 14, 1801.

25. William G. McLoughlin, New England Dissent, 1630–1833: The Baptists and the Separation of Church and State, 2 vols. (Cambridge, Mass.: Harvard University Press, 1971), vol. 2, pp. 920, 986 (footnote omitted).

26. See M. Louise Greene, The Development of Religious Liberty in Connecticut (Boston: Houghton, Mifflin, and Co., 1905), pp. 394, 407 ("[F]rom 1793 the dissenters began to lean towards affiliation with the [Jeffersonian] Democratic-Republican party, the successors to the Anti-Federal; yet it was not until toward the close of the War of 1812 that the Republican party made large gains in Connecticut and the dissenters began to feel sure that the dawn of religious liberty was at hand. . . . [T]he Republican [party] gains were greater among the Methodists and Baptists. This was partly because not a few among these dissenters associated Jefferson's party with his efforts towards disestablishment in Virginia in 1785."); Forrest McDonald, The Presidency of Thomas Jefferson (Lawrence, Kans.: University Press of Kansas, 1976), p. 17 ("[R]eligious dissenters supported Jefferson because of his well-known championship of the cause of religious liberty. New England Baptists, for instance, having fought long and vainly for disestablishment, virtually idolized Jefferson.").

27. See McLoughlin, New England Dissent, vol. 2, pp. 1004–1005 (commenting on the Connecticut Baptists' affiliation with the Republicans at the turn of the century); Merrill D. Peterson, Thomas Jefferson and the New Nation: A Biography (New York: Oxford University Press, 1970), p. 671 (Republicans in Connecticut "were few, outcasts of society, and systematically excluded from the state government.").

28. Letter from a committee of the Danbury Baptist association to Thomas Jefferson, 7 October 1801. A notation in the margin of the letter preserved in the Thomas Jefferson Papers at the Library of Congress indicates that the letter, which was dated 7 October 1801, was received on 30 December 1801.

29. Letter from Thomas Jefferson to Levi Lincoln, 1 January 1802. By the early 1800s, Americans had come to expect that presidential "replies to addresses" would be used as the "prime vehicles for the dissemination of partisan views." James Hutson, "'A Wall of Separation': FBI Helps Restore Jefferson's Obliterated Draft," *The Library of Congress Information Bulletin* 57, no. 6 (June 1998): 137.

30. A careless reading of Jefferson's letter to Levi Lincoln is the source of the frequently repeated error that the Danbury Baptists requested Jefferson to designate a day of public fasting and national thanksgiving. Jefferson wrote to Lincoln: "the Baptist address . . . furnishes an occasion too . . . of saying why I do not proclaim fastings & thanksgivings, as my predecessors did. [*T*]*he address to be sure does not point at this*" (emphasis added). Letter from Thomas Jefferson to Levi Lincoln, 1 January 1802.

31. For a discussion on the practices of Jefferson's two presidential predecessors in appointing days for public thanksgiving and religious observance, see Anson Phelps Stokes, *Church and State in the United States,* 3 vols. (New York: Harper and Brothers, 1950), vol. 1, pp. 486–491.

32. For examples of Federalist complaints concerning Republican opposition to the designation of days for public thanksgiving, see *Newport Mercury* (Rhode Island), 24 November 1801, p. 2; *United States Oracle, and Advertiser* (Portsmouth, N.H.), 28 November 1801, p. 2.

33. Schulz, "'Of Bigotry in Politics and Religion,'" pp. 85–86.

34. Edward S. Corwin, "The Supreme Court as National School Board," in *A Constitution of Powers in a Secular State* (Charlottesville, Va.: Michie Co., 1951), p. 106.

35. See Laurie Goodstein, "Fresh Debate on 1802 Jefferson Letter," *New York Times,* 10 September 1998, p. A20; Diego Ribadeneira, "New Debate Flares Over Jefferson's View of Church and State," *Boston Globe,* 1 August 1998, p. B2; Warren Fiske, "Test on Letter by Jefferson Fuels Debate on Church, State," *Virginian-Pilot* (Norfolk, Va.), 4 July 1998, p. A1; Carl Hartman, "Jefferson's Stance on Religion Fuels Debate," *USA Today,* 31 July 1998, p. 6A; Irvin Molotsky, "One of Jefferson's Enigmas, so Finally the F.B.I. Steps In," *New York Times,* 30 May 1998, p. A15; Larry Witham, "Very Political Jefferson Built 'Wall of Separation,'" *Washington Times,* 1 June 1998, p. A1; Bill Broadway, "One Nation Under God," *Washington Post,* 6 June 1998, p. B9; Carl Hartman, "Line Uncovered in Historic Letter," *Dayton Daily News,* 6 June 1998, p. 7C; Martin Kettle, "Sacred Ideal Founded on Jefferson's Fudge," *Guardian* (London), 8 June 1998, p. 12.

36. Hutson, "'A Wall of Separation,'" p. 138.

37. Letter from Thomas Jefferson to Levi Lincoln, 1 January 1802.

38. See text accompanying notes 32, 63–64.

39. Malone, *Jefferson the President: First Term,* p. 109. See also Peterson, *Thomas Jefferson and the New Nation,* p. 672 (Levi Lincoln was "the President's chief liaison with the New England Republicans").

Jefferson's solicitation of advice from his cabinet officers controverts the claims of critics who discount or belittle the Danbury letter as a hastily drafted "little address of courtesy," lacking deliberation or precision. J. M. O'Neill, *Religion and Education Under the Constitution* (New York: Harper and Brothers, 1949), p. 83. See also ibid., pp. 79, 81, 136 ("little letter of courtesy"), p. 242 ("little note of courtesy"); *Wallace v. Jaffree,* 472 U.S. 38, 92 (1985) (Rehnquist, J., dissenting) ("a short note of courtesy"); Joseph H. Brady, *Confusion Twice Confounded: The First Amendment and the*

Supreme Court (South Orange, N.J.: Seton Hall University Press, 1954), p. 32 ("the short courtesy note"), p. 70 ("offhand little metaphor"). See also Leonard W. Levy, *The Establishment Clause: Religion and the First Amendment,* rev. ed. (Chapel Hill, N.C.: University of North Carolina Press, 1994), pp. 247–248 (denouncing the tendency of critics to belittle the letter); Leo Pfeffer, *Church, State, and Freedom* (Boston: Beacon Press, 1953), pp. 118–121 (arguing that it is difficult to characterize the Danbury letter as lacking in deliberation).

40. Draft letter from Thomas Jefferson to Messrs. Nehemiah Dodge, Ephraim Robbins, and Stephen S. Nelson, a committee of the Danbury Baptist association in the state of Connecticut, 1 January 1802, Presidential Papers Microfilm, Thomas Jefferson Papers (Manuscript Division, Library of Congress), Series 1, Reel 25, November 15, 1801–March 31, 1802.

41. See note 18.

42. Letter from Thomas Jefferson to Levi Lincoln, 1 January 1802.

43. Hutson, "'A Wall of Separation,'" pp. 137, 163.

44. Letter from Thomas Jefferson to Levi Lincoln, 1 January 1802.

45. Letter from Thomas Jefferson to Levi Lincoln, 1 January 1802.

46. Rodney K. Smith, *Public Prayer and the Constitution: A Case Study in Constitutional Interpretation* (Wilmington, Del.: Scholarly Resources, Inc., 1987), p. 62 (Jefferson's letter to Lincoln "made it very evident that he understood that his response articulated a principle that had not yet germinated into an accepted legal or political tenet."). See text accompanying notes 98–102.

47. Letter from Levi Lincoln to Thomas Jefferson, 1 January 1802, Presidential Papers Microfilm, Thomas Jefferson Papers (Manuscript Division, Library of Congress), Series 1, Reel 25, November 15, 1801–March 31, 1802.

48. Draft letter from Thomas Jefferson to Messrs. Nehemiah Dodge, Ephraim Robbins, and Stephen S. Nelson, a committee of the Danbury Baptist association in the state of Connecticut, 1 January 1802. See note 55.

49. *Dictionary of American Biography,* ed. Allen Johnson and Dumas Malone (New York: Charles Scribner's Sons, 1931–1932), vol. 4, p. 483.

50. Letter from Gideon Granger to Thomas Jefferson, [31] December 1801, Presidential Papers Microfilm, Thomas Jefferson Papers (Manuscript Division, Library of Congress), Series 1, Reel 25, November 15, 1801–March 31, 1802. A notation on the reverse side of the manuscript reads: "Granger. Gideon. recd. Dec. 31. 1801."

51. In the preliminary draft of this letter, the first letter of "God" is not capitalized.

52. Most published collections of Jefferson's writings incorrectly transcribe this word as "legislative." See, for example, *The Writings of Thomas Jefferson,* ed. H. A. Washington, 9 vols. (Washington, D.C.: Taylor & Maury, 1853–1854), vol. 8, pp. 113–114; *The Writings of Thomas Jefferson,* ed. Andrew A. Lipscomb and Albert Ellery Bergh, Library Edition, 20 vols. (Washington, D.C.: Thomas Jefferson Memorial Association, 1903–1904), vol. 16, pp. 281–282 [hereinafter *Writings of Jefferson*]; *The Life and Selected Writings of Thomas Jefferson,* ed. Adrienne Koch and William Peden (New York: The Modern Library; Random House, 1944), p. 332; *The Complete Jefferson,* ed. Saul K. Padover (New York: Duell, Sloan and Pearce, 1943), pp. 518–519; *The Portable Thomas Jefferson,* ed. Merrill D. Peterson (New York: Penguin Books, 1975), p. 303; *Writings,* notes and selections by Merrill D. Peterson (New York: Literary Classics of the United States, The Library of America, 1984), p. 510.

53. U.S. Constitution, amend. I.

54. In the preliminary draft of this letter, Jefferson inked out the word *eternal* between the words *wall of* and *separation*. James H. Hutson suggested that Jefferson removed *eternal* as a modifier of *wall* because the original phrase "sounded so uncompromisingly secular," "too antireligious to pious New England ears." Hutson, "'A Wall of Separation,'" p. 163.

55. In the preliminary draft of this letter, this sentence is followed by the following sentence, which was omitted from the final draft: "Congress thus inhibited from acts respecting religion, and the Executive authorised only to execute their acts, I have refrained from prescribing even occasional performances of devotion, prescribed indeed legally where an Executive is the legal head of a national church, but subject here, as religious exercises only to the voluntary regulations and discipline of each respective sect." In the preliminary draft, Jefferson inked out what appears to be the word *those* between the words *even* and *occasional*. In the preliminary draft, the clause reading, "prescribed indeed legally where an Executive is the legal head of a national church," had initially read, "practised indeed by the Executive of another nation as the legal head of it's [sic] church." In the preliminary draft, a line is drawn around this entire sentence and the following comment in the same hand is written in the left margin: "this paragraph was omitted on the suggestion that it might give uneasiness to some of our republican friends in the eastern States where the proclamation of thanksgivings etc [?] by their Executive is an antient habit, & is respected."

56. The preliminary draft of this letter reveals that Jefferson wrote and rewrote this sentence before settling on the final language. He first wrote: "confining myself therefore to the duties of my station, which are merely temporal, be assured that your religious rights shall never be infringed by any act of mine, and that I shall see with friendly dispositions the progress of those sentiments which tend to restore to man all his natural rights, convinced he has no natural right in opposition to his social duties." He then apparently amended this sentence to read: "concurring with this great act of national legislation in behalf of the rights of conscience." (Jefferson apparently intended this sentence to continued with "I shall see with friendly dispositions the progress of those sentiments . . ." from the initial draft). The opening words *concurring with* were replaced with *adhering to*. Each of these versions were inked out before Jefferson wrote the final version. At some point, he also replaced *friendly dispositions* in the initial version with *sincere satisfaction*.

57. In the preliminary draft of this letter, Jefferson initially wrote "the Danbury Baptist association" before replacing this with "your religious association."

58. Letter from Thomas Jefferson to Messrs. Nehemiah Dodge, Ephraim Robbins, and Stephen S. Nelson, a committee of the Danbury Baptist Association in the state of Connecticut, 1 January 1802. In 1998, the preliminary draft of this handwritten letter was scientifically analyzed by the Federal Bureau of Investigation in their state-of-the-art laboratory in order to ascertain words and phrases Jefferson apparently inked out. This annotated transcription of the Danbury letter with specific references to the preliminary draft relies on the FBI examination of the draft manuscript. For an excellent analysis of the preliminary draft that draws on the FBI report, see Hutson, "'A Wall of Separation,'" pp. 136–139, 163.

59. Compare Jefferson's language here with that in the *Notes on the State of Virginia:* "The legitimate powers of government extend to such acts only as are injuri-

ous to others." Jefferson, "Query XVII," *Notes on Virginia*, in *Writings of Jefferson*, vol. 2, p. 221. This comparison, along with a commentary on the Danbury letter, is noted in Richard P. McBrien, *Caesar's Coin: Religion and Politics in America* (New York: Macmillan, 1987), p. 64. See also Jefferson's language in his draft of "A Bill for Establishing Religious Freedom," which was subsequently deleted by legislative amendment: "that the opinions of men are not the object of civil government, nor under its jurisdiction." *Papers of Jefferson*, vol. 2, p. 546.

60. Jefferson's public actions as president were not always consistent with a policy of strict separation between religion and civil government. For example, on January 3, 1802, the Sunday following the New Year's Day Jefferson wrote the Danbury Baptist Association, the president attended a religious service in the U.S. Capitol. The sermon was preached by Elder John Leland who was in town to present the president with a mammoth Cheshire cheese. See letter from Manasseh Cutler to Dr. Joseph Torrey, 4 January 1802, in William Parker Cutler and Julia Perkins Cutler, *Life, Journals and Correspondence of Rev. Manasseh Cutler, LL.D.* (Cincinnati: Robert Clarke and Co., 1888), vol. 2, pp. 66–67; see also ibid., vol. 2, pp. 58–59 (diary entry for 3 January 1802); Stokes, *Church and State in the United States*, vol. 1, p. 499; Butterfield, "Elder John Leland, Jeffersonian Itinerant," pp. 226–227; Hutson, "'A Wall of Separation,'" p. 163.

61. Jon Butler, "Coercion, Miracle, Reason: Rethinking the American Religious Experience in the Revolutionary Age," in *Religion in a Revolutionary Age*, ed. Ronald Hoffman and Peter J. Albert (Charlottesville: University Press of Virginia; United States Capitol Historical Society, 1994), pp. 29–30.

62. Jefferson's final version of the Danbury letter did not explicitly mention the issue of "fastings & thanksgivings," and it would not be apparent from the text that this was the original object of the address were it not for his letter to Levi Lincoln. The "performances of devotion" is an oblique reference to the practice of public "fastings & thanksgivings" mentioned in the preliminary draft.

63. "Proclamation for a National Fast," 6 March 1799, in *The Works of John Adams, Second President of the United States*, ed. Charles Francis Adams (Boston: Little, Brown and Co., 1854), vol. 9, pp. 172–174.

64. Letter from John Adams to Benjamin Rush, 12 June 1812, in *The Spur of Fame: Dialogues of John Adams and Benjamin Rush, 1805–1813*, ed. John A. Schutz and Douglass Adair (San Marino, Calif.: Huntington Library, 1966), p. 224. See generally Edwin S. Gaustad, *Sworn on the Altar of God: A Religious Biography of Thomas Jefferson* (Grand Rapids, Mich.: William B. Eerdmans, 1996), pp. 94–96.

65. See John G. West, Jr., *The Politics of Revelation and Reason: Religion and Civic Life in the New Nation* (Lawrence, Kans.: University Press of Kansas, 1996), p. 57.

66. Thomas Jefferson, First Annual Message, 8 December 1801, *Writings of Jefferson*, vol. 3, p. 327.

67. Thomas Jefferson, Second Annual Message, 15 December 1802, *Writings of Jefferson*, vol. 3, p. 340. Jefferson concluded his second inaugural address by asking Americans to join with him in prayer that the "Being in whose hands we are . . . will so enlighten the minds of your servants, guide their councils, and prosper their measures, that whatsoever they do, shall result in your good, and shall secure to you the peace, friendship, and approbation of all nations." Jefferson, Second Inaugural Address, 4 March 1805, *Writings of Jefferson*, vol. 3, p. 383.

68. "Resolution of the House of Burgesses Designating a Day of Fasting and Prayer," 24 May 1774, *Papers of Jefferson,* vol. 1, p. 105. See also Thomas Jefferson and John Walker to the Inhabitants of the Parish of St. Anne, before 23 July 1774, *Papers of Jefferson,* vol. 1, p. 116.

69. Thomas Jefferson, *Autobiography, Writings of Jefferson,* vol. 1, pp. 9–10.

70. See Robert M. Healey, *Jefferson on Religion in Public Education* (New Haven, Conn.: Yale University Press, 1962), p. 135; Gaustad, *Sworn on the Altar of God,* pp. 102–103 (commenting on Jefferson's role in this proclamation).

71. "Proclamation Appointing a Day of Thanksgiving and Prayer," 11 November 1779, *Papers of Jefferson,* vol. 3, pp. 177–179.

72. *Report of the Committee of Revisors Appointed by the General Assembly of Virginia in MDCCLXXVI* (Richmond, Va.: printed by Dixon & Holt, 1784), pp. 59–60 [hereinafter *Report of the Revisors*]. The bill is reprinted in *Papers of Jefferson,* vol. 2, p. 556. This bill was part of a legislative package that included Jefferson's "Bill for Establishing Religious Freedom" and "Bill for Punishing Disturbers of Religious Worship and Sabbath Breakers." The three bills were apparently framed by Jefferson and sponsored in the Virginia legislature by James Madison. See Daniel L. Dreisbach, "A New Perspective on Jefferson's Views on Church-State Relations: The Virginia Statute for Establishing Religious Freedom in Its Legislative Context," *American Journal of Legal History* 35 (1991): 172–204.

73. Julian P. Boyd, editor of the Jefferson papers, did not explicitly attribute authorship of this bill to Jefferson. He did not, however, reject the possibility that Jefferson drafted "A Bill for Appointing Days of Public Fasting and Thanksgiving." Boyd noted that Jefferson apparently endorsed the bill. *Papers of Jefferson,* vol. 2, p. 556. Other scholars have described Jefferson as the author of this bill. See, for example, Robert L. Cord, *Separation of Church and State: Historical Fact and Current Fiction* (New York: Lambeth Press, 1982), pp. 220–221; Healey, *Jefferson on Religion in Public Education,* p. 135; Donald L. Drakeman, "Religion and the Republic: James Madison and the First Amendment," *Journal of Church and State* 25 (1983): 441; Comment, "Jefferson and the Church–State Wall: A Historical Examination of the Man and the Metaphor," *Brigham Young University Law Review* 1978 (1978). 657, 666.

74. *Report of the Revisors,* p. 60; *Papers of Jefferson,* vol. 2, p. 556. The punitive feature of "A Bill for Appointing Days of Public Fasting and Thanksgiving" is difficult to reconcile with that portion of Jefferson's "Bill for Establishing Religious Freedom" declaring "that no man shall be compelled to frequent or support any religious worship, place, or ministry whatsoever." *Report of the Revisors,* p. 58; *Papers of Jefferson,* vol. 2, p. 546; William Waller Hening, ed., *The Statutes at Large; Being a Collection of all the Laws of Virginia, from the First Session of the Legislature, in the Year 1619* (Richmond, Va.: J. & G. Cochran, 1823), vol. 12, p. 86.

75. *Papers of Jefferson,* vol. 2, p. 556.

76. Mark DeWolfe Howe, *The Garden and the Wilderness: Religion and Government in American Constitutional History* (Chicago: University of Chicago Press, 1965), pp. 19–20. In *The Federalist Papers,* No. 45, James Madison observed that "[t]he powers delegated by the proposed Constitution to the federal government are few and defined. Those which are to remain in the State governments are numerous and indefinite. . . . The powers reserved to the several States will extend to all the objects which, in the ordinary course of affairs, concern the lives, liberties, and properties of

the people, and the internal order, improvement, and prosperity of the State." *The Federalist Papers,* ed. Clinton Rossiter (New York: Mentor Books, 1961), pp. 292–293.

77. See Note, "Rethinking the Incorporation of the Establishment Clause: A Federalist View," *Harvard Law Review* 105 (1992): 1706–1707 (the word *Congress* emphasizes the federalism component of the First Amendment). See also Corwin, "The Supreme Court as National School Board," p. 109 ("the First Amendment, taken by itself, is binding only on Congress").

78. Joseph Francis Thorning, *Religious Liberty in Transition* (Washington, D.C.: The Catholic University of America, 1931), p. 4.

79. The First Amendment, it should be noted, denied the national government jurisdiction over religion not because religion was thought unimportant or because governmental support for religion was generally regarded as improper, but rather because jurisdiction in issues pertaining to "establishment" and government regulation of religion were thought appropriately reserved by the states.

80. James McClellan, *Joseph Story and the American Constitution: A Study in Political and Legal Thought* (Norman: University of Oklahoma Press, 1971), p. 146. Note also the view of Thomas Jefferson who wrote to James Madison in July 1788: "I hope therefore a bill of rights will be formed to guard the people against the federal government, as they are already guarded against their state governments in most instances." Letter from Thomas Jefferson to James Madison, 31 July 1788, *Papers of Jefferson,* vol. 13, p. 443.

81. James McClellan, "The Making and the Unmaking of the Establishment Clause," in *A Blueprint for Judicial Reform,* ed. Patrick B. McGuigan and Randall R. Rader (Washington, D.C.: Free Congress Research and Education Foundation, 1981), pp. 295, 314–315 (footnote omitted).

82. Corwin, "The Supreme Court as National School Board," p. 106. See also Howe, *The Garden and the Wilderness,* p. 29 ("the federalism of the First Amendment may be even more important than its libertarianism."). For other works that argue that the specific purpose of the First Amendment religion provisions was to preserve state sovereignty over religious matters, see Chester James Antieau, Arthur T. Downey, and Edward C. Roberts, *Freedom from Federal Establishment: Formation and Early History of the First Amendment Religion Clauses* (Milwaukee: Bruce, 1964); Clifton B. Kruse, Jr., "The Historical Meaning and Judicial Construction of the Establishment of Religion Clause of the First Amendment," *Washburn Law Journal* 2 (1962): 65–141; William K. Lietzau, "Rediscovering the Establishment Clause: Federalism and the Rollback of Incorporation," *DePaul Law Review* 39 (1990): 1191–1234; Note, "Rethinking the Incorporation of the Establishment Clause: A Federalist View," *Harvard Law Review* 105 (1992): 1700–1719; Joseph M. Snee, "Religious Disestablishment and the Fourteenth Amendment," *Washington University Law Quarterly* 1954 (1954): 371–407; Steven D. Smith, *Foreordained Failure: The Quest for a Constitutional Principle of Religious Freedom* (New York: Oxford University Press, 1995), pp. 17–54.

83. *Barron v. Baltimore,* 32 U.S. (7 Peters) 243, 250 (1833).

84. *Permoli v. Municipality,* 44 U.S. (3 Howard) 589, 609 (1845).

85. Joseph Story, *Commentaries on the Constitution of the United States,* 3 vols. (Boston: Hilliard, Gray, and Co., 1833), vol. 3, p. 730, sec. 1873.

86. Story, *Commentaries on the Constitution of the United States,* vol. 3, p. 731, sec. 1873. See also ibid., vol. 3, p. 728, sec. 1871 ("The real object of the [first] amendment

was . . . to exclude all rivalry among Christian sects, and to prevent any national ecclesiastical establishment, which should give to an hierarchy the exclusive patronage of the national government.").

87. Letter from Thomas Jefferson to the Reverend Samuel Miller, 23 January 1808, *Writings of Jefferson*, vol. 11, p. 428. See also James Madison's argument in the Virginia ratifying convention: "There is not a shadow of right in the general [federal] government to intermeddle with religion. Its least interference with it would be a most flagrant usurpation." Jonathan Elliot, ed., *The Debates in the Several State Conventions on the Adoption of the Federal Constitution*, 2d ed., 5 vols. (Philadelphia: J. B. Lippincott, 1836), vol. 3, p. 330.

88. Letter from Thomas Jefferson to Mrs. John Adams, 11 September 1804, *Writings of Jefferson*, vol. 11, p. 51.

89. U.S. Constitution, amend. X.

90. See letter from Thomas Jefferson to Monsieur Destutt de Tracy, 26 January 1811, *Writings of Jefferson*, vol. 13, p. 19 ("the true barriers of our liberty in this country are our State governments").

91. As early as 1798, Jefferson elaborated on this theme in his draft of "The Kentucky Resolutions" written in opposition to the Alien and Sedition Laws:

> *Resolved,* That it is true as a general principle, and is also expressly declared by one of the amendments to the Constitution, that "the powers not delegated to the United States by the Constitution, nor prohibited by it to the States, are reserved to the States respectively, or to the people"; and that no power over the freedom of religion, freedom of speech, or freedom of the press being delegated to the United States by the Constitution, nor prohibited by it to the States, all lawful powers respecting the same did of right remain, and were reserved to the States or the people: that thus was manifested their determination to retain to themselves the right of judging how far the licentiousness of speech and of the press may be abridged without lessening their useful freedom, and how far those abuses which cannot be separated from their use should be tolerated, rather than the use be destroyed. And thus also they guarded against all abridgment by the United States of the freedom of religious opinions and exercises, and retained to themselves the right of protecting the same, as this State, by a law passed on the general demand of its citizens, had already protected them from all human restraint or interference. And that in addition to this general principle and express declaration, another and more special provision has been made by one of the amendments to the Constitution, which expressly declares that "Congress shall make no law respecting an establishment of religion, or prohibiting the free exercise thereof, or abridging the freedom of speech or of the press": thereby guarding in the same sentence, and under the same words, the freedom of religion, of speech, and of the press: insomuch, that whatever violates either, throws down the sanctuary which covers the others, and that libels, falsehood, and defamation, equally with heresy and false religion, are withheld from the cognizance of federal tribunals.

Thomas Jefferson, "Drafts of the Kentucky Resolutions of 1798" [November 1798], in *The Works of Thomas Jefferson*, ed. Paul Leicester Ford, Federal Edition, 12 vols. (New York: G. P. Putnam's Sons, 1904–1905), vol. 8, pp. 463–465. Significantly, Jefferson coupled the Tenth and First Amendments and argued that power over religion, speech, and press was reserved to the state governments or the people. See generally Snee, "Religious Disestablishment and the Fourteenth Amendment," pp. 390–392; Comment, "Jefferson and the Church–State Wall," pp. 654–655.

92. Edward S. Corwin described this portion of the second inaugural address, perhaps offered in response to criticisms of Jefferson's refusal to appoint days for national religious observances, as a "more deliberate, more carefully considered evalu-
ation by Jefferson of the religious clauses of the First Amendment" than the Danbury
letter. Corwin, "The Supreme Court as National School Board," p. 106.

93. Thomas Jefferson, Second Inaugural Address, 4 March 1805, *Writings of Jefferson,* vol. 3, p. 378. See Stokes, *Church and State in the United States,* vol. 1, p. 335
(stating that in this passage of the address Jefferson "doubtless had in mind particularly his well-known objection to presidential Thanksgiving Day proclamations");
Gaustad, *Sworn on the Altar of God,* pp. 99–100 (indicating that this passage of the
address explicitly reaffirmed Jefferson's opposition to "presidential proclamations
pertaining to religion").

94. In the light of the text and structure of the First Amendment, it is also appropriate to think of the First Amendment religion provisions as a restriction on civil government only and not a restraint on religion (or the role of religion in public life).
Inasmuch as a wall is a bilateral, rather than unilateral, barrier that not only prevents
civil government from invading the ecclesiastical domain, as intended by the archi-
tects of the First Amendment, but also prohibits religion and the church from influencing the conduct of civil government, then the "wall" metaphor mischaracterizes
the First Amendment. The various guarantees in the First Amendment were entirely
a check or restraint on civil government, specifically the national legislature. The free
press guarantee, for example, was not written to protect the civil state from the press;
rather, it was designed to protect a free and independent press from control or interference by the federal government. Similarly, the religion provisions were added to
the Constitution to protect religion and religious institutions from rough or corrupting interference by the federal government, and not to protect the civil state from the
influence of, or overreaching by, religion. In other words, the First Amendment prohibition on religious establishment was a clear restraint on the power of civil government (i.e., the federal government) to give legal preference to any single sect or
combination of sects or to invade the religious domain. Any construction of Jefferson's "wall" that imposes restraints on entities other than civil government exceeds
the limitations imposed by the First Amendment, from which the "wall" metaphor
was explicitly derived.

95. See O'Neill, *Religion and Education Under the Constitution,* pp. 67–69, 79–83
(arguing that Jefferson's "wall" separated the federal government and one religion);
Snee, "Religious Disestablishment and the Fourteenth Amendment," p. 389 (arguing
that Jefferson's "wall" affirmed the principle of federalism); Cord, *Separation of
Church and State,* p. 115 ("By this phrase Jefferson could only have meant that the
'wall of separation' was erected 'between church and State' in regard to possible federal action. . . . Therefore, to leave the impression that Jefferson's 'separation' statement was a universal one concerning the whole of the federal and state political system is extremely misleading."); M. Stanton Evans, *The Theme Is Freedom: Religion,
Politics, and the American Tradition* (Washington, D.C.: Regnery Publishing Inc.,
1994), p. 288 ("The wall of separation, instead, was *between the federal government
and the states,* [and was] meant to make sure the central authority didn't meddle with
the customs of local jurisdictions."); Comment, "Jefferson and the Church–State Wall,"
pp. 645, 656–659 (arguing that Jefferson's "wall" was a study in federalism, and the

"wall" described in the Danbury letter was erected only against the federal government).

96. Jefferson was concerned about the lack of presidential authority, under the federal Constitution, to appoint days for religious devotion. Comment, "Jefferson and the Church–State Wall," p. 656.

97. Draft letter from Thomas Jefferson to Messrs. Nehemiah Dodge, Ephraim Robbins, and Stephen S. Nelson, a committee of the Danbury Baptist association in the state of Connecticut, 1 January 1802. This sentence parallels an acknowledgment made in the letter from the Baptists: "we are sensible that the President of the united States, is not the national Legislator, & also sensible that the national government cannot destroy the Laws of each State." Thus, language in both the Baptists' letter and Jefferson's response confirms that it was generally understood and unchallenged, as a principle of federalism, that religion was a subject of state jurisdiction.

98. See Kurt T. Lash, "The Second Adoption of the Establishment Clause: The Rise of the Nonestablishment Principle," *Arizona State Law Journal* 27 (1995): 1096–1097.

99. *The Debates and Proceedings in the Congress of the United States,* ed. Joseph Gales, 42 vols. (Washington, D.C.: Gales and Seaton, 1834–1856), 1st Cong., 1st sess., vol. 1, p. 914 (25 September 1789); *Documentary History of the First Federal Congress of the United States of America, March 4, 1789–March 3, 1791,* ed. Linda Grant De Pauw, vol. 1, *Senate Legislative Journal* (Baltimore: Johns Hopkins University Press, 1972), vol. 1, p. 197; *Journal of the First Session of the Senate of the United States of America* (New York: Thomas Greenleaf, 1789), p. 154 (26 September 1789).

100. *U.S. Statutes at Large* 1 (1789): 71.

101. See note 31.

102. See Smith, *Public Prayer and the Constitution,* p. 62; Daniel L. Dreisbach, "'Sowing Useful Truths and Principles': The Danbury Baptists, Thomas Jefferson, and the 'Wall of Separation,'" *Journal of Church and State* 39 (1997): 465–466.

103. In *Cantwell v. Connecticut,* 310 U.S. 296, 303 (1940), and *Everson v. Board of Education,* 330 U.S. 1, 15 (1947), the First Amendment free exercise and nonestablishment of religion provisions respectively were incorporated into the "liberties" protected by the Fourteenth Amendment due process of law clause, thereby guarding these First Amendment provisions from infringement by the states. The present discussion is about Jefferson's construction of his "wall" and not about post-Fourteenth Amendment interpretations of the metaphor. It should be noted that if the jurisdictional interpretation of the First Amendment, and hence the "wall," is correct, then not only is it impossible (not to mention illogical) to "incorporate" into the "liberty" protected by the Fourteenth Amendment that which is essentially the structural assignment of authority over a specific subject matter to a particular level or branch of government (as opposed to a libertarian device that confers judicially enforceable, substantive rights upon individuals), but also the First Amendment "cannot be incorporated without eviscerating its raison d'etre." Note, "Rethinking the Incorporation of the Establishment Clause," p. 1709. See also Donald L. Drakeman, *Church-State Constitutional Issues: Making Sense of the Establishment Clause* (Westport, Conn.: Greenwood Press, 1991), p. 111 (incorporation "may have stood the eighteenth-century framers' decision on its head"); Smith, *Foreordained Failure,* pp. 49–50; *Abington School District v. Schempp,* 374 U.S. 203, 309–310 (1963) (Stewart, J., dissenting) ("As a matter of history, the First Amendment was adopted solely as a limitation upon the

newly created National Government. The events leading to its adoption strongly suggest that the Establishment Clause was primarily an attempt to insure that Congress not only would be powerless to establish a national church, but would also be unable to interfere with existing state establishments. . . . Each State was left free to go its own way and pursue its own policy with respect to religion. . . . [I]t is not without irony that a constitutional provision evidently designed to leave the States free to go their own way should now have become a restriction upon their autonomy."). Pursuant to this view, incorporating the nonestablishment provision (and Jefferson's "wall") is as nonsensical as incorporating the Tenth Amendment.

104. In the last sentence of the second paragraph of the Danbury letter, Jefferson wrote: "adhering to this expression of the supreme will of the nation in behalf of the rights of conscience, I shall see with sincere satisfaction the progress of those sentiments which tend to restore to man all his natural rights, convinced he has no natural right in opposition to his social duties." "[T]his expression of the supreme will of the nation" is a reference to the First Amendment, which was cited in the preceding two sentences of the preliminary draft and, as previously noted, applied only to the federal government. In the second clause of the sentence, it is not clear whether Jefferson was referring to a "progress of those sentiments" promoting the rights of conscience among individuals vis-à-vis the federal regime only, *pursuant to the First Amendment*, or whether he was looking forward to the "progress of those sentiments" among citizens in the states because state governments voluntarily adopted the First Amendment model. He certainly did not believe the states were subject to the First Amendment "wall."

105. James McClellan made this same point, forcefully repudiating the Supreme Court's "incorporation" of the First Amendment and, by extension, Jefferson's "wall" in recent church–state jurisprudence: "To apply Jefferson's wall of separation theory to present cases, as the Supreme Court has done, is to lift it wholly out of context. Jefferson believed that the states were free to prescribe the nature of religious liberty within their respective jurisdictions. . . . The application of the Jeffersonian theory *against* the states, and its utilization by the federal courts in deciding how a state should behave with respect to civil liberties, is wholly contrary to the very basis of the Jeffersonian philosophy of states' rights; and it is incompatible with Jefferson's strong desire to resist the increasing powers of the Supreme Court. To say that the national courts instead of the various state courts should possess final authority in the enforcement of an absolute wall of separation between church and state is similar to arguing that the powers of the states are best preserved by transferring those powers to the federal government." McClellan, *Joseph Story and the American Constitution,* pp. 143–144 (footnote omitted).

106. Jefferson was concerned that a civil magistrate's recommendation for a day of public fasting and prayer would be, in effect, indistinguishable from a mandatory prescription for such exercises, and thereby would impose penalties on those who for reasons of conscience failed to comply. This argument applies equally to state and federal magistrates. Jefferson further argued that it is in the interests of religion to direct its own exercises, discipline, and doctrines and not to vest such matters in the hands of civil government.

107. This language is borrowed from Steven D. Smith's commentary on the First Amendment religion clauses. Smith, *Foreordained Failure,* p. 17. The framers and ratifiers of the religion clauses, Smith argued, deliberately declined to adopt a principle or theory of religious liberty. "They consciously chose not to answer the religion

question, and they were able for the most part to avoid it . . . because of the way in which they answered the jurisdiction question—that is, by assigning the religion question to the states." Accordingly, it is futile to locate in or extrapolate from the original meaning of the religion clauses a substantive right or principle of religious liberty. In other words, the First Amendment was calculated not to articulate a principle or theory of religious liberty but merely to specify who (or what level or branch of civil government) shall substantively address this subject matter. Ibid., pp. 21, 25.

108. See Howe, *The Garden and the Wilderness,* pp. 5–31.

109. See generally Irwin H. Polishook, ed., *Roger Williams, John Cotton and Religious Freedom: A Controversy in New and Old England* (Englewood Cliffs, N.J.: Prentice-Hall, 1967); Sacvan Bercovitch, "Typology in Puritan New England: The Williams–Cotton Controversy Reassessed," *American Quarterly* 19 (Summer 1967): 166–191; Richard M. Gummere, "Church, State and Classics: The Cotton–Williams Debate," *Classical Journal* 54 (1958): 175–183; Elisabeth Feist Hirsch, "John Cotton and Roger Williams: Their Controversy Concerning Religious Liberty," *Church History* 10 (1941): 38–51; Henry Bamford Parkes, "John Cotton and Roger Williams Debate Toleration, 1644–1652," *New England Quarterly* 4 (1931): 735–756; Jesper Rosenmeier, "The Teacher and the Witness: John Cotton and Roger Williams," *William and Mary Quarterly,* 3d ser., 25 (1968): 408–431; George Albert Stead, "Roger Williams and the Massachusetts-Bay," *New England Quarterly* 7 (1934): 235–257.

110. Roger Williams, "Mr. Cotton's Letter Lately Printed, Examined and Answered," in *The Complete Writings of Roger Williams* (Providence, R.I.: Providence Press, 1866), vol. 1, p. 392. The quotation is taken from Perry Miller's modernized version in Miller, *Roger Williams: His Contribution to the American Tradition* (Indianapolis, Ind.: Bobbs-Merrill, 1953; reprinted New York: Atheneum, 1962), p. 98.

The motif of a protective "hedge" or "wall" was ubiquitous in the rhetoric of colonial New England. See A. W. Plumstead, ed., *The Wall and the Garden: Selected Massachusetts Election Sermons, 1670–1775* (Minneapolis: University of Minnesota Press, 1968).

111. Roger Williams, *The Bloody Tenent Yet More Bloody,* ed. Samuel L. Caldwell, *Complete Writings of Williams,* vol. 4, p. 333.

112. Howe, *The Garden and the Wilderness,* p. 19. Quoting Perry Miller, Arlin M. Adams and Charles J. Emmerich similarly opined: "In contrast to Enlightenment rationalists, Roger Williams and others in the pietistic tradition built a wall of separation 'not to prevent the state from becoming an instrument of "priestcraft," but in order to keep the holy and pure religion of Jesus Christ from contamination by the slightest taint of earthly support.'" Adams and Emmerich, *A Nation Dedicated to Religious Liberty: The Constitutional Heritage of the Religion Clauses* (Philadelphia: University of Pennsylvania Press, 1990), p. 56, quoting Perry Miller, "Roger Williams: An Essay in Interpretation," in *The Complete Writings of Roger Williams* (Russell and Russell, 1963), vol. 7, p. 6.

113. Howe, *The Garden and the Wilderness,* p. 6. Justice Harry Blackmun quoted this passage in *Lee v. Weisman,* 505 U.S. 577, 608, n. 11 (1992) (Blackmun, J., concurring).

114. Howe, *The Garden and the Wilderness,* p. 2.

115. Howe, *The Garden and the Wilderness,* p. 9. See generally Tom Gerety, "Legal Gardening: Mark DeWolfe Howe on Church and State: A Retrospective Essay," *Stanford Law Review* 38 (1986): 595–614.

116. David Little, "Roger Williams and the Separation of Church and State," in *Religion and the State: Essays in Honor of Leo Pfeffer,* ed. James E. Wood, Jr. (Waco, Tex.: Baylor University Press, 1985), pp. 15–16; William Lee Miller, *The First Liberty: Religion and the American Republic* (New York: Alfred A. Knopf, 1986), pp. 182–183.

117. Timothy L. Hall, "Roger Williams and the Foundations of Religious Liberty," *Boston University Law Review* 71 (1991): 482 (footnote omitted), quoting Roger Williams, *The Bloudy Tenet, of Persecution,* in *Complete Writings of Williams,* vol. 3, p. 178. Hall further noted that "Williams defined for the state a sphere of existence untroubled by religious disputes. He thus created a notion of the secular, not as antagonistic to religion, but as occupied with fundamentally different concerns from religion. Williams respected the secular city because he believed that God had instituted it and that its existence was not hostile to the existence of the Church." Ibid. (footnote omitted).

118. Howe, *The Garden and the Wilderness,* pp. 1–2. See also John Witte, Jr., "The Essential Rights and Liberties of Religion in the American Constitutional Experiment," *Notre Dame Law Review* 71 (1996): 400, n. 144. For a useful comparison between the perspectives of Jefferson and various Baptists on church-state separation, see William G. McLoughlin, *Soul Liberty: The Baptists' Struggle in New England, 1630–1833* (Hanover, N.H.: Brown University Press, 1991), pp. 249–269.

119. Gaustad, *Sworn on the Altar of God,* p. 72. See also LeRoy Moore, "Roger Williams as an Enduring Symbol for Baptists," *Journal of Church and State* 7 (1965): 185 (there is little question but that Jefferson and Madison never read works by Williams).

120. Moore, "Roger Williams as an Enduring Symbol for Baptists," p. 185; LeRoy Moore, "Roger Williams and the Historians," *Church History* 32 (December 1963): 432–451 (emphasizing the unavailability of Williams's writings in America before the nineteenth century). For other useful historiographical essays on Williams's contributions to American traditions, see Raymond D. Irwin, "A Man for All Eras: The Changing Historical Image of Roger Williams, 1630–1993," *Fides et Historia: Journal of the Conference on Faith and History* 26, no. 3 (1994): 6–23; Nancy E. Peace, "Roger Williams—A Historiographical Essay," *Rhode Island History* 35 (1976): 103–113.

121. Miller, "Roger Williams: An Essay in Interpretation," in *Complete Writings of Williams,* vol. 7, p. 10. Perry Miller also wrote that "although Williams is celebrated as the prophet of religious freedom, he actually exerted little or no influence on institutional developments in America; only after the conception of liberty for all denominations had triumphed on wholly other grounds did Americans look back on Williams and invest him with his ill-fitting halo." Miller, *Roger Williams: His Contribution to the American Tradition,* p. 29. Miller further opined that Williams "exerted little or no direct influence on theorists of the Revolution and the Constitution, who drew on quite different intellectual sources." Ibid., p. 254.

122. Carla H. Hay, *James Burgh, Spokesman for Reform in Hanoverian England* (Washington, D.C.: University Press of America, 1979), pp. 30, 41–44.

123. Hay, *James Burgh,* p. 3. See generally Caroline Robbins, *The Eighteenth-Century Commonwealthman: Studies in the Transmission, Development and Circumstance of English Liberal Thought from the Restoration of Charles II until the War with the Thirteen Colonies* (Cambridge, Mass.: Harvard University Press, 1959). For a more recent discussion of the Real Whigs or Commonwealthmen and their influence

on American political and constitutional thought in the revolutionary era, see David N. Mayer, "The English Radical Whig Origins of American Constitutionalism," *Washington University Law Quarterly* 70 (1992): 131–208. Mayer places Burgh squarely within this tradition. Ibid., p. 170.

124. Oscar and Mary Handlin, "James Burgh and American Revolutionary Theory," *Proceedings of the Massachusetts Historical Society* 73 (1961): 43. See also Hay, *James Burgh,* pp. 28–30.

125. Caroline Robbins described the work as "perhaps the most important political treatise which appeared in England in the first half of the reign of George III." Robbins, *The Eighteenth-Century Commonwealthman,* p. 365.

126. Hay, *James Burgh,* p. 49. Carla H. Hay briefly traced the evolution of Burgh's religious beliefs from his early Calvinist training as the son of a Church of Scotland clergyman to a conversion "to some form of unitarianism." In his later works he rejected Trinitarianism and other doctrines of orthodox Christianity. However, "[t]here was never any question in Burgh's mind that organized Christianity was the most valid expression of man's religious needs and duties. . . . Moreover, Burgh always believed that Protestantism was the only legitimate manifestation of the Christian faith." Hay, *James Burgh,* pp. 49–55.

127. Colin Bonwick, *English Radicals and the American Revolution* (Chapel Hill: University of North Carolina Press, 1977), pp. 14–15.

128. Hay, *James Burgh,* p. 51. The Real Whigs were early and zealous advocates of religious liberty. Mayer, "The English Radical Whig Origins of American Constitutionalism," p. 163.

129. [James Burgh], *Crito, or Essays on Various Subjects,* 2 vols. (London, 1766, 1767), vol. 2, p. 68, as quoted in Isaac Kramnick, *Republicanism and Bourgeois Radicalism: Political Ideology in Late Eighteenth-Century England and America* (Ithaca, N.Y.: Cornell University Press, 1990), p. 232. Carla H. Hay pointed out that "[a]lthough Burgh heartily endorsed private religious devotions, he maintained that the public expression of such sentiments was especially useful in inculcating a sense of one's obligations to God." Hay, *James Burgh,* p. 50 (endnote omitted).

130. *Crito,* vol. 1, p. 7.

131. *Crito,* vol. 2, p. 119 (emphasis in the original).

132. *Crito,* vol. 2, pp. 117–119 (emphasis in the original).

133. Letter from Thomas Jefferson to Thomas Mann Randolph, 30 May 1790, *Writings of Jefferson,* vol. 8, pp. 31–32. Nearly a quarter of a century later, Jefferson gave the same advice to Bernard Moore; see letter from Thomas Jefferson to Bernard Moore, 30 August 1814, in Henry S. Randall, *The Life of Thomas Jefferson,* 3 vols. (New York: Derby and Jackson, 1857), vol. 1, p. 55.

134. H. Trevor Colbourn, "Thomas Jefferson's Use of the Past," *William and Mary Quarterly,* 3d ser., 15 (1958): 65, n. 47; Hay, *James Burgh,* p. 43.

135. See letter from John Adams to James Burgh, 28 December 1774, *Works of Adams,* vol. 9, p. 351 (Adams wrote that he had "contributed somewhat to make the [Political] Disquisitions more known and attended to in several parts of America," and reported that the work was "held in as high estimation by all my friends as they are by me."). See also [Adams], "Novanglus," in *Works of Adams,* vol. 4, p. 21, n. * (Burgh's *Political Disquisitions* is "[a] book which ought to be in the hands of every American who has learned to read.").

136. Hay, *James Burgh*, p. 42.

137. James Burgh, *Political Disquisitions: or, An Enquiry into Public Errors, Defects, and Abuses*, 3 vols. (Philadelphia, 1775), vol. 3, "Names of the Encouragers."

138. Oscar and Mary Handlin, "James Burgh and American Revolutionary Theory," p. 57. Carla H. Hay argued that Burgh's "tome [*Political Disquisitions*] quickly secured the status in England and in America of a monumental reference work with the authority of a political classic. An impressive number of America's founding fathers and virtually all the key figures in the English reform movement were indebted to the work." Hay, *James Burgh*, p. 105.

139. Isaac Kramnick and R. Laurence Moore identified Burgh as "the original source of the metaphor, which Jefferson would use, that captures in a phrase this entire liberal secular view of the relationship between politics and religion—the wall of separation." Kramnick and Moore, *The Godless Constitution: The Case Against Religious Correctness* (New York: W. W. Norton, 1996), p. 82. See also Kramnick, *Republicanism and Bourgeois Radicalism*, p. 232 (Burgh "could well be the source of Jefferson's" metaphor).

140. *Crito*, vol. 2, dedication, pp. 1, 3 (emphasis in the original). See also Hay, *James Burgh*, p. 34; Kramnick, *Republicanism and Bourgeois Radicalism*, p. 228.

141. See Joseph F. Costanzo, "Thomas Jefferson, Religious Education and Public Law," *Journal of Public Law* 8 (1959): 98 ("Years before all the states cancelled their church establishments and decades before the Supreme Court would make the First Amendment meaning of religious liberty operative upon the states through the Fourteenth Amendment, Jefferson is looking forward to the day when state governments would follow the example of the federal Constitution and guarantee by law equality of religious freedom.").

142. See note 18.

143. *Memoir, Correspondence and Miscellanies, from the Papers of Thomas Jefferson*, ed. Thomas Jefferson Randolph, 4 vols. (Charlottesville, Va.: F. Carr and Co., 1829).

144. *The Writings of Thomas Jefferson*, ed. Henry A. Washington, 9 vols. (Washington, D.C.: Taylor and Maury, 1853–1854).

145. Jeremiah S. Black, "Religious Liberty," An Address to the Phrenakosmian Society of Pennsylvania College, Delivered at the Annual Commencement, September 17, 1856, in *Essays and Speeches of Jeremiah S. Black* (New York: D. Appleton, 1885), p. 53 (emphasis in the original). Black's remark was quoted in *McCollum v. Board of Education*, 333 U.S. 203, 219–220, n. 8 (1948) (opinion of Frankfurter, J.).

146. Philip Schaff, *Church and State in the United States; or the American Idea of Religious Liberty and Its Practical Effects* (New York: G. P. Putnam's Sons; American Historical Society, 1888), p. 29, n. 1. Schaff reprinted excerpts from *Reynolds v. United States* (1878) in which the Supreme Court for the first time cited the Danbury letter. Ibid., p. 121. It is likely that this Court case exposed Schaff to the metaphor. In his 1857 biography of Jefferson, Henry S. Randall referenced, but did not quote, Jefferson's response to the Baptists and reproduced in full the letter to Levi Lincoln. Randall, *The Life of Thomas Jefferson*, vol. 3, p. 2.

147. *Reynolds v. United States*, 98 U.S. 145, 164 (1878). Robert M. Hutchins observed that the "wall" metaphor "played no role" in the Supreme Court's decision in *Reynolds v. United States*. Chief Justice Morrison R. Waite, who authored the opinion,

"wanted to use another phrase in Jefferson's letter to support his decision: he could not edit the letter to leave out the wall. The remark of Jefferson on which the Chief Justice relied was that the powers of government could reach only the actions of men, not their opinions." Hutchins, "The Future of the Wall," in *The Wall Between Church and State*, ed. Dallin H. Oaks (Chicago: University of Chicago Press, 1963), p. 17.

148. *Everson v. Board of Education*, 330 U.S. 1, 16, 18 (1947). Justice Hugo L. Black wrote the majority opinion in *Everson*. For a useful discussion of Justice Black's attraction to Jefferson's metaphor as a theme of his church–state views, see Barbara A. Perry, "Justice Hugo Black and the 'Wall of Separation Between Church and State,'" *Journal of Church and State* 31 (1989): 55–72

149. *McCollum v. Board of Education*, 333 U.S. 203, 247 (1948) (Reed, J., dissenting).

150. *Engel v. Vitale*, 370 U.S. 421, 445–446 (1962) (Stewart, J., dissenting).

151. *McCollum*, 333 U.S. at 238 (Jackson, J., concurring). But see *Committee for Public Education and Religious Liberty v. Nyquist*, 413 U.S. 756, 761 (1973) (Justice Lewis F. Powell, Jr. disputing that Jefferson's metaphoric "wall" has become as winding as his famous serpentine walls). See also Justice Jackson's admission in *Zorach v. Clauson:* "The wall which the Court was professing to erect between Church and State has become even more warped and twisted than I expected." *Zorach*, 343 U.S. 306, 325 (1952) (Jackson, J., dissenting). It is significant that Jackson credited the Court, not Jefferson or the framers of the First Amendment, with erection of the "wall." Gerard V. Bradley, *Church-State Relationships in America* (Westport, Conn.: Greenwood, 1987), p. 189.

152. *Gillette v. United States*, 401 U.S. 437, 450 (1971).

153. *Lemon v. Kurtzman*, 403 U.S. 602, 614 (1971).

154. *Wallace v. Jaffree*, 472 U.S. 38, 92, 106–107 (1985) (Rehnquist, J., dissenting). Jefferson, in fact, returned to America in November 1789, after the First Congress drafted the First Amendment, but before formal ratification of the Bill of Rights. For a scathing critique of Rehnquist's use of history in his dissenting *Jaffree* opinion, see Leo Pfeffer, "The Establishment Clause: An Absolutist's Defense," *Notre Dame Journal of Law, Ethics and Public Policy* 4 (1990): 720–729.

155. *Hyde v. United States*, 225 U.S. 347, 391 (1912) (Holmes, J., dissenting).

156. *Berkey v. Third Avenue Railroad Co.*, 244 N.Y. 84, 94, 155 N.E. 58, 61 (1926). See also William A. Stanmeyer, "Free Exercise and the Wall: The Obsolescence of a Metaphor," *George Washington Law Review* 37 (1968): 223–224 (footnote omitted) ("In recent controversies over the meaning of the American Constitution, there is probably no figure of speech more famous than the 'Wall of Separation between Church and State.' . . . Yet because of its very popularity, this metaphor endangers public understanding of the policy it aims to express, for frequent repetition of any shorthand phrase can, if we are not careful, reduce it to the status of a slogan. And slogans are poor tools with which to fashion public policy or Constitutional doctrine. If Justice Cardozo's comment is correct, if metaphors are indeed fickle friends which 'end often by enslaving' the very thought they started out to free, then the site, contours, foundation, and usefulness of this 'Wall' must be 'narrowly watched.'").

157. Letter from George Washington to the United Baptist Churches of Virginia, May 1789, *The Papers of George Washington*, Presidential Series, ed. Dorothy Twohig

(Charlottesville, Va.: University Press of Virginia, 1987), vol. 2, p. 423. For commentary on this letter, see Conrad Henry Moehlman, *The Wall of Separation Between Church and State: An Historical Study of Recent Criticism of the Religious Clause of the First Amendment* (Boston: Beacon Press, 1951), pp. 86–87 ("Washington's phrase 'effectual barriers against the horrors of spiritual tyranny' was the forerunner of Jefferson's 'wall of separation between church and state.' Both loved figures of speech: Washington, the military man, thought of 'barriers'; Jefferson, the man of home life, thought of a substantial, separating, secure wall around his estate. A barrier is the equivalent of a wall, especially when it is 'effectual.'"); Paul F. Boller, Jr. "George Washington and Religious Liberty," *William and Mary Quarterly,* 3d ser., 17 (1960): 498 (some Baptists "look upon [Washington's metaphor] as the forerunner of Jefferson's 'wall of separation between church and state.'").

158. James Madison, "Memorial and Remonstrance," in *The Papers of James Madison,* ed. Robert A. Rutland et al. (Chicago: University of Chicago Press, 1973), vol. 8, p. 299. See Eva T.H. Brann, "Madison's 'Memorial and Remonstrance': A Model of American Eloquence," in *Rhetoric and American Statesmanship,* ed. Glen E. Thurow and Jeffrey D. Wallin (Durham, N.C.: Carolina Academic Press, 1984), p. 21 ("That barrier, the limitation of legislative jurisdiction, is the political palisade before the 'wall of separation,' in Jefferson's famous metaphor for the First Amendment, which is to be erected between church and state.").

159. Letter from James Madison to the Reverend Jasper Adams, September 1833, in *Religion and Politics in the Early Republic: Jasper Adams and the Church-State Debate,* ed. Daniel L. Dreisbach (Lexington: University Press of Kentucky, 1996), p. 120 (emphasis added). In the same letter immediately following the "line" metaphor, Madison wrote: "The tendency to a usurpation on one side, or the other, or to a corrupting coalition or alliance between them, will be best guarded against by an entire abstinence of the Government from interference, in any way whatever, beyond the necessity of preserving public order, & protecting each sect against trespasses on its legal rights by others." Ibid. It would be a mistake to construe his "line of separation" as support for something less than a separation between church and state.

160. Sidney E. Mead, "Neither Church nor State: Reflections on James Madison's 'Line of Separation,'" *Journal of Church and State* 10 (1968): 350.

161. McBrien, *Caesar's Coin,* p. 66. See also ibid., pp. 176–177. See Terry Eastland, "In Defense of Religious America," *Commentary* 71, no. 6 (June 1981): 39 ("in today's usage the idea of a wall connotes antagonism and suspicion between the two sides thus separated.").

162. Cf. *McCollum,* 333 U.S. at 231 (opinion of Frankfurter, J.) ("Separation means separation, not something less. Jefferson's metaphor in describing the relation between Church and State speaks of a 'wall of separation,' not of a fine line easily overstepped."). See also Gaustad, *Sworn on the Altar of God,* p. 99 (according to Jefferson, the First Amendment "did not draw pale lines in invisible ink between the civil and ecclesiastical estates: it built a *wall.*"). McBrien noted that "theoretical appeals to the 'wall of separation' notwithstanding, the Court has adopted, in practice, the Madisonian rather than the Jeffersonian metaphor." For a discussion on the Supreme Court's references to the "line" metaphor and a comparison between Madison's "line" and Jefferson's "wall," see McBrien, *Caesar's Coin,* pp. 66–67.

163. The late Erwin N. Griswold, former dean of the Harvard Law School and U.S. Solicitor General, remarked: "Jefferson is often cited as the author of views leading to the absolutist approach. His 'wall of separation' is the shibboleth of those who feel that all traces of religion must be barred from any part of public activity. . . . What Jefferson wrote was a powerful way of summarizing the effect of the First Amendment. But it was clearly neither a complete statement nor a substitute for the words of the Amendment itself. Moreover, the absolute effect which some have sought to give to these words is belied by Jefferson's own subsequent actions and writings." Griswold, "Absolute is in the Dark—A Discussion of the Approach of the Supreme Court to Constitutional Questions," *Utah Law Review* 8 (1963): 174 (footnote omitted).

164. See Robert M. Hutchins, "The Future of the Wall," p. 18 (the "wall" "has not produced those instant solutions which its apparent clarity and directness lead its devotees to expect."); ibid., p. 19 ("The wall has done what walls usually do: it has obscured the view. It has lent a simplistic air to the discussion of a very complicated matter. Hence it has caused confusion whenever it has been invoked. Far from helping to decide cases, it has made opinions and decisions unintelligible. The wall is offered as a reason. It is not a reason; it is a figure of speech."); Paul G. Kauper, "Everson v. Board of Education: A Product of the Judicial Will," *Arizona Law Review* 15 (1973): 321 ("The use of any metaphor as a substitute for reasoning and principle is suspect, and this was early found to be the case with respect to the wall."); Ronald F. Thiemann, *Religion in Public Life: A Dilemma for Democracy* (Washington, D.C.: Georgetown University Press, 1996), pp. 42–43 ("Principles derived from metaphors have the advantage of capturing with vividness and felicity the essential elements of a complicated situation. They have the distinct disadvantage, however, of encouraging simplicity instead of precise analysis or fostering caricature when detailed portraiture is needed. At a time when our nation is struggling to define the proper role of religion and religiously based moral convictions within public life, the phrase 'the separation of church and state' and its attendant metaphor 'a wall of separation between church and state' serve not to clarify but to confuse. While the phrases identify one aspect of government's relation to religion, they deflect our attention from other fundamental features of the first amendment guarantees.") (endnote omitted).

165. Kauper, "Everson v. Board of Education: A Product of the Judicial Will," pp. 321–322, citing Wilber G. Katz, "Freedom of Religion and State Neutrality," *University of Chicago Law Review* 20 (1953): 428.

166. Robert Frost, "Mending Wall," in *Collected Poems of Robert Frost* (New York: Henry Holt and Co., 1930), p. 48.

167. See *Lemon v. Kurtzman*, 403 U.S. 602, 614 (1971).

168. *Larkin v. Grendel's Den*, 459 U.S. 116, 122–123 (1982). See also *Lynch v. Donnelly*, 465 U.S. 668, 673 (1984) ("The concept of a 'wall' of separation is a useful figure of speech probably deriving from [the] views of Thomas Jefferson.").

169. *Everson*, 330 U.S. at 59 (Rutledge, J., dissenting).

170. Levy, *The Establishment Clause*, p. 250.

171. Frost, "Mending Wall," p. 48. Justice Felix Frankfurter quoted Frost's poem in *McCollum*, 333 U.S. at 232 (opinion of Frankfurter, J.) ("If nowhere else, in the relation between Church and State, 'good fences make good neighbors.'"). But see O'Neill, *Religion and Education Under the Constitution*, p. 243 ("True enough! But only fences that allow for cooperation, friendly intercourse. Fences so 'high and im-

pregnable' as not to permit the slightest breach *never* make good neighbors. They are called 'spite fences' and are *never* built by good neighbors. They are only the instruments of extreme unneighborliness.") (emphasis in the original).

172. It is reported that these were the last words of John Adams who, unaware that Jefferson had expired five hours earlier at Monticello, died on July 4, 1826, the fiftieth anniversary of the American Declaration of Independence. See Merrill D. Peterson, *The Jefferson Image in the American Mind* (New York: Oxford University Press, 1960), pp. 3–6.

4

The Revolution in the Churches: Women's Religious Activism in the Early American Republic

Catherine A. Brekus

In 1801, a Connecticut woman who identified herself only as a "Female Advocate" published an angry treatise demanding greater equality for women. Writing twenty-five years after the American Revolution, she protested that men had unjustly deprived women of their religious, political, and legal rights. "Why ought the one half of mankind, to vault and lord it over the other?" she asked. Why should men have the power "to teach, to construe, to govern without the voice of women, or the least regard to the judgment or assent of the other sex"? Despite her loyalty to the new republic, she complained that it had not yet fulfilled its revolutionary promise. The problem, she explained, was simple: "men engross all the emoluments, offices, honors and merits of church and state."[1]

Like this anonymous female writer, one of the first public defenders of women's rights, many recent historians have lamented that women were excluded from the republican vision of liberty and equality. Even though the Founding Fathers were committed to creating a new social and political order, they never questioned women's subordination to men. Despite a few small gains, including the liberalization of divorce laws, women in the new republic still had few concrete rights: they were not allowed to vote, hold public office, make contracts, or if married, own their own property. (The first married women's property acts were not passed until the late 1830s.) With regret, many women's historians have concluded that the American Revolution was *not* revolutionary for women: it failed to dismantle the oppressive structures that confined them, offering them few of the precious freedoms celebrated by their sons, husbands, and fathers. More bleakly, other scholars have suggested that the Revolution not only excluded women, but was actively constructed against them. As the Founding Fathers faced the daunting task of creating one nation out of thirteen separate colonies, they chose to define citizenship against the subordinate position of women and slaves. A true republic, John Adams wrote, would be an exemplar of "all great, manly, and warlike virtues." As historian Linda Kerber has explained, "the construction of the autonomous, patriotic, male citizen required that the traditional relationship of women with unreliability, unpredictability, and lust be emphasized. Women's weakness became a foil for republican manliness." A citizen was independent, strong, and assertive—in other words, the opposite of a woman. In order to unify all white men in a single American identity, Revolutionary leaders insisted that women were too irrational, too passionate, and, in a word, too "feminine" to be trusted in the public world of men.[2]

There is no question that this dark interpretation of the Revolution's exclusionary character holds a disturbing grain of truth, but, as this chapter will argue, it would be a mistake to underestimate how deeply the Revolution affected American women. When historians have searched for evidence of a women's "revolution," they have often looked in the wrong places. Since women could not vote or hold public office until the passage of the Nineteenth Amendment in 1920, historians have assumed that they were utterly excluded from the public sphere. Yet the public realm encompassed more than the government, and the most momentous development for eighteenth-century women did not take place in politics, but in religion. In 1791, when the Bill of Rights declared that "Congress shall make no law respecting an establishment of religion or prohibiting the free exercise thereof," women gained new, unexpected opportunities to participate with men in public religious life. Far from remaining in a separate, domestic "sphere," they devoted themselves to building America into a virtuous, moral nation—a nation with the soul of a church.[3]

Historians have written countless number of books and articles about the separation of church and state, but few have asked how it affected American women. Even though the Founding Fathers probably never intended to cause a revolution in the churches, especially not a revolution that undermined traditional assumptions about gender roles, they inadvertently did just that. As churches lost their formal connection to the state, they no longer seemed as much like public institutions that should be governed by men alone. Forced to rely on persuasion, not coercion, to survive in the new republic, churches became simply one more kind of voluntary association competing for members. Because churches bridged the gap between the public and the private, the "masculine" world of the government and the "feminine" world of the family, many Americans believed that women as well as men could become public evangelists. Instead of obeying the biblical injunction to "keep silence in the churches," thousands of women in the early republic—white and black, northern and southern, Protestant, Catholic, and Jewish—organized home mission societies, distributed religious tracts, and founded charities and orphanages. Most remarkable of all, more than one hundred evangelical women crisscrossed the country as itinerant preachers. Few of these women were as politically radical as the contentious Female Advocate, but after the separation of church and state, they insisted that public religious activism was not outside of their "sphere." Before there was a political revolution for American women in the early republic, there was a religious revolution.

WOMEN, CHURCH, AND STATE IN COLONIAL AMERICA

It is impossible to understand the magnitude of the First Amendment without first understanding the close relationship between church and state in colonial America. As John Murrin has noted, one of the most persistent myths about the nation's founding is that the first settlers fled to the New World in order to defend the principle of religious liberty. Persecuted by English authorities, as schoolchildren learn today, the Puritans and Pilgrims built a new world in the wilderness where they could worship freely. One hundred and fifty years later, when Thomas Jefferson and James Madison supported the free exercise of religion, they were simply defending ideals that were essentially "American." Like most myths, this one certainly contains elements of truth: the Puritans strongly defended liberty of conscience, and because of their commitment to reform, they barred clergymen from holding public office. Nevertheless, the Puritans insisted that the government should be built on religious foundations, and they believed that political leaders had a duty to defend biblical truth. In the words of historian Harry Stout, the government "existed primarily for religious reasons and represented, in effect, the coercive arm of the churches." In seventeenth-century Massachusetts and Connecticut, for example, only male church members could vote in civil elections or hold political office, and everyone was legally required to pay taxes to support ministers and churches. Religious dissenters were fined, whipped, shipped out of the colony, or even put to death—grim proof of the government's commitment to preserving religious conformity. Between 1659 and 1661, four Quakers were hanged on the Boston Common for the crime of blasphemy.[4]

Church and state were closely linked in other seventeenth-century colonies as well. Although Southern Anglicans did not persecute dissenters as strenuously as the Puritans, they, too, believed that religion was crucial to maintaining political and social order. In Virginia, all colonists—no matter what their personal beliefs—were required to attend church and pay assessments for ministers' salaries. In Maryland, which was originally founded as a haven for Roman Catholics, Anglicans seized power and forbade Catholics to vote, hold office, or worship outside of private homes. "They deprive us of all the Advantages promised our Ancestors on their Coming into this Province," complained a group of Catholic petitioners. Of the original thirteen colonies, only four—Pennsylvania, Delaware, Rhode Island, and New Jersey—did not have established churches, and yet even there, political leaders assumed that Christianity was the bedrock of civil virtue. In 1701, for example, Pennsylvania's Charter of Privileges required all officeholders to affirm their belief in Christ.[5]

As America became more religiously pluralistic in the eighteenth century, most colonies became more tolerant, and the number of dissenting churches—Baptists, Methodists, Quakers, Separates—grew rapidly. Especially after the divisive evangelical revivals of the 1740s and 1750s, as Elizabeth Clark has explained, "there flourished a large measure of toleration and of support for free exercise of religion throughout the colonies." Yet religious tolerance was not the same as true religious liberty, and most Americans remained deeply suspicious of Catholic "Papists," whom they identified with the "Beast" of the Book of Revelation, and atheists, or, as they called them, "Nothingarians." "Allowing atheists Liberty of Conscience," objected the Reverend Moses Dickinson in 1775, would be "absurd." On the eve of the American Revolution, few colonists imagined that they would soon create a republic in which they would be free to worship—or *not* to worship—as they pleased.[6]

Partially because of this close relationship between church and state in colonial America, women were almost universally excluded from positions of religious leadership. Although there were many reasons why established churches tried to restrict women's public religious activism, including biblical precedent, they were also influenced by political considerations. With the power to collect state taxes for their support, both the Anglicans in the South and the Puritans in New England prided themselves on being the guardians of public order, and they believed that religion and politics were inextricably connected. Like colonial governments, which were built upon hierarchy and exclusion, they forbade women to "rule": women could not vote in church elections, speak publicly, or be ordained. On one hand, ministers praised women for their "*Zeal,* Faith, Purity, Charity, [and] Patience," and as growing numbers of women swelled the pews during the seventeenth century, they began to argue that women were inherently more pious than men.[7] According to available records, women dominated membership lists in virtually all Protestant churches. In the words of Cotton Mather, a Puritan minister, there seemed to be "far more Godly Women in the World, than there are Godly Men." Yet despite this language of female piety, clergymen also described women as sinfully weak and passionate, and echoing Paul's words to the Corinthians, they ordered them to "keep silence in the churches." When

William Secker, a Puritan minister, wrote an advice book for young men, he urged them to choose wives who would accept their "natural" subordination in the family, church, and state. "Our Ribs were not ordained to be our Rulers," he explained. "The Woman was made for the mans comfort, but the man was not made for the womans command. Those shoulders aspire too high, that content not themselves with a room below the head."[8]

When women in established churches dared to "aspire too high," they were often subjected to civil as well as church discipline. Anne Hutchinson, for example, the most celebrated female evangelist in the seventeenth century, was convicted of sedition after accusing her ministers of preaching a covenant of works rather than a covenant of grace—a serious charge in a culture that prized its Calvinist heritage. During a contentious court battle, Hutchinson repeatedly insisted that she had not broken any law, but her accusers knew better: her "ayme," Governor John Winthrop wrote, was nothing less than "the utter subversion both of Churches and civill state." Not only had she "infected" others with her heretical opinions by holding large religious meetings in her home, but she had violated codes of womanly modesty. "You have stept out of your place," complained Hugh Peters. "You have rather bine a Husband than a Wife and a preacher than a Hearer; and a Magistrate than a Subject." Her challenge to Puritan orthodoxy was perceived as a threat to men's authority in the state as well as the family and the church. Maligned as an "American Jezebel," she was excommunicated from her church and exiled to the wilderness of Rhode Island, "the Sinke into which all the Rest of the Colonyes empty their Hereticks."[9]

Using strikingly political language, ministers accused Hutchinson and other outspoken women of trying to "rule" over men or, in an even more common phrase, trying to "govern" them. For example, when a "cunning" woman in North Haven, Connecticut, claimed to have been divinely inspired to speak as a religious leader, she was disciplined for "contending and wanting to govern." Echoing this political rhetoric, a conservative minister accused Moravian, Quaker, and Separate Baptist women of wanting to be "Queens for Life." Because women in these sects were allowed to organize separate female meetings, participate in disciplinary hearings, and speak publicly, he saw them as an alarming threat to political as well as religious stability. In reality, few (if any) of these women claimed the power to "govern Men," but he assumed they were secretly plotting to reduce their husbands and fathers to a state of *"tame Subjection"* and "abject Submission."[10] In his opinion, churches could not expand women's religious rights without endangering the structure of the entire social order.

The only churches in colonial America that did not equate female religious activism with political disorder were composed of dissenters who received no financial support from the state. In contrast to the established churches, which saw themselves as virtually a branch of the government, sects such as the Baptists, Quakers, and Strict Congregationalists (more popularly known as the Separates) were opposed to the principle of religious establishment, and they thought it was possible to defend women's *gospel* liberty without raising questions about their *political* liberty as well. On the negative side, none of these churches treated women as the full equals of men, and despite their egalitarian rhetoric, they never questioned women's legal, economic, and political subordination. Even though Ebenezer Frothingham, a Separate clergyman, defended women's right to speak as public evangelists, he also waxed poetic in his descriptions of the patriarchal family: "What a beautiful, good, and ravishing sight it would be, to see a family well ordered and governed," he exulted. "The man in his place, in right government from love to God, and his dear family.—The woman in dutiful subjection to her husband." Despite their hostility to established churches, dissenters shared the popular disdain for women who tried to "rule" over men. More positively, however, they also gave women unprecedented freedom to vote in church meetings, serve on disciplinary committees, choose new ministers, and speak as evangelists.[11] Because they severed the connection between religion and politics, they saw no reason why women could not participate in the public life of the church.

The Quakers, the most theologically and socially radical sect in colonial America, allowed large numbers of women to serve as religious leaders. Because the Quakers believed that all people—no matter what their sex or race—have an "inner light" that allows them to receive revelations from God, they licensed women as well as men to spread God's word as "Public Friends." By 1800, almost half of the Quaker ministers in the Philadelphia Yearly Meeting were female. Besides the countless numbers of women who "witnessed" during local meetings, there were also dozens who traveled as itinerant ministers in both America and abroad. Between 1700 and 1800, at least forty-two American women crossed the ocean to visit Quaker meetings in Britain, often leaving their families for months or even years at a time. (Charity Cook, a Quaker minister from North Carolina, once left her husband and children for more than five years while she traveled through America, Great Britain, and Germany.[12]) Committed to religious liberty, the Quakers deliberately set themselves apart from the established churches that ordered women to "learn in silence with all subjection."

Although no other colonial sect was as egalitarian as the Quakers, both the Separates and Baptists allowed women to vote on church elections and to speak publicly as exhorters. As defined in the eighteenth century, an "exhorter" was an informal evangelist who admonished or encouraged others to repent. Unlike ordained clergymen, exhorters had no institutional authority: they did not have the right to deliver formal sermons explaining biblical texts, and they usually spoke from the pew rather than the pulpit. Nevertheless, female exhorters often spoke to large crowds of curious spectators, and the most daring did not hesitate to do battle with established clergymen. In 1742, when the Reverend Joseph Fish, a Congregationalist, arrived to preach at a meeting in New London, Connecticut, he was shocked to find several female exhorters boldly leading the congregation in prayer. Even after he stepped into the pulpit, one particularly contentious woman tried to drown out his voice with her own.[13]

As the examples of the Baptists, Quakers, and Separates illustrate, dissenting churches were far more likely than established churches to entrust women with public religious authority. Yet it is important to note that *all* of the churches that stood outside of the religious establishment were not so tolerant. Even though there was a strong correlation between dissent and female religious leadership, it was not absolute. For example, even though Roger Williams founded Rhode Island as a monument to religious liberty, he described female preaching as "a business all sober and modest Humanity abhor to think of."[14] Nor did Catholics and Jews—the quintessential religious outsiders in colonial America—ever encourage women to become public evangelists. Because Catholics were forced to hold meetings in private homes, Catholic laywomen seem to have been particularly influential within their communities, but there is no evidence that they were given the same authority as men. Later in the nineteenth century, Protestants would express shock (and disgust) at the sight of Catholic sisters, who seemed dangerously independent, but there were no female religious orders in British America until 1790. Even though Catholics, like Separates and Baptists, were a minority religion that stood apart from the state, they did not allow women to vote on church business or speak publicly during worship.

In sum, then, there was a strong correlation between religious dissent and female leadership in colonial America, but it was not absolute. The groups that gave women the greatest religious freedoms were shaped not only by their distinctive relationship to the state, but by their distinctive theologies and eschatologies. Yet even though there was no *single* factor that decisively determined attitudes toward women's religious activism, church–state relations were a significant influence.

FEMALE EVANGELISM IN THE EARLY REPUBLIC

In 1791, when the Bill of Rights shattered the traditional relationship between religion and politics, Americans were forced to rethink all of their assumptions about the role of churches in civic life. Historians debate over whether the founders intended to erect a "wall of separation" between church and state, or whether they simply intended to leave the question of religious establishments to state legislatures, but all agree that the "free exercise" clause was nothing short of revolutionary. As Jon Butler has explained, most colonial assemblies had "restricted legitimate religious opinion and practice to Christianity, or at best, to the Judeo-Christian tradition," but the founders defined religious freedom much more broadly. Influenced by the Enlightenment, they stripped the federal government of any power to coerce religious belief. Under Article Six of the Constitution—"No religious test shall ever be required as a qualification to any office or public trust under the authority of the United States"—even the nation's highest elected officials were not compelled to profess their belief in Christianity.[15]

Despite this dramatic legal break with the past, however, older attitudes about church and state died slowly. Ever since the fourth century, when Constantine had established Christianity as the Roman Empire's official religion, most Westerners had assumed that governments could not exist without strong religious foundations. Even though Americans knew they were too pluralistic to ever agree on a single national church, they also believed that the republic would collapse if it ever lost its distinctive Christian identity. "Statesmen . . . may plan and speculate for liberty," John Adams explained, "but it is religion and morality alone which can establish the principles upon which Freedom can securely stand." Following this logic, many Americans demanded that state legislatures follow a different course from the federal government. In Pennsylvania, officeholders were forced to "acknowledge the Scriptures of the old and new testaments to be given by divine inspiration," and in New Jersey, they were required to be Protestant. In the Puritan strongholds of Massachusetts, Connecticut, and New Hampshire, state legislatures did not begin disestablishing the churches until more than twenty years after the Bill of Rights. Despite the new rhetoric of religious freedom, most Americans still assumed that Protestantism should be the religion of the republic. In the famous words of Joseph Story, a Supreme Court justice, the "great basis" of the republic was "the Christian religion."[16]

Nevertheless, the separation of church and state represented a fundamental restructuring of American religion around the principles of freedom and competition. In the new republic, churchgoing would be voluntary, not required, and the churches that wanted to survive had to compete against one another for new converts. Even Massachusetts finally disestablished the Congregational church at the late date of 1833. Although churches continued to exert an enormous influence on American culture, they were helpless to enforce theological conformity in a new, pluralistic religious marketplace. Religious authority had now shifted from the state to voluntary institutional bodies.[17]

Even the definition of the word *church* changed: Americans no longer imagined churches as comprehensive, unifying institutions that undergirded the political order, but as voluntary devotional communities where people could worship with other believers. Quoting from John Locke, Thomas Jefferson defined a church as:

"a *voluntary* society of men, joining themselves together of their own accord, in order to the public worshipping of God in such a manner as they judge acceptable to him and effectual to the salvation of their souls." It is *voluntary* because no man is *by nature* bound to any church. The hope of his salvation is the cause of his entering into it. If he find anything wrong in it, he should be as free to go out as he was to come in.

Persuasion, not coercion, had become the dominant metaphor of religious life.[18]

Cut off from government support, churches in the early republic no longer enjoyed the privileges of formal state authority. Contrary to what some historians have argued, however, this does not mean that they were entirely stripped of their political and intellectual power. In her controversial 1977 book *The Feminization of American Culture,* Ann Douglas charged that the disestablishment of the churches transformed them into "feminine," privatized institutions that were peripheral to American culture. Without the power to enforce religious conformity, ministers increasingly depended on women, the majority of their congregants, for financial and psychological support, and in order to attract more converts, they substituted a cheap sentimentalism for theological rigor. By the mid-nineteenth century, according to Douglas, churches had lost their former stature as the custodians of public morality.[19]

Yet even though nineteenth-century churches were not as powerful as their seventeenth- and eighteenth-century predecessors, they still retained vestiges of their former power. Churches could not collect state taxes or force people into the pews, but they continued to influence American culture throughout the nineteenth and twentieth centuries. Indeed, they were centrally involved in both the abolitionist and civil rights movements. After disestablishment, churches occupied a new space in American culture, a space that was neither entirely public nor entirely private. Standing between the private world of the family and the public world of the government, they had become part of what we now call "civil society": "the many forms of community and association that dot the landscape of a democratic culture," including neighborhood groups, trade unions, and charities.[20] Occupying a middle ground between the public and the private, churches were no longer any different from all the other voluntary societies competing for members in the vast marketplace of American culture. Rather than the state-supported guardians of public order, they had become simply another kind of independent association.

As churches ceased to be public, political institutions in the same sense as they had been in colonial America, ministers began to give women greater opportunities for involvement and leadership. Following in the footsteps of eighteenth-century Separates, Quakers, and Baptists, who had never been formally connected to the state, they no longer feared that female religious activism would necessarily lead to political disorder. If churches occupied a middle ground between the family and the government, then women as well as men could take an active role in church affairs without appearing too "masculine" or commanding. In churches across the country, women worked side by side with men to build a more religious society. In an address to the Female Cent Society of Bedford, New Hampshire, a minister explained, "it is the will of our Lord, to make use of the exertions of women, and to receive their friendly aid, in support of his cause on the earth."[21]

In the tumultuous years after the nation's founding, ministers and politicians particularly welcomed women's religious activism because of their fears that the republic might be too fragile to survive. From the vantage point of the late twentieth century, it is easy to forget how precarious America's great democratic experiment must have seemed in the early 1800s: Federalists and Republicans argued bitterly over the centralization of power; the New England states briefly toyed with the idea of secession at the 1814 Hartford Convention; and the Southern states, intent on preserving the "peculiar institution" of slavery, only reluctantly agreed to abide by the Missouri Compromise of 1819. Fearful of what the future might hold, many Americans predicted that the nation would endure only if it nurtured an ethic of republican and Christian virtue. After Andrew Reed, an English minister, visited the United States in the early 1830s, he warned that Americans would prosper only if *"they remain[ed] under the influence of religion."* "AMERICA WILL BE GREAT ONLY IF AMERICA IS GOOD," he proclaimed. "If not, her greatness will vanish away like a morning cloud." According to Alexis de Tocqueville, the most perceptive nineteenth-century critic of American democracy, Americans believed that religion was "indispensable to the maintenance of republican institutions." The nation would thrive only as long as ordinary people—women as well as men—were willing to work together on behalf of the common good.[22]

For a number of reasons, including the growth of a market economy, the influence of Scottish moral philosophers and British sentimental novelists, and the new ideology of republican motherhood, nineteenth-century Americans increasingly turned to women rather than men to sustain the values of a Christian culture. After the American Revolution, the popular understanding of the word "virtue" changed: "virtu"—the "masculine" quality of public spirit—became "virtue"—the "feminine" quality of morality. Even though ministers still described women as the weaker sex, they also published countless numbers of sermons and tracts praising their natural piety and goodness. "Their feelings are more exquisite than those of men," one author wrote, "and their sentiments greater and more refined."[23] By 1825, it was common wisdom that women's Christian morality was the glue that held the republic together. "What though females cannot stand in the sacred desk, nor sit on the bench of justice?" a Baptist asked. "What though they cannot be employed in framing laws, nor in conducting diplomatic missions, nor in organizing or governing nations? They can contribute more by their virtues and their influence to bind society together, than all the laws that legislators ever formed."[24] Women, according to ministers and politicians, were the guardians of civic virtue.

The drawbacks of this seemingly positive language are immediately obvious to anyone who has studied the Victorian "cult of true womanhood." However much women may have been praised for their morality, they still had few concrete political or legal rights, and their virtue was closely tied to their domesticity. Indeed, one historian has suggested that men stressed women's inherent differences in order to claim political participation as a masculine prerogative. The more that women seemed to differ from men, the easier it was to justify their exclusion from the government.[25] In popular magazines, novels, and advice books, women read that they were too pure and innocent to participate in the aggressive world of party politics. Instead of exercising power, they were supposed to be satisfied with radiating "influence."

Yet even though women sometimes chafed against this ideology of female virtue, they also transformed it into a powerful justification of their right to participate in the public sphere. As one evangelical woman explained in 1806, "the Lord has permitted our sex to step out of the narrow path of domestic life, and employ their talents of grace, whether great or small, in doing all in their power to assist in the glorious cause of his spiritual kingdom established on earth."[26] Armed with the faith that they were more virtuous and pious than men, women organized temperance societies, raised money for widows and orphans, and, risking scandal, launched purity campaigns to close down local brothels. Margaret Prior, a devout Methodist and a member of the Moral Reform Society in New York City, shocked many of her friends by visiting "houses of infamy" to hand out religious tracts and encourage prostitutes to convert. Besides being condemned by polite society, she was also harassed by the women whom she supposedly wanted to help. On one occasion when she exhorted a group of prostitutes to repent, they imprisoned her in a locked room. Refusing to be intimidated, she called out:

> Well, if I'm a prisoner I shall *pray* here, and would sing praises to God if I were not so hoarse. Yes, bless the Lord! his presence can make me happy here or anywhere, and you can have no power to harm me unless he gives it. This is a dreadful place, to be sure, but it is not so bad as hell; for there, there is no hope. The smoke of their torment ascendeth up for ever and ever! What a mercy that we are not all there!

As Prior later explained, "I talked to them in this way until they were glad to open the door as a signal for my release."[27] By the 1820s and 1830s, female reformers such as Prior were a familiar (and often irritating) presence on American streets.

Many historians have celebrated women's religious activism in the new republic, but they have often been uncertain over whether to characterize it as "public." Not only have they assumed that churches were private institutions, but they have also tended to equate the public realm with formal politics. As a result, they have sometimes described women's religious associations as part of a separate female "sphere" that stood outside of civic culture. According to Mary Ryan, for example, female religious reformers were on "the sidelines of the public sphere." Their work was "conducted just off the public stage. . . ." To be sure, most of the women who joined women's associations did not try to directly influence the political process, and they did not demand political rights. Nevertheless, churches and other religious associations belonged to the public realm as well as the private, and they numbered among the most powerful institutions in civil society. Even though most women denied that their religious work was political, they helped shape public debates about children's welfare, slavery, temperance, and sexual morality.[28]

Most of the women who founded charitable and reform organizations in the early republic were white, middle-class, northern, and Protestant, but their dominance did not go uncontested. Instead of one single public sphere where all women worked together on behalf of the common good, there were multiple publics where women competed with one another for authority. Not surprisingly, black and white women, middle and lower-class women, and Catholic, Jewish, and Protestant women often had different visions of what might constitute true religion, and they founded separate organizations to further their goals. In response to zealous home missionaries such as Margaret Prior, who hoped to promote America's identity as a Protestant nation, Catholic and Jewish women created their own distinctive institutions. In 1819, for example, Rebecca Gratz helped found the first Female Hebrew Benevolent Society in Philadelphia.[29]

Competition between Catholic and Protestant women was especially fierce during these years. As Irish and German immigrants flooded America's ports during the 1820s and 1830s, Catholic sisters came with them, founding charities, orphanages, and schools to ease the hardships of urban life. Although these women were praised by Catholics for their self-sacrificing devotion to the needy, they were condemned by Protestants who were deeply suspicious of their celibacy and their seeming independence from male authority. On one hand, nuns were criticized for being too manly and aggressive, while on the other, they were decried as submissive, obedient dupes who mindlessly followed the orders of their bishops and the pope. Fueled by inflammatory exposés such as Maria Monk's *Awful Disclosures,* the bestselling book in America before the publication of *Uncle Tom's Cabin,* rumors swirled that Catholic convents were nothing more than "harems" for sexually voracious priests. According to Monk, whose tale was promoted by several prominent Protestant ministers, the babies born of these illicit liaisons were buried in basement pits.[30] At a time when Protestants were fearful that Catholics were plotting nothing less than the overthrow of the republic, Protestant and Catholic women aggressively competed with one another for public respect. While Protestant women urged impressionable "young ladies" not to be seduced by the illusion of sisters' religious independence, Catholic sisters waged a smear campaign of their own: one Catholic woman denigrated Protestantism as "a mere chaos; dark and void, and shapeless like the original nothing from which the world was founded."[31] These public disputes raged throughout the rest of the century, bringing Catholic and Protestant women into the public sphere to promote their own distinctive understandings of Christianity.

The sheer variety of women's religious activism in the early republic is staggering, crossing boundaries of denomination, class, race, and even region. To mention just a few examples: the Oblate Sisters of Providence, the first black religious order in America, taught free black children to read; more than five hundred Protestant women served as missionaries to the Indians between 1815 and 1865; and scores of middle-class white women sailed to the South Seas to save the "heathen."[32] According to Elizabeth Varon, who has studied white women's activism in Virginia, even respectable Southern "ladies" fought to influence public debates. Contrary to what most historians have assumed, elite Southern women were energetically involved in missionary associations, charities, and especially the American Colonization Society. In the years before the Civil War, women such as Ann Page, the widow of a wealthy planter, raised thousands of dollars to send slaves back to Africa. "The evils of slavery," she warned, "can not be seen by human powers." Mixing religion with politics, Southern women also sent petitions to the state legislature demanding a government-sponsored plan of gradual emancipation.[33] Despite the rhetoric of female domesticity, southern as well as northern women were visible participants in an extraordinary number of national organizations, including the American Colonization Society, the American Tract Society, the American Bible Society, and the American Sunday School Union.

Of all the religious women who made their voices heard in the public sphere, perhaps none were more visible or controversial than evangelical female preachers. During the revivals of the Second Great Awakening (1790–1845), several new sects—including the Methodists, the African Methodists, the Freewill Baptists, the Christian Connection, and the Millerites—allowed more than one hundred women to crisscross the country as itinerant evangelists. Rather than exhorters (like eighteenth-century Baptist and Separate women), these women were preachers who stood in the pulpit to deliver formal sermons on biblical texts. With a few notable exceptions, including Sojourner Truth, almost all of these women have been forgotten, but they were immensely popular among lower-class evangelicals in the early nineteenth century. Harriet Livermore, one of the most charismatic (and affluent), was invited to preach in front of Congress four times between 1827 and 1843. "It savored more of inspiration than anything I ever witnessed," one woman marveled. "And to enjoy the frame of mind which I think she does, I would relinquish the world. Call this rhapsody if you will; but would to God you had heard her!" More negatively, President John Quincy Adams, who sat on the steps leading up to her feet because he could not find a free chair, slighted Livermore as a religious fanatic. "There is a permanency in this woman's monomania which seems accountable only from the impulse of vanity and love of fame," he wrote later.[34]

In the eyes of the American public, female preachers symbolized both the benefits and the dangers of the growing acceptance of public womanhood. According to their supporters, especially the clergymen in their own sects, female preachers were pious "Mothers in Israel" and "Sisters in Christ" who had been divinely inspired to preach the gospel. Like male ministers, they were committed to creating a Christian nation, and they had "succeeded in turning many to RIGHTEOUSNESS." According to their critics, however, these same women were "jezebels" who had sacrificed their "feminine" modesty for public glory. "Wherever you find a female public teacher," warned the Reverend Thomas Andros, "there in general you will find a jezebel, who comes as the advocate of some deadly corruption of Christianity." As Harriet Livermore and other female preachers traveled from town to town, they were locked out of meetinghouses, slandered as "crazy" or "shameless," and sometimes even threatened with physical harm. Like Catholic sisters, they were also accused of being sexually promiscuous. Dorothy Ripley, a female preacher from England, was so renowned for her evangelism to slaves that she met with Thomas Jefferson, but despite her fame, she was suspected of being a "lewd woman." On a stagecoach trip to Virginia, one man tried "to take undue liberties" with her.[35]

Generally speaking, the churches that were still established by law, or only recently disestablished, tended to be the most opposed to female preaching. Like their eighteenth-century forebears, they still assumed that church and state were closely connected (or *should* be closely connected), and they viewed women's religious leadership as a threat to men's political as well as religious authority. For example, even though New England Congregationalists believed that women could become missionaries or Sunday school teachers, they insisted that women could not "rule" over men as preachers. In 1817, the Reverend Matthew Perrine warned his female congregants to set their sights on more humble forms of religious service. "Women have a work to do in the house of God," he assured his listeners, but that work did not include "teaching" or "governing" men. Although women could organize benevolent societies, they could not "perform the office of public teachers, or . . . exercise rule, or . . . dictate in matters of faith and discipline."[36] Even though women could evangelize sinners informally, they could not "govern" men by usurping their exclusive right to the pulpit.

Many ministers seem to have viewed female preaching as a symbol of their crumbling authority in the wake of church disestablishment. In 1832, when Massachusetts became the last state to sever the link between church and state, no church in America could claim to be part of the formal public of the government, but only the informal public of reform organizations, charities, and missions—a truncated public that seemed to carry far less power and prestige. Even though the Congregationalists and Anglicans accepted the principle of religious liberty, they seem to have longed for the political and intellectual authority that their colonial forefathers had taken for granted.[37] Cut off from state support, they resented having to compete in a new spiritual marketplace with upstart Methodists and Baptists, uneducated immigrant Catholics, and, last but not least, crusading "jezebels." In the angry words of Parsons Cooke, a Congregationalist minister, "To a well-balanced mind there is something revolting in the spectacle of a woman . . . intruding upon the theatres of masculine ambition, trampling under foot the commands of God, and the decencies of her sex, under a mistaken zeal for God."[38] In his opinion, only educated Protestant ministers were qualified to be the religious leaders of the new nation.

To defend themselves against their critics, female preachers denied having any intention of undermining men's authority in the family, church, or state. On one hand, they held a more expansive view of womanhood than middle-class female reformers, and they angrily defended women's right to proclaim the gospel. God had created woman to be "'a help meet'—an equal—a partner—a companion—an assistant," Harriet Livermore wrote, not "a servant, to sit at the feet of man, and do him homage." Yet these women also never demanded the right to be ordained, and instead of questioning their subordination to men, they affirmed their secondary place in the hierarchy of creation. Even though Deborah Peirce published an entire book defending women's right to spread "the good news of salvation," she agreed that only *men* had the right to "rule and go forward."[39] In a culture that separated church and state, she claimed that women's religious authority did not give them the right to political power. Women could preach to men, but not govern them.

Given this conservative rhetoric, it may seem like an exaggeration to describe women's religious activism in the early republic as "revolutionary." Even though women took a more visible role in civil society after the separation of church and state, they did not gain any legal or political rights, and even their religious rights remained limited. In 1820, as in 1776, women made up the majority of most Protestant churches, but they still could not vote, own their own property, or be ordained to the ministry. If, as many historians have argued, the founders could not imagine a society where women would be truly equal to men, they were not alone: most Americans in the early republic assumed that women had been created subordinate by nature. The separation of church and state, it could be argued, did little to improve the political rather than religious status of American women.

Yet whatever the founders originally intended, women constructed their own meanings and their own possibilities out of the republican language they inherited, and as conservative critics had long feared, the most radical began to question why they were allowed to participate in public religious life but not in the government. If women could be reformers and missionaries, then why couldn't they also vote or hold public office? When the first women's rights convention met in Seneca Falls, New York, in 1848, women insisted that they were politically as well as religiously equal to men. Since God intended women to be "man's equal," they declared, they had a "sacred right to the elective franchise." The early women's rights movement, as we have only recently begun to understand, had deep religious roots. Although early feminists phrased many of their arguments in the abstract language of natural rights, they also claimed that God had specially "anointed," "sanctified," and "baptized" them to fight for a "sacred cause." As one woman explained, God had called her "to restore the divine order to the world."[40]

By separating church and state, the founders set in motion a religious revolution that brought countless numbers of women into the public sphere as home and foreign missionaries, moral reformers, temperance activists, preachers, and, last but not least, women's rights activists. As we have seen, it was a revolution that was sadly incomplete, contested, and flawed, but despite its limitations, it laid the foundation for a new acceptance of women's religious and political equality to men. Future generations of American women, looking backward with both hope and regret, would have to struggle to finish the work that the founders had never intended to begin.

NOTES

1. *The Female Advocate, Written by a Lady* (New Haven, Conn.: Thomas Green and Son, 1801), reprinted in *Early American Women: A Documentary History 1600–1900,* ed. Nancy Woloch (Belmont, Calif.: Wadsworth Publishing, 1992), pp. 186–189. See also Linda K. Kerber, *Women of the Republic: Intellect and Ideology in Revolutionary America* (Chapel Hill: University of North Carolina Press, 1980), p. 277.

2. John Adams quoted in Sara M. Evans, *Born for Liberty: A History of Women in America* (New York: Free Press, 1989), p. 47. Linda K. Kerber, "'I have Don . . . much to Carrey on the Warr': Women and the Shaping of Republican Ideology After the American Revolution," in *Women and Politics in the Age of the Democratic Revolution,* ed. Harriet B. Applewhite and Darline G. Levy (Ann Arbor: The University of Michigan Press, 1990), p. 251. On women in the Revolution, see Kerber, *Women of the Republic;* Mary Beth Norton, *Liberty's Daughters: The Revolutionary Experience*

of American Women, 1750–1800 (Boston: Little, Brown, and Company, 1989); Susan Juster, *Disorderly Women: Sexual Politics and Evangelicalism in Revolutionary New England* (Ithaca, N.Y.: Cornell University Press, 1994), pp. 135–144; Ronald Hoffman and Peter J. Albert, eds., *Women in the Age of the American Revolution* (Charlottesville: the University Press of Virginia, 1989); Joan Hoff-Wilson, "The Illusion of Change: Women and the American Revolution," in *The American Revolution: Explorations in the History of American Radicalism,* ed. Alfred F. Young (Dekalb, Ill.: Northern Illinois University, 1976), pp. 383–445; and Marylynn Salmon, "'Life, Liberty, and Dower': The Legal Status of Women after the American Revolution," in *Women, War, and Revolution,* ed. Carol R. Berkin and Clara M. Lovett (New York: Holms and Meier, 1980), pp. 85–106. Several historians have argued that the republic was constructed against women. See Carroll Smith-Rosenberg, "Dis-Covering the Subject of the 'Great Constitutional Discussion,' 1786–1789," *The Journal of American History* 79 (December 1992): 841–873; and Cynthia Jordan, "'Old Worlds' in 'New Circumstances': Language and Leadership in Post-Revolutionary America," *American Quarterly* 40, no. 4 (December 1988): 491–513. Joan Landes has made a similar argument about the essentially exclusionary nature of the French republic. See Joan B. Landes, *Women and the Public Sphere in the Age of the French Revolution* (Ithaca, N.Y.: Cornell University Press, 1988). In contrast, Rosemarie Zagarri argues that women's exclusion from the republic was "contingent, not essential." See Rosemarie Zagarri, "The Rights of Man and Woman in Post-Revolutionary America," *William and Mary Quarterly* 55, no. 2 (April 1998): 229.

3. G. K. Chesterton described America as a "nation with the soul of a church." See Sidney E. Mead, *The Nation with the Soul of a Church* (New York: Harper and Row, 1975).

4. John M. Murrin, "Religion and Politics in America from the First Settlements to the Civil War," in *Religion and American Politics: From the Colonial Period to the 1980s,* ed. Mark A. Noll (New York: Oxford University Press, 1990), pp. 19–43. Harry S. Stout, *The New England Soul: Preaching and Religious Culture in Early New England* (New York: Oxford University Press, 1986), p. 20. On seventeenth-century attitudes toward religious freedom, see James H. Hutson, *Religion and the Founding of the American Republic* (Washington, D.C.: Library of Congress, 1998), pp. 3–18.

5. The Catholic petitioners are quoted in Jay Dolan, *The American Catholic Experience: A History from Colonial Times to the Present* (Garden City, N.J.: Doubleday, 1985), p. 85. See Thomas J. Curry, *The First Freedoms: Church and State in America to the Passage of the First Amendment* (New York: Oxford University Press, 1986), pp. 31–53, 75; J. William Frost, *A Perfect Freedom: Religious Liberty in Pennsylvania* (Cambridge: Cambridge University Press, 1990), and Anson Phelps Stokes, *Church and State in the United States: Historical Development and Contemporary Problems of Religious Freedom Under the Constitution* (New York: Harper and Brothers, 1950), vol. 1, pp. 206–208.

6. Elizabeth B. Clark, "Church–State Relations in the Constitution-Making Period," in *Church and State in America: A Bibliographical Guide,* vol. 1: *The Colonial and Early National Periods,* ed. John F. Wilson (New York: Greenwood Press, 1986), p. 155. Moses Dickinson, *A Sermon* (New London, 1775), p. 35, quoted in Curry, *First Freedoms,* p. 79. For examples of the growing religious toleration in the eighteenth century, see the documents reprinted in *Church and State in American History: The*

Burden of Religious Pluralism, second ed., ed. John F. Wilson and Donald L. Drakeman (Boston: Beacon Press, 1987), pp. 32–82.

7. Benjamin Colman, *The Duty and Honour of Aged Women* (Boston: B. Green, 1711), p. 5. Emphasis in the original. On positive images of women in Puritan sermons, see Laurel Thacher Ulrich, "Vertuous Women Found: New England Ministerial Literature, 1688–1735," in *A Heritage of Her Own,* ed. Nancy F. Cott and Elizabeth H. Pleck (New York, 1979), pp. 58–80; and Lonna M. Malmsheimer, "Daughters of Zion: New England Roots of American Feminism," *New England Quarterly* (September 1977): 484–504.

8. Cotton Mather, *Ornaments for the Daughters of Zion* (Cambridge, Mass., 1692), pp. 44–45. William Secker, *A Wedding Ring for the Finger, the Salve of Divinity on the Sore of Humanity. Directions to Those Men Who Want Wives, How to Choose* (Boston: Samuel Green, 1690), quoted in Lyle Koehler, *A Search for Power: The Weaker Sex in Seventeenth-Century New England* (Chicago: University of Chicago Press, 1980), p. 31. For statistics on membership by gender, see Harry S. Stout and Catherine A. Brekus, "A New England Church: Center Church, New Haven, 1639–1989," in *American Congregations,* ed. James P. Wind and James W. Lewis (Chicago: University of Chicago Press, 1994), pp. 14–102, and Richard D. Shiels, "The Feminization of American Congregationalism, 1730–1835," *American Quarterly* 33 (1981): 48.

9. John Winthrop, *A Short Story,* in *The Antinomian Controversy, 1636–1638: A Documentary History,* ed. David D. Hall (Durham: Duke University Press, 1990), pp. 263–265. "A Report of the Trial of Mrs. Anne Hutchinson before the Church in Boston," in *The Antinomian Controversy,* pp. 382–83. The description of Rhode Island comes from John Woodbridge, Jr., to Richard Baxter, in "Woodbridge-Baxter Correspondence," ed. Raymond Phineas Stearns, *New England Quarterly* 10 (1937), p. 573, quoted in Carla Pestana, *Quakers and Baptists in Colonial Massachusetts* (Cambridge: Cambridge University Press, 1991), p. 2. On Hutchinson, see Ben Barker-Benfield, "Anne Hutchinson and the Puritan Attitude toward Women," *Feminist Studies* 1, no. 2 (1972–73): 65–96; Lyle Koehler, "The Case of the American Jezebels: Anne Hutchinson and Female Agitation during the Years of Antinomian Turmoil, 1636–1640," *William and Mary Quarterly* 31 (1974): 55–78; Amy Scrager Lang, *Prophetic Woman: Anne Hutchinson and the Problem of Dissent in the Literature of New England* (Berkeley: University of California Press, 1987); and Jane Kamensky, *Governing the Tongue: The Politics of Speech in Early New England* (New York: Oxford University Press, 1997), pp. 71–81.

10. Barbara E. Lacey, "Women and the Great Awakening in Connecticut," Ph.D. dissertation, Clark University, 1982, p. 152. Robert Ross, *A Plain Address to the Quakers, Moravians, Separatists* (New Haven: Parker and Company, 1762), pp. 146–148, 151, emphasis in the original.

11. Ebenezer Frothingham, *A Key to Unlock the Door, That Leads in, to Take a Fair View of the Religious Constitution, Established by Law, in the Colony of Connecticut* (New Haven: n.p., 1767), p. 199. On voting, see Juster, *Disorderly Women,* pp. 41–42. On the Baptists and Separates, see William G. McLoughlin, *New England Dissent, 1630–1883: The Baptists and the Separation of Church and State,* 2 vols. (Cambridge: Harvard University Press, 1971), and C. C. Goen, *Revivalism and Separatism in New England, 1740–1800: Strict Congregationalists and Separate Baptists in the Great Awakening* (New Haven: Yale University Press, 1962).

12. Joan M. Jensen, *Loosening the Bonds: Mid-Atlantic Farm Women, 1750–1850* (New Haven: Yale University Press, 1986), pp. 150–151. Margaret Hope Bacon, *Mothers of Feminism: The Story of Quaker Women in America* (San Francisco: Harper and Row, 1986), p. 34. On Cook, see Algie I. Newlin, *Charity Cook: A Liberated Woman* (Richmond, Ind.: Friends United Press, 1981), p. 63. See also Mary Maples Dunn, "Latest Light on Women of Light," in *Witnesses for Change: Quaker Women Over Three Centuries,* ed. Elisabeth Potts Brown and Susan Mosher Stuard (New Brunswick: Rutgers University Press, 1989); Barry Levy, *Quakers and the American Family: British Settlement in the Delaware Valley* (New York: Oxford University Press, 1988), pp. 193–230; and Rebecca Larson, *Daughters of Light: Quaker Women Preaching and Prophesying in the Colonies and Abroad, 1700–1775* (New York: Knopf, 1999).

13. On Fish, see Joshua Hempstead, *The Diary of Joshua Hempstead of New London, Connecticut* (New London, 1901), pp. 402–403. On female exhorters, see Catherine A. Brekus, *Strangers and Pilgrims: Female Preaching in America, 1740–1845* (Chapel Hill: University of North Carolina Press, 1998), pp. 44–61.

14. Roger Williams, *George Fox Digg'd Out of His Burrowes* (Boston: John Foster, 1676), p. 12, quoted in Koehler, *Search for Power,* p. 306.

15. Jon Butler, *Awash in a Sea of Faith: Christianizing the American People* (Cambridge: Harvard University Press, 1990), p. 265. For a sampling of the debate over the founders' intentions, see John F. Wilson, "Religion, Government, and Power in the New American Nation," in *Religion and American Politics: From the Colonial Period to the 1980s,* ed. Mark A. Noll (New York: Oxford University Press, 1990), pp. 77–91; Winthrop S. Hudson, *The Great Tradition of the American Churches* (New York: Harper and Brothers, 1953); Edwin S. Gaustad, "Religious Tests, Constitutions, and 'Christian Nation,'" in *Religion in a Revolutionary Age,* ed. Ronald Hoffman and Peter J. Albert (Charlottesville: University Press of Virginia, 1994), pp. 218–235; Loren P. Beth, *The American Theory of Church and State* (Gainesville: University of Florida Press, 1958), pp. 61–76; Robert T. Handy, *A Christian America: Protestant Hopes and Historical Realities,* 2d ed. (New York: Oxford University Press, 1984); and Mark A. Noll, *One Nation Under God? Christian Faith and Political Action in America* (San Francisco: Harper and Row, 1988), pp. 54–74.

16. Handy, *A Christian America,* p. 4; John Adams to Zabdiel Adams, June 21, 1776, quoted in Edwin S. Gaustad, *Neither King Nor Prelate: Religion and the New Nation, 1776–1826* (Grand Rapids, Mich.: Eerdmans, 1993), p. 92; Mark A. Noll, *A History of Christianity in the United States and Canada* (Grand Rapids, Mich.: W. B. Eerdmans, 1992), p. 145, and Robert Baird, *Religion in America* (New York: Harper & Brothers, 1856), p. 268. For Joseph Story, see *The Founders' Constitution,* ed. Philip B. Kurland and Ralph Lerner (Chicago: University of Chicago Press, 1987), Vol. 5, p. 108. Several historians have pointed out the persistence of official or unofficial Protestant establishments. See Paul Conkin, *The Uneasy Center: Reformed Christianity in Antebellum America* (Chapel Hill: University of North Carolina, 1995), pp. 116–118; Butler, *Awash in a Sea of Faith,* p. 257; Martin E. Marty, "Living with Establishment and Disestablishment in Nineteenth-Century Anglo America," *Journal of Church and State* 18, no. 1 (1976): 61–77; and Clark, "Church–State Relations," p. 161. For a discussion of Federalist clergy who continued to link religion and politics, see Harry S. Stout, "Rhetoric and Reality in the Early Republic: The Case of the Federalist Clergy," in *Religion and American Politics: From the Colonial Period to the 1980s,*

ed. Mark A. Noll (New York: Oxford University Press, 1990), pp. 62–76. See also Louis P. Masur, "Religion and Reform in America, 1776–1860," in *Church and State in America: A Bibliographical Guide,* vol. 1: *The Colonial and Early National Periods,* ed. John F. Wilson (New York: Greenwood Press, 1986), p. 226.

17. Butler, *Awash in a Sea of Faith,* p. 268.

18. Thomas Jefferson, "Notes on Religion, October (1776?)," quoted in Sidney E. Mead, *The Lively Experiment: The Shaping of Christianity in America* (New York: Harper and Rowe, 1963), p. 58, emphasis in the original. On the transformation from coercion to persuasion, see Mead, *Lively Experiment,* pp. 16–37. Jon Butler points out that many historians have ignored "the redefinition of the term 'religion' in public discourse." See Butler, *Awash in a Sea of Faith,* p. 258. E. Brooks Holifield offers a useful overview of the changing definition of congregations in "Toward a History of American Congregations," in *American Congregations,* Volume 2: *New Perspectives in the Study of Congregations,* ed. James P. Wind and James W. Lewis (Chicago: University of Chicago Press, 1994), pp. 23–53.

19. Ann Douglas, *The Feminization of American Culture* (New York: Knopf, 1977), especially 17–43. For a challenge to Douglas, see David S. Reynolds, "The Feminization Controversy: Sexual Stereotypes and the Paradoxes of Piety in Nineteenth-Century America," *New England Quarterly* 53 (March 1980): 96–106.

20. Martin E. Marty argues that religion is both public and private. See his "Religion: A Private Affair, in Public Affairs," *Religion and American Culture* 3, no. 2 (Summer 1993): 115–128. See also Clarke E. Cochran, *Religion in Public and Private Life* (New York: Routledge, 1990). The definition of "civil society" comes from Jean Bethke Elshtain, *Democracy on Trial* (New York: Basic Books, 1995), p. 6. The literature on voluntarism and civil society is vast. For a sampling, see Robert Wuthnow, ed., *Between States and Markets: The Voluntary Sector in Comparative Perspective* (Princeton: Princeton University Press, 1991); Max L. Stackhouse, "Religion and the Social Space for Voluntary Institutions," in *Faith and Philanthropy in America: Exploring the Role of Religion in America's Voluntary Sector,* ed. Robert Wuthnow and Virginia A. Hodgkinson (San Francisco: Jossey-Bass Publishers, 1990), pp. 22–37; and Mary Ann Glendon and David Blankenhorn, *Seedbeds of Virtue: Sources of Competence, Character, and Citizenship in American Society* (Lanham, Md.: Madison Books, 1995). Robert Handy equated churches with voluntary societies in *A Christian America,* p. 37.

21. Walter Harris, *A Discourse to the Members of the Female Cent Society in Bedford, New Hampshire, July 18, 1814* (Concord, New Hampshire: George Hough, 1814), p. 5.

22. Andrew Reed, *American Churches* (1835), reprinted in *The Voluntary Church: American Religious Life (1740–1865) Seen Through the Eyes of European Visitors* (New York: Macmillan, 1967), p. 108. Alexis de Tocqueville, *Democracy in America* (1835; rpt. New York: Knopf, 1945), I, p. 316.

23. On the transformation from "virtu" to "virtue," see Ruth H. Bloch, "The Gendered Meanings of Virtue in Revolutionary America," *Signs* 13 (Autumn 1987): 37–58. "Comparison of the Sexes," *American Museum* (January 1789), p. 59, cited in Bloch, "Gendered Meanings," p. 51.

24. "The Influence of the Female Character," *The Western New York Baptist Magazine,* 4, no. 10 (May 1825): 311. See also Amos Chase, *On Female Excellence* (Litchfield, Conn., 1792); Nathan Strong, *The Character of a Virtuous and Good Woman* (Hartford, 1809); Joseph Richardson, *A Sermon on the Duty and Dignity of Woman*

Delivered April 22, 1832 (Hingham, Mass.: Jedidiah Farmer, 1833); Thomas Brana-gan, *The Excellency of the Female Character Vindicated* (New York: Samuel Wood, 1807); and Gardiner Spring, *The Excellence and Influence of the Female Character,* 2d ed. (New York, 1825).

25. Barbara Welter, "The Cult of True Womanhood, 1820–1860," *American Quarterly* 18 (1966): 151–174. Thomas Laquer, *Making Sex: Body and Gender from the Greeks to Freud* (Cambridge: Harvard University Press, 1990), p. 196.

26. "An Address to All the Benevolent Female Associations in the United States," *Newport Female Evangelical Miscellany,* no. 1 (January 1, 1806).

27. Sarah R. Ingraham, compiler, *Walks of Usefulness, or Reminiscences of Mrs. Margaret Prior* (New York: American Female Moral Reform Society, 1843), p. 143.

28. Mary Ryan, *Women in Public: Between Banners and Ballots, 1825–1880* (Baltimore: Johns Hopkins University Press, 1990), p. 53. Kathy Peiss criticizes Ryan for ignoring that "the world of churches, camp meetings, Sunday schools, and missionary societies—a world dominated by women—must be understood as an alternative public arena." See Kathy Peiss, "Going Public: Women in Nineteenth-Century Cultural History," *American Literary History* 3, no. 4 (Winter 1991): 820. Elizabeth Varon describes benevolent associations as "political" even though women themselves hesitated to use this word. See Elizabeth R. Varon, *We Mean to Be Counted: White Women and Politics in Antebellum Virginia* (Chapel Hill: University of North Carolina Press, 1998), pp. 2–3.

29. On the existence of multiple public spheres, see Nancy Fraser, "Rethinking the Pubic Sphere: A Contribution to the Critique of Actually Existing Democracy," in *Habermas and the Public Sphere,* ed. Craig Calhoun (Cambridge: Massachusetts Institute of Technology Press, 1992), pp. 123–124. On Jewish women, see Susan Hill Lindley, *"You Have Stept Out of Your Place": A History of Women and Religion in America* (Louisville, Ky.: Westminster John Knox Press, 1996), pp. 230–232, and Ann Braude, "Women and Religious Practice in American Judaism," in *In Our Own Voices: Four Centuries of American Women's Religious Writing,* ed. Rosemary Radford Ruether and Rosemary Skinner Keller (San Francisco: Harper San Francisco, 1994), pp. 111–152.

30. Maria Monk, *Awful Disclosures, by Maria Monk, of the Hotel Dieu Nunnery of Montreal* (New York: DeWitt and Davenport, 1855). For a good discussion of Monk, see Jenny Franchot, *Roads to Rome: The Antebellum Protestant Encounter with Catholicism* (Berkeley: University of California Press, 1994), pp. 135–145.

31. Mary Sadlier, *Con O'Regan; or, Emigrant Life in the New World,* quoted in *American Catholic Women: A Historical Exploration,* ed. Karen Kennelley (New York: Macmillan, 1989), p. 27. On Catholic women, see Mary Ewens, *The Role of the Nun in Nineteenth Century America* (New York: Arno Press, 1978); Joseph G. Mannard, "'Maternity. . . of the Spirit': Nuns and Domesticity in Antebellum America," *U.S. Catholic Historian* 5 (1986): 305–324; Carol K. Coburn and Martha Smith, *Spirited Lives: How Nuns Shaped Catholic Culture and American Life, 1836–1920* (Chapel Hill: The University of North Carolina Press, 1998); and Suellen Hoy, "Walking Nuns: Chicago's Irish Sisters of Mercy," in *At the Crossroads: Old Saint Patrick's and the Chicago Irish,* ed. Ellen Skerett (Chicago: Wild Onion Books, 1997), pp. 39–52.

32. On the variety of women's public religious work, see Dana L. Robert, *American Women in Mission: A Social History of Their Thought and Practice* (Macon, Ga.: Mercer University Press, 1996); Nancy A. Hewitt, *Women's Activism and Social*

Change: Rochester, New York 1722–1872 (Ithaca, N.Y.: Cornell University Press, 1984); Lindley, *"You Have Stept Out of Your Place,"* pp. 70–116; Mary P. Ryan, *Cradle of the Middle Class: The Family in Oneida County, New York, 1790–1865* (Cambridge: Cambridge University Press, 1981), pp. 105–144; and Lydia Huffman Hoyle, "Missionary Women Among the American Indians, 1815–1865," diss., University of North Carolina at Chapel Hill, 1992.

33. Varon, *We Mean to Be Counted*, pp. 10–70; and Charles Andrews, *Memoir of Mrs. Ann R. Page* (New York: Protestant Episcopal Society for the Promotion of Evangelical Knowledge, 1856), p. 26.

34. *National Intelligencer* (January 9, 1827); *Newburyport Herald* (January 19, 1827); *The New York Commercial Advertiser* (January 11, 1827); and Charles Francis Adams, ed., *Memoirs of John Quincy Adams, Comprising Portions of His Diary from 1795 to 1848* (Philadelphia: J. B. Lippincott, 1876), vol. 10, pp. 7–8. See also Catherine A. Brekus, "Harriet Livermore, the 'Pilgrim Stranger': Female Preaching and Biblical Feminism in Early-Nineteenth-Century America," *Church History* 65 (September 1996): 389–404; Cynthia Jürisson, "Federalist, Feminist, Revivalist: Harriet Livermore (1788–1868) and the Limits of Democratization in the Early Republic," diss., Princeton Theological Seminary, 1994; and Brekus, *Strangers and Pilgrims*.

35. *Christian Palladium* (Union Mills, New York), vol. 1, no. 5 (September 1832): 109; Thomas Andros, *Discourses on Several Important Theological Subjects* (Boston 1817), p. 169; and Dorothy Ripley, *The Extraordinary Conversion and Religious Experience of Dorothy Ripley, with Her First Voyage and Travels in America* (New York: G. & R. Waite, 1810), pp. 64, 77, and 68.

36. Matthew La Rue Perrine, *Women Have a Work to Do in the House of God* (New York: Edward W. Thompson, 1817), p. 10. See also Joseph Richardson, *A Sermon on the Duty and Dignity of Woman Delivered April 22, 1832* (Hingham, Mass.: Jedidiah Farmer, 1833).

37. On this theme, see Douglas, *Feminization*, pp. 17–43.

38. Parsons Cooke, *Female Preaching, Unlawful and Inexpedient: A Sermon* (Lynn, Mass.: James R. Newhall, 1837), p. 17.

39. Harriet Livermore, *Addresses to the Dispersed of Judah* (Philadelphia: L. R. Bailey, 1849), p. 113; and Deborah Peirce, *A Scriptural Vindication of Female Preaching* (Carmel, N.Y.: E. Burroughs, 1820), p. 13.

40. Elizabeth Cady Stanton, Susan B. Anthony, and Matilda Joslyn Gage, *History of Woman Suffrage*, vol. 1, 1848–1861 (1881; rpt. New York: Arno Press, 1969), p. 383, 523. On the religious roots of the nineteenth-century woman's rights movement, see Elizabeth Clark, "Religion, Rights and Difference: The Origins of American Feminism, 1848–1860," Institute for Legal Studies *Working Papers* 2:2 (February 1987); Elizabeth Battelle Clark, "The Politics of God and the Woman's Vote: Religion in the American Suffrage Movement, 1848–1895," diss., Princeton University, 1989; Nancy Gale Isenberg, "'Coequality of the Sexes': The Feminist Discourse of the Antebellum Women's Rights Movement in America," diss., The University of Wisconsin-Madison, 1990; and Catherine A. Brekus, "'Restoring the Divine Order to the World': Religion and the Family in the Antebellum Woman's Rights Movement," in *Religion, Feminism, and the Family*, ed. Anne Carr and Mary Stewart Van Leeuwen (Westminster: John Knox Press, 1995), pp. 166–182.

5

Evangelicals in the American Founding and Evangelical Political Mobilization Today

Mark A. Noll

As the story goes, the Constitutional Convention was deadlocked and rapidly approaching a point of no return. It was Thursday, June 28, 1787. Small states refusing to give way on the principle of "one state—one vote" and large states refusing to give way on the principle of representation apportioned by population were at loggerheads. At this critical juncture, Benjamin Franklin, aged eighty-two and mostly silent to that point, arose to speak. Franklin's brief address implored the delegates to find a compromise and then asked why it was that "this Assembly, groping as it were in the dark . . . [has] not hitherto once thought of humbly applying to the Father of lights to illuminate our understandings?" He reminded the delegates that during the contest with Great Britain, the Continental Congress had daily prayed "in this room for divine protection" and that "all of us who were engaged in the struggle must have observed frequent instances of a superintending providence in our favor." Franklin told the assembly that "the longer I live, the more convincing proofs I see of this truth—*that God Governs in the affairs of men*" and he reminded them of the assurance "in the sacred writings" that "except the Lord build the House they labour in vain that build it." And so he moved that the assembly institute "prayers imploring the assistance of heaven, and its blessings on our deliberations, [to] be held in this Assembly every morning before we proceed to business."[1]

The motion was immediately seconded by Roger Sherman, a cagey veteran of Connecticut politics who was also a strong ally of his minister at the Second Congregational Church in New Haven, the Rev. Jonathan Edwards, Jr.[2]

Thus far, this account is recorded in James Madison's *Notes* on the Constitutional Convention. Now, however, the story takes on an interesting twist as recorded in two books by Peter Marshall and David Manuel, which in various editions have sold over 850,000 copies in the past twenty years and which have become mainstays in the historical consciousness of many evangelical Protestants. Their titles are *The Light and the Glory: Discovering God's Plan for America from Christopher Columbus to George Washington* and *From Sea to Shining Sea: Discovering God's Plan for America in Her First Half-Century of Independence, 1787–1837.*

Franklin's appeal for prayer "marked the turning point." It was "clearly the most extraordinary speech anyone had delivered in the entire three months the delegates had been meeting. . . . They immediately declared three days of prayer and fasting, to seek God's help in breaking the deadlock among them. At the end of that time, all the resentment and wrangling were gone. . . . Why does [the Constitution] work so well? One reason is that it was divinely inspired. A second is that it was the completion of nearly two hundred years of Puritan political thought. Those early church covenants recognized the sinfulness of man. They anticipated the possibility of human wrong. The Constitution does exactly the same thing. In effect, it documents the Covenant Way on national paper."[3]

Much of the force as well as much of the confusion in and about evangelical political mobilization in the United States at the end of the twentieth century is illustrated by the farrago of fact and fantasy surrounding Franklin's appeal for prayer at the 1787 convention. The facts, as provided by the manuscript sources closest to the incident and clarified by careful historians, are these:

—First, Franklin did make such a motion.

—Second, this same Franklin only a short time later wrote at some length to the Rev. Ezra Stiles about his own religion. Franklin believed in God but concerning "Jesus of Nazareth," he had, "with most of the present Dissenters in England . . . some Doubts as to his Divinity."[4]

—Third, Franklin's motion was not approved but tabled; there was no three-day recess; and the Convention never did begin its sessions with prayer.

—Fourth, the story that the Convention acted positively on Franklin's motion, that it recessed to fast, and that it was miraculously guided in writing the Constitution was first published in the mid-1820s. Only in 1833, in a tract by Thomas S. Grimké, did this account begin to figure in broader assessments of the American founding. But that tract was explicitly repudiated by James Madison, by then one of the few surviving members of the Constitutional Convention, who told Grimké with great assurance that Franklin's motion had never been enacted.[5]

The matters that are pertinent for a consideration of evangelical political mobilization today are the relative absence of an explicitly evangelical discourse in the founding era itself and the emergence of an evangelical discourse about the sacred character of the founding only in the 1830s. In order to link this early American history to contemporary concerns, however, it is necessary to be clear on the use of terms. After briefly discussing terminology and after briefly summarizing the major features of evangelical political mobilization today, this chapter returns to the first century of the United States' history in order to make several arguments. First, although Christian faith of a generally Protestant variety played a large part in the founding era of the United States, this form of Christianity was not primarily what is usually meant today by the term "evangelical." Second, evangelical Christianity became important in the early United States only after 1800 and only in national situations quite different from those prevailing during the founding period. Third, attention to the historical circumstances in which Protestant evangelicals became active in American politics in distinctly evangelical ways during the period 1815 to 1860 offers more insight concerning evangelical political mobilization today than does attention to the evangelical stake in the American founding.

* * *

Dwelling on questions of definition, though only a preliminary exercise, is important because of the appalling lack of precision in much contemporary discussion of religion and politics. For the word "evangelical," the most important discrimination is whether it is being applied as a term in the history of Christianity or as a term in the assessment of modern political life.

In the former case, "evangelicalism" refers to a set of religious beliefs and practices that emerged out of Northern European and British Protestantism at the start of the eighteenth century. Since that time, variations of those beliefs and practices have been carried around the world by European Pietist and English-speaking evangelical missionaries and now constitute the identifying marks of the majority of the world's Protestants. Over the passage of time, however, the beliefs and practices that were once relatively distinct to evangelical Protestants have found a home as well in other main religious traditions. Eighteenth-century evangelicalism was guided by many potent leaders, including John and Charles Wesley, founders of Methodism; the grand itinerant George Whitefield; the brilliant Congregational theologian Jonathan Edwards; Hannah More, an active Anglican publicist; the hymnwriter John Newton; William Wilberforce, who was renowned for his opposition to the slave trade; Isaac Backus, leader of Baptists in America; and Samuel Davies, Backus's counterpart as leader of American Presbyterians. It was a movement within Protestantism that, although riven by many internal fissures, could nonetheless be distinguished easily from Roman Catholicism and Eastern Orthodoxy as well as from traditional forms of Protestantism in which the evangelical distinctives were rejected or subordinated. Those historic differences are not now as clear-cut as was the case 250 years ago.

The most serviceable general definition of "evangelical," for the purposes of the history of Christianity, has been provided by the British historian David Bebbington, who highlights four key defining characteristics: biblicism (a reliance on the Bible as ultimate religious authority), conversionism (a stress on the New Birth), activism (an energetic, individualistic approach to religious duties and social involvement), and crucicentrism (a focus on Christ's redeeming work as the heart of essential Christianity).[6]

The problem such a definition poses for analyses of contemporary American society is that surveys find these evangelical characteristics spread widely in the population. A major survey by the Angus Reid Group in October 1996, for example, used Bebbington's characteristics in drawing up questions about religion. It asked 3,000 randomly selected Americans (as well as 3,000 Canadians) about a wide range of social and religious matters, including many related to the traditional concerns of evangelical Protestants. Four of the most important of those concerns are the Bible, conversion, the forgiveness of sins, and the mandate to spread the Christian message.[7] For the purposes of measuring the modern situation, I counted responses as "evangelical" if

1. a respondent strongly agreed that "the Bible is the inspired word of God"; or agreed to whatever degree that "the Bible is God's word, and is to be taken literally, word for word";
2. a respondent strongly agreed that "I have committed my life to Christ and consider myself to be a converted Christian";
3. a respondent strongly agreed that "through the life, death, and resurrection of Jesus, God provided a way for the forgiveness of my sins"; and
4. a respondent agreed or agreed strongly that "it is important to encourage non-Christians to become Christians."

For the population of the United States as a whole, 33.2 percent of respondents affirmed all four of these evangelical characteristics and another 19.7 percent affirmed three out of the four.

In order to make more sense out of the responses to the Angus Reid Poll, a framework of categories developed by the political scientists John Green, James Guth, Lyman Kellstedt, and Corwin Smidt is of great help.[8] For reasons that will soon be evident, they find it useful to divide the American population into six broad religious groups:

Conservative Protestants. This category is for those who said they were affiliated with the following churches: Adventist, Alliance, Baptist, Brethren, Church of Christ, Church of God, Mennonite, or who identified their church as charismatic, evangelical, fundamentalist, holiness, or pentecostal. These Protestants resemble what the paper will later refer to as the antiformalists of the antebellum era.

Mainline Protestants. This designation is for those identified as Anglican, Episcopal, United Church of Christ, Methodist, most Lutherans, most Presbyterians, and most Reformed. These are close to what the paper will describe as the formalists of the early United States.

Black Protestants. Even though African-American Protestants share many doctrinal and behavioral characteristics with those in conservative Protestant denominations, they are treated as a separate category because their responses to almost all social, political, or cultural questions set them apart dramatically from the conservative Protestant denominations.[9]

Roman Catholics.

Secular/Nominal. These people responded that they were agnostic, atheist, or nothing in particular. Also added to this category are those who, though they responded with a religious affiliation, showed no or virtually no religious commitment.

Other. This is a grabbag category that includes Mormons, Jehovah's Witnesses, Eastern Orthodox, Unitarian-Universalists, Jews, and others not readily classifiable with the other larger groups. (The numbers for all such groups, as well as for members of other religions, even in a survey of 6,000 respondents, is very low.)

Green, Guth, Kellstedt, and Smidt have also found that the three largest of these broad categories can be usefully divided into high and low levels of active religious participation. For the purposes of this division, "low" designates those who, though self-identified with a religious tradition, rank at the bottom of a Religious Commitment scale that measures prayer, attendance at church, belief that religion is important, and belief that God is needed in modern times. Those who measure "low" may show positive on a couple of these variables, but no more than a couple. By contrast, the "high" category is for those who pray and attend church at least monthly, who believe in traditional views of God, and who say religion is important in their lives.

With these divisions, then, the United States population breaks down as follows:

Table 5.1   Proportion of U.S. Population by Religious Tradition and Commitment

% of U.S. Population			
ConProt—hi	19.9	Catholic—hi	12.9
ConProt—lo	6.2	Catholic—lo	7.3
MainProt—hi	9.5	Sec/Nominal	19.9
MainProt—lo	5.2	Other	9.8
BlackProt	9.2		

For the history of Christianity, the really interesting question is where the traditionally evangelical convictions are found. The answer is surprising.

Table 5.2 Percentages Within Religious Traditions Holding to Three or Four of the Evangelical Beliefs

ConProt—hi	92	Catholic—hi	53
ConProt—lo	66	Catholic—lo	33
MainProt—hi	70	Sec/Nominal	14
MainProt—lo	26	Other	34
BlackProt	77		

It is significant that the High and Low categories of Religious Commitment reflect a considerable difference with respect to traditional evangelical concerns. Even more significant is the fact that, while we would expect high percentages of evangelical belief among active conservative Protestants, the percentage of evangelical belief among active mainline Protestants and active Roman Catholics is also quite substantial. For the history of Christianity, this kind of information cries out for explorations of the religious overlap between conservative Protestants and other varieties of Christians.

But when religion and American politics are the issues, other questions become more important. It turns out, in fact, that measures of religious belief and practice are not the most revealing indicators for connections between religion and politics.

What does turn out to be more meaningful for almost every possible relationship is the addition of measures concerning Belonging and Behaving alongside the measures for Believing.[10] That is, when the question is not only what you believe, but also how you act and what movements, churches, or other agencies you support, the answers have an immediate political implication. In particular, when people belong to an organization like a specific church and also behave in ways fitting the patterns of the church, that combination of behavior and belonging turns out to make a much greater difference for political purposes than the mere profession of belief.

To show this difference, it is possible to compare political connections to beliefs alone with political connections to beliefs as well as affiliations. Again, as taken from the October 1996 Angus Reid Poll, the differences are striking.

Table 5.3 Percentages of Support for Presidential Candidates (October 1996) Divided by Numbers of Evangelical Beliefs They Affirm

	Clinton	*Dole*	*Perot*
All four beliefs	48	46	6
Three	62	30	8
Two	63	28	9
One	63	28	9
Zero	68	22	10

Table 5.4 Percentages of Support for Presidential Candidates (October 1996)
Divided by Religious Traditions

	Clinton	*Dole*	*Perot*
ConProt—hi	37	57	6
ConProt—lo	48	41	11
MainProt—hi	46	47	11
MainProt—lo	57	34	9
BlackProt	96	1	3
Catholic—hi	60	33	7
Catholic—lo	63	26	7
Sec/Nominal	68	22	10
Other	63	27	9

To drive home the difference that affiliation makes, it is useful to present one more table from a different poll. Green, Kellstedt, Guth, and Smidt carried out their own survey of American voters in 1996. By using a scale measuring traditional religious adherence, they found even higher levels of support for Republican candidates among traditional conservative Protestants.

Table 5.5 Percentages of Support for Presidential and House Vote (1996) Divided
by Religious Groups and Loyalty to Religious Traditions

	% of Pop.	*Clinton*	*Dole*	*Perot*	*House GOP*
WhiteConProt—traditionalist	(12)	22	74	4	79
WhiteConProt—modernist	(10)	42	48	10	60
WhiteMainProt—traditionalist	(6)	31	63	6	79
WhiteMainProt—modernist	(7)	54	42	4	60
WhiteCatholic—traditionalist	(8)	39	52	9	63
WhiteCatholic—modernist	(7)	57	31	12	37
BlackProt	(9)	95	5	1	13
Sec/Nominal	(28)	56	29	16	36

Source: Adapted from John Green, Lyman Kellstedt, James Guth, and Corwin Smidt, "Who Elected Clinton: A Collision of Values," *First Things* Aug./Sept. 1997, 35–40, esp. 37.

Tables 5.3, 5.4, and 5.5 drive home the following conclusion: Narrowly considered in strictly religious terms, evangelicalism turns out to have an interesting, but not overwhelming connection with political choice. By contrast, evangelical convictions that take shape in a conservative Protestant environment have a much stronger political connection.

The conclusion to be drawn from such tables is that when people speak of the evangelical political mobilization of the past quarter century, the discussion almost always concerns not just evangelical beliefs and practices *per se,* but evangelical beliefs and practices combined with adherence to conservative Protestant denominational groups.

Have we labored like an elephant to bring forth only a mouse of a distinction? No. For an accounting of religion, it is important to see that belief in the Bible as authoritative divine revelation or belief in the need to be converted to Christ cannot in fact be as easily clustered with a particular political movement as the bare use of the term "evangelical" often implies. Even when considering evangelicals in conservative Protestant denominations, it is necessary to remember that a substantial minority oppose the main political drift of their fellow conservative Protestants.[11]

Nonetheless, among white evangelical adherents of conservative Protestant denominations there has decidedly occurred a political mobilization during the past quarter century. That mobilization is now most easily seen in the extraordinarily high electoral support provided to Republican candidates at the state and federal levels. Less obviously, the mobilization is noticeable in a series of changes that have taken place since 1950 among white conservative Protestant evangelicals:

—First, there has been a notable politicization of subject matter in evangelical periodicals.[12] More articles address politics and more of these articles do so with engaged or adversarial language.

—Second, entire religious families that were once largely apolitical have entered into political activity. Pentecostal denominations like the Assemblies of God are the most prominent examples, but within many other Holiness, Baptist, or even Anabaptist denominations there is now a degree of political activity that was unknown two generations ago.

—Third, conservative Protestants follow a new set of leaders who have embraced political partisanship. In the early 1950s Billy Graham's sermons fully exploited the rhetoric of the Cold War, but he remained mostly nonpartisan in his domestic politics (Graham's closest presidential friends were Lyndon Johnson and Richard Nixon).[13] No widely known evangelical in the 1950s addressed political issues and named political names with the frankness exhibited by James Dobson, Jerry Falwell, and Pat Robertson during the past twenty years.

—Fourth, political changes in the South have affected evangelical politics since that is the region with the most white conservative Protestants. The movement of the South from a mainstay of the Democratic party to an active shaper of the Republican party—and during a period when the largest conservative Protestant denomination in the South, the Southern Baptist Convention, has witnessed a successful, but heatedly contested, effort by self-styled conservatives to control their denomination—has contributed greatly to evangelical political mobilization in the nation as a whole.

The political mobilization of evangelical conservative Protestants is evident on every hand. Almost as evident are the basic reasons for that mobilization. Even after well-publicized debacles like the Scopes Trial of 1925 or setbacks in northern Protestant denominations like the Presbyterians and the

Baptists about the same time, Protestant conservatives did not vanish, as some notable commentators at the time asserted they would. Rather, conservative Protestant efforts were turned to local situations and the effort to preserve their own churches and voluntary agencies.[14] The British sociologist Steve Bruce, one of the shrewdest observers of such matters, has put his finger on the key factor that transformed these local actions into national mobilization. Conservative Protestants, Bruce writes, "were working to create social institutions which would permit them to reproduce their own culture sheltered from modernizing influences. The problem was that such boundary-maintaining activity depended on a weak (or benign) federal government which would permit the regions (and pockets of fundamentalists more centrally located) to go their own way."[15]

As others, like Robert Wuthnow, have also noted, the mobilization of evangelical Protestant conservatives coincides with the expansion of federal authority and the consequent resentment of the conservatives at the imposition of what are in effect national standards of moral practice.[16] The issues at stake are various—racial desegregation of the schools, destruction of racial barriers to the franchise, national funding for science education, discovery of a right to abortion in the right to privacy, elimination of prayers in public schools, judicial erection of a wall of separation between religion and society, mandates for equality between men and women in higher education, and assertions of civil protection for nontraditional sexual preferences—but the result is the same. Local situations where it had once been possible to work at (or neglect) solutions to morally charged issues locally were now being addressed by federal actions. National efforts to legislate morality struck many conservative Protestants as so instinctively wrong-headed as to justify their own counter-attempts at legislating an alternative morality.

We will note a historical irony to that resentment shortly, but here it is important to record two aspects of evangelical political mobilization that are securely rooted in American history. First was the application of the Manichean vocabulary of revival to the political arena. Conservative Protestants had grown accustomed over the preceding two centuries to preaching in apocalyptic terms about the battle between God and Satan for the souls of human beings. It was, thus, only second nature to enter politics with a similar vocabulary in which apocalyptic rhetoric was applied to the struggle between godliness and the evil forces of big government, secular humanism, the Supreme Court, the National Education Association, or the Democratic party.

The second characteristic was a sense of historical violation. Part of the animus behind evangelical political mobilization is the deep conviction that the United States was once a Christian country in a meaningful, if nonestablishmentarian, sense of the term, which in the fairly recent past has been hijacked by secularists in a great conspiracy to negate that historical reality. The widespread historical grievance that energizes the labors of Marshall and

Manuel, David Barton, Tim LaHaye, Francis Schaeffer, and John White-head[17]—to mention only some of the best-selling authors who share this historical opinion—can be summarized as a paraphrase of the words of Mary Magdalene from the twentieth chapter of the Gospel of John: They have taken away my country and we do not know where they have laid it.

*   *   *

At this point, it is appropriate to return to the past that conservative Protestants think has been stolen from them. A clearer, nonmythological picture of evangelical involvement in the early period of American history will be helpful, in the first instance, for correcting a picture regularly misconstrued by partisans of the New Christian Right—and also, it must be said, by partisan opponents of the New Christian Right, as in the provocative recent polemic *The Godless Constitution,* by R. Laurence Moore and Isaac Kramnick.[18]

In the second instance, a clearer picture of the evangelical place in early America will make it possible to understand current evangelical attitudes as a complex continuation of historic positions and by so doing may also promote a clearer assessment of religion and politics more generally in American society today.

The central historical points concern the role of evangelicals in the founding period, the rise of evangelicalism after 1800, the appropriation by evangelicals of the founders' expectations for church–state interaction, and the fragmented character of evangelical politics in the early United States.

(1) Evangelicalism as defined by its conservative Protestant exponents today played at best a negligible role in the founding era of the 1770s and 1780s. Almost all the leading Protestants who were politically active in the period of the Declaration of Independence, the Revolutionary War, and the Constitutional Convention differed substantially from modern evangelical conservative Protestants. Several of the leaders whose beliefs came closest to the modern meaning of evangelical, like John Witherspoon of New Jersey and Patrick Henry of Virginia, were advocates of religious establishments who thought that state support of the churches was essential for their health and the health of society. Others like the Episcopalians Madison, Washington, and James Wilson were office-holders in Protestant churches but either so reticent about their own religious convictions or so obviously deistic in their beliefs as to represent a kind of Enlightenment religion. Still other Protestants of a traditional European sort were sincere supporters of their churches but innocent of the stress on conversion or the practices of pietism that distinguish modern evangelicals. Historian John Murrin may overstate matters, but only slightly, when he claims that "the Federal Constitution was, in short, the eighteenth-century equivalent of a secular humanist text. The delegates were not a very orthodox group of men in any doctrinal sense. The

only born-again Christian among them was probably Richard Bassett of Delaware, a Methodist who generously supported the labors of Francis Asbury and other missionaries but who said nothing at the convention. One cliché often applied to the Constitution is not correct in any literal sense— that at least the Founders, unlike the wildly optimistic French, believed in original sin and its implications for government and politics. Quite possibly not a single delegate accepted Calvinist orthodoxy original sin."[19]

In light of what happened later in the United States, where Methodists and Baptists supplied a very high proportion of the great army of evangelical activists, it is significant that the Constitutional Convention of fifty-five delegates included only two Methodists and not a single Baptist.[20]

To assert rather than to argue carefully through a complicated historiographical thicket, it is also possible to suggest that the public discourse on display in the Declaration of Independence, the Articles of Confederation, and the Constitution, while respectful of the deity in general, was hardly evangelical in any specific sense of the term. The most careful studies of religion in the founding era make strong claims for the presence of Protestant elements in the politics of the Revolutionary period, but none claims an overwhelmingly Protestant ethos, and none claims for the founding a specifically evangelical influence.[21] The well-documented debates on the ratification of the Constitution were not entirely devoid of interest in religion, since those debates included concern for protecting religious liberty as later specified in the First Amendment. But the overwhelmingly this-worldly character of those debates reveals no preoccupation with explicitly Christian, much less explicitly evangelical, concerns.[22]

To be sure, Americans during the 1780s and 1790s continued to herald the divine blessing on the United States, but they did so with at least as much attention to an Enlightenment deity as to an explicitly evangelical God. In a word, the political discourse of the founders was not atheistic, but neither did it represent a repristination of vigorous Puritan Calvinism nor an anticipation of activist Protestant evangelicalism.

(2) One of the reasons why the evangelical engagement with politics in the founding era was so slight is that American evangelicalism was in a parlous state of transition precisely in the half century surrounding 1776. In that period most forms of Protestantism in North America were undergoing a momentous shift. They were moving beyond a territorial Protestantism dominated by establishmentarian Congregationalists, Episcopalians, and Presbyterians, where evangelical impulses and sectarian forms of church organization were distinctly at the margin. They were evolving toward a distinctly evangelical Protestantism dominated by Methodists and Baptists who used sectarian modes of church organization and voluntary organization outside the churches to accomplish their spiritual and social mission.

The Great Awakening of the 1740s had injected an evangelical element into the American churches and had succeeded in shaking up inherited Eu-

ropean patterns of church establishment, but it had not succeeded in transforming American Protestantism into a thoroughly evangelical religion. It
was more successful at ending Puritanism than inaugurating evangelicalism.
The magnitude of the change under way in the later Revolutionary era is suggested by shifting ecclesiastical demography. In 1776, fully 55 percent of all
adherents to churches in the United States were Congregationalists, Presbyterians, and Episcopalians, almost all of whom continued to favor
church–state establishments and of whom only a minority would have identified with the newer evangelical impulses. By 1850, these three groups
made up less than 19 percent of all church adherents, while the proportion
of Methodists and Baptists had risen from virtually nowhere to constitute
about 55 percent of the churched population.[23]

During the 1770s and 1780s, the newer configuration of overtly evangelical, sectarian, and voluntaristic American Protestantism could be glimpsed in
a wide range of frontier revivals and also in the beginnings of systematic
Methodist organization.[24] But the flourishing of evangelical Protestantism did
not occur until after the turn of the new century.

One of the reasons for that later flourishing, however, is relevant to politics. It was in part by adapting to the American political environment as
shaped by the Revolution that the largely European Protestantism of the
colonial period evolved into the evangelicalism of the national period. Perceptive historians like Nathan Hatch and Russell Richey have shown that the
story of the evangelicalization of Protestantism in the new United States is
also the story of how American Protestantism came to embrace the democratic, republican, commonsensical, liberal, and providential conceptions by
which the founders had defined America in the 1770s and 1780s.[25]

The links between internal developments within Protestantism and Protestant investment in the new American values are numerous. For instance,
English-language Protestants moved away from Calvinist notions of God
(which had been the dominant view in the colonial period) at the same time
that they joined the American outrage against arbitrary imperial authority.
Protestants likewise moved rapidly away from established churches exercising their authority by inherited right to voluntary churches exercising authority through the charisma of individual leadership at the same time that
they embraced the new principles of American democracy. Similarly, the
shift from reliance on the Bible as interpreted by learned, properly educated
authorities to reliance on the Bible as interpreted by individuals exercising
their democratic rights coincided with the spread of American notions of
self-reliance.

These changes in Protestantism led to two important results: First, evangelicalism, in part because it knew how to exploit the new American vocabulary, emerged as the overwhelmingly dominant form of religion in the national period. Second, evangelical Protestantism, exploiting both its internal

religious energies and its synergistic adaptation to the new American values, grew like wildfire. Absolute church statistics are a problem in the national period, since membership requirements were stiff and churches enrolled far fewer formal members than the much larger number affected by their work. But absolute numbers are not the key thing about antebellum American Protestantism. Rather, the key is that in comparative terms the United States possessed no alternative ideology that came anywhere close to the influence of evangelical Protestantism from the early years of the nineteenth century through the Civil War.[26]

The important chronological point is that a form of evangelical conservative Protestantism reasonably similar to what is known as evangelical conservative Protestantism today did not emerge in the United States until a generation or more after the founding period. This Protestantism combined a radical religious individualism (especially in notions of conversion) with a strong communal sense, expressed through voluntary organization of churches and parachurch special-purpose agencies. It tended to stress the family as a sacred space insulated from the hustling confusions of the marketplace, but nonetheless participated vigorously and with discipline in that marketplace. This singular form of what might be called proprietary sectarianism was the immediate ancestor of contemporary evangelical conservative Protestantism.

(3) To note the timing of the evangelical surge is to realize that as expansionary-minded evangelicals went about the conversion of both Americans and American society in the early national period, they did so within a framework for religion and society handed down from the founding generation. This point is worth repeating: Protestants like today's evangelicals came into existence only in the early nineteenth century. By that time, the basic guidelines for church–state, religious–social interaction had been set by the founding generation to which evangelicalism as we know it had contributed very little. But since wholehearted accommodation to public values propounded by the founders was one of the means by which evangelicalism surged on many fronts in the early nineteenth century, evangelicals were also quick to baptize the founders' framework for religious–political interaction as their own. Evangelical attachment to the Constitution was, therefore, by adoption rather than by natural birth. This sequence explains why it was not until the 1820s and the 1830s that evangelicals began to construct, with the aid of Benjamin Franklin, a very strange ally, a distinctly evangelical account of the constitutional convention.

But since evangelicals did come to embrace fully the founders' framework as their own, it is important to review the nature of that framework. To do so, the arguments of a fine recent book by John G. West, *The Politics of Revelation and Reason: Religion and Civic Life in the New Nation,* are especially valuable.[27]

The major founding fathers, though they differed among themselves on many questions of religion as well as politics, did come to a basic agreement on the place of religion in society. West, for example, documents a wide range of agreement on such questions among John Jay and John Witherspoon, who were evangelicals in something like the modern sense of the term; James Wilson and Alexander Hamilton, whose attachment to Christian orthodoxy varied throughout their lives; George Washington and James Madison, who shared devotion to the republic and an extreme reticence about declaring their personal faith; and Benjamin Franklin, John Adams, and Thomas Jefferson, deists or Unitarians who, if only for pragmatic reasons, did not rule out public activities by more traditional believers. All nine of these founders wanted the new United States to promote religious liberty and none wanted the national government to dictate religious beliefs or practices to its citizens. The surprising degree of agreement among those whose own religious convictions differed so considerably rested on two shared assumptions: first, that the moral goods promoted by the churches largely coincided with the moral goods promoted by the government, and, second, that the churches had a role to play in making the moral calculus of republicanism actually work.

This moral calculus of republicanism was, and remains, an extraordinarily significant assumption for many Americans, evangelicals included. As the calculus was expressed in the first century of the United States, it embraced two separate convictions: that morality was necessary to create the virtuous citizens without which a republic could not survive, and that the churches should contribute to the promotion of that morality. The practical challenge inherited from the founding era was how a new-fangled kind of church, which had given up the rights of establishment, might insert itself as a promoter of morality into a public sphere from which the founders' commitment to religious freedom had excluded the old style of established churches.

Evangelical Protestants responded to that challenge vigorously. To be sure, the first explicitly evangelical political engagement—an attack on Jefferson as a dangerous infidel in the run-up to the election of 1800—was a flop.[28] This first evangelical mobilization failed in part because Jefferson turned out to be a moral president and even supported a wide range of religious practices, like attending Sunday services of Christian worship in the Capitol building and authorizing federal support for military chaplains and Christian missions to the Indians. The attack on Jefferson failed also because evangelicals seem instinctively to have grasped that they were treating Jefferson as a monarch who might set up an alternative state religion rather than what he really was, a democratically elected official whose job was to preside over free, competitive public space.

Evangelicals hit their stride after about 1812 by turning to voluntary societies as the way of promoting public morality. Petition drives against Sunday mails and missionary mobilization against Cherokee removal were two of the earliest efforts.[29] In these efforts, the main evangelical groups were largely successful in meeting the challenge posed by the founders by aiming, not at establishment, but at provision of private moral capital to sustain the republic.

The fact that evangelicals failed in their efforts to stop the transport of mail on Sunday and to halt the removal of the Cherokee from Georgia does not negate the conclusion that these campaigns illustrated successful evangelical adaptation to a nonestablishmentarian, yet still vigorously religious, effort to provide the morality without which a republic would collapse.

The proof that they had learned how to function as openly Christian advocates in a republic defined by constitutional freedom of religion is found in the extraordinary role that evangelicals played in the sectional antagonism leading to the Civil War. That role has recently been documented in a magisterial book by Richard J. Carwardine, *Evangelicals and Politics in Antebellum America*.[30] The point that it makes, along with many other outstanding recent studies, is that, as powerful as evangelical public influence was in the full generation before Fort Sumter, it was, of course, an influence divided starkly by the Mason and Dixon Line.

(4) The final historical point, therefore, is that evangelical politics in the first century of the United States was in fact never unitary. While virtually all evangelicals and all organized forms of evangelicalism embraced the founders' framework for religion and politics, deep internal fissures divided evangelicals from one another with respect to how, where, and with what means public action should proceed within those guidelines. A fine recent survey of antebellum evangelicalism by Curtis D. Johnson provides a vocabulary for summarizing those differences.[31]

In Johnson's picture, antebellum evangelicals were divided into three distinct groups, Formalists, Antiformalists, and African Americans. Formalists, mostly Congregationalists and Presbyterians, with some Episcopalians and Reformed, flavored their evangelical convictions with a dose of establishmentarian principle. These formalists were the key agents in establishing the most visible voluntary societies. They were central in high-profile religious events like the Businessman's Revival of 1857–58.[32] They were also the ones who enjoyed the highest profiles in national leadership: for example, the preacher-reformer Lyman Beecher; Beecher's children, the golden-throated Henry Ward, and the best-selling author Harriet Beecher Stowe; Theodore Frelinghuysen, the "Christian Statesman" who ran as the vice presidential candidate on Henry Clay's 1844 Whig ticket; and the abolitionist Theodore Dwight Weld, who was a protégé of the revivalist Charles Grandison Finney. Formalist evangelicals were concentrated in Northern towns and cities. They were natural allies of the Federalist, Whig, and Republican parties. From among them came many leading abolitionists as well as most of the public voices for moderation on the questions of slavery and states' rights. The irony of the formalists' contribution to American evangelicalism is that they favored the kind of active, moralistic government that most white evangelicals after World War II have denounced.

Another three-fifths of American evangelicals were what Johnson calls antiformalists, generally Methodists, Baptists, and adherents of the new-minted American restorationist denominations, "Christians," Disciples, and Churches of Christ.[33] They tended to come from middle and lower classes, to be stronger in the West and South, and to live in small towns and rural areas. Antiformalist religion was frankly sectarian, emotional, apocalyptic, and determinedly conversionist. Leading figures were the Baptist preacher John Leland, who was as fervent in his support for Jefferson as he was faithful as an itinerant revivalist; Alexander Campbell, the dominant force in the Restorationist movement; and the Methodist Nathan Bangs (in the earlier, revivalist stage of his career). Antiformalists were marked by great solicitude for spiritual liberty, and so they were often in the forefront of opposition to the formalists' national plans for promoting education, distributing the Bible, and encouraging social reforms. They tended to be anti-Yankee, anti-Whig, and anti-Republican, and thus Democrats (except in regions where strife with other antiformalist Democrats pushed some into the arms of Whigs or Republicans). This group is less well studied than the Formalists but quite significant. From it came also a number of evangelical anti-abolitionists who held with ever-increasing determination that the Bible sanctioned the black chattel slavery of the Southern states.

Johnson suggests that African Americans made up about one-fifth of the total evangelical population in the antebellum period. African Americans were primarily Methodists and Baptists who shared most of the evangelical convictions and many evangelical habits of piety. The politics of African Americans were, of course, severely restricted. The evangelicalism of African Americans was the faith of the disinherited and was so very different from either of the two main white segments.

The rest of the Protestants in antebellum America probably did not total as many as the African Americans. But some of them, especially from among the Lutherans but also from smaller German groups of Pietists, were also being pulled into the orbit of formalist evangelicals. Mostly, however, these other Protestants remained isolated by language and their distinctive religious practices. (By 1850, the Roman Catholic church was growing rapidly, but it still counted fewer adherents than either the Methodists or the Baptists, and it was still decades away from exerting a national political influence.)

The crucial historical point is that evangelicals in the national and antebellum periods overwhelmingly accepted the founders' guidelines for religious-political interaction, but differed considerably among themselves as to how best to act within those guidelines. To be sure, a movement did arise toward mid-century promoting the passage of a "Christian Amendment" to the Constitution in order to rectify what especially Presbyterians with strong Scottish connections thought was a mistake in the original that did not acknowledge God's sovereignty over the United States. But support for this amendment never caught on.

If most evangelicals agreed that the founders had acted wisely in the Constitution, they nonetheless regularly failed to rally around a single strategy. Internal differences were sharpest on questions pitting local and individual values against national and communal values. For example, every presidential election from the early 1830s onward featured an effort to portray the candidates as godly individuals. While this effort was more of a challenge for some candidates than for others, the remarkable thing is that Whigs, Republicans, Democrats, Free Soilers and Know Nothings all were eager for religious, often specifically evangelical, sanction for their contrasting policies. Formalist evangelicals organized massive voluntary activity aimed at rectification of social wrongs, especially intemperance and slavery. But many of these campaigns for social reform were themselves contentious, with antiformalists resisting the national programs of the formalists. Further disagreement arose when some of the formalists sought government action against intemperance and slavery. The most dramatic illustration of evangelical divisions was the aggressive evangelical support for both Northern Unionism and the Southern Confederacy. Evangelical certainty about the virtue of the North, or of the South, was one of the prime factors making resort to arms such a fearful step.

A summary is now in order to clarify several matters concerning the past, which contemporary evangelical Protestant conservatives think has been stolen:

1. Evangelicals are mistaken in thinking of the founding period as strongly influenced by the kind of religion that they hold dear.
2. Evangelicalism began to exert a large presence in America, in fact, only a generation or more after the founding.
3. But the voluntaristic, non-, or antiestablishmentarian forms of evangelicalism that came to prevail widely in the nineteenth century were closely bound to the ideals of the founders about the relationship of religion and society.
4. That commitment to the founders' guidelines, which very early on, as in the story of Benjamin Franklin at the Constitutional Convention, became a distinctly religious commitment, did not yield a unified evangelical approach to public life. Regional, class, hermeneutical, and intra-evangelical denominational differences created several opposing evangelical political tendencies in the antebellum period.

* * *

If these historical conclusions are even approximately correct, they bear in several ways on the recent political mobilization of evangelical conservative Protestants. First, for analysis of the constitutional warrants often applied to public disagreements today, better history shows how much it complicates issues to view the founders in their own historical context. The founders' guidelines for religion and society came out of a situation that was much more theistic than some modern liberals admit, but also out of a situation that was much less explicitly Christian than modern evangelicals wish it had been. The founders wanted much less specific religious influence on politics than contemporary evangelical conservative Protestants seek, but they looked to religion for much more support for republican morality than opponents of contemporary evangelicals can tolerate.

While giving due weight to the normative character of the Constitution's reasoning on religion and society, historically informed exegesis of the Constitution requires great finesse. The founders' guidelines for religion and society were written in a situation where it was assumed that denominations in the European fashion wanted a formal stake in ordering government, where religious activity was organized primarily through the churches, where very few institutions of national government touched the daily lives of ordinary citizens, and where almost all varieties of religion in America were either Protestant or Enlightenment modifications of Protestantism. Now we live in a situation where no denominations seek establishment, where tremendous amounts of religious activity are organized outside the churches, where institutions of national government regularly touch day-to-day life in many ways, and where the range of Christian varieties, of other religions, and of no religion is much broader than in the founding period.

These historical realities mean that there is no constitutional silver bullet to be fired by evangelical conservative Protestants, or by anyone else, for questions of religion and public life. Romantic evangelical re-creations of a godly constitutional elysium undercut honest political debate as much as do procedural libertarian dismissals of the founders' presuppositional theism. The extent that evangelical political mobilization, or mobilization by any other interest, rests on fraudulent views of real historical situations, to that extent responsible political debate is compromised.

A second conclusion concerns evangelicalism more directly. For analysis of the evangelical conservative Protestantism that has mobilized so vigorously over the last generation, better history shows how this mobilization is both traditional and novel. It is traditional for American evangelicals to mobilize for political action. It is novel to synthesize antiformalist and formalist impulses. In the early nineteenth century, formalist and antiformalist evangelicals opposed each other and so defused the impact of evangelical political energy. Over the past several decades, however, formalist and antiformalist evangelical tendencies have united. The result is a more concentrated political vision among evangelicals than ever existed in the national or antebellum periods. Contemporary evangelical mobilization is, therefore, fueled by both proprietary and sectarian concerns. The proprietary concern seeks means to coerce Americans to do good. The sectarian concern wants Americans to be left alone. These two impulses are both historically evangelical, but in the early period they often canceled each other out. Today they are joined and so create a movement with a confused political philosophy, but also with an unusual potential for concentrated action. Race continues to divide evangelical Protestants for political purposes, even as region did in the antebellum period. But unlike the earlier period, the political mobilization of evangelical conservative Protestants today is now both a formalist and an antiformalist mobilization.

Third, for analysis of evangelicalism as a religious expression, better history shows how dangerous political involvement can be. It would be especially useful for contemporary evangelical conservative Protestants to realize that evangelical political activity in an earlier United States peaked in the 1850s. In the words of Richard Carwardine: "When during the climax of the campaigns of 1856 and 1860 ministers officiated with equal enthusiasm at revival meetings and at Republican rallies, it was clear that religion and politics had fused more completely than ever before in the American republic."[34] In other words, evangelical religion provided much of the impetus that led to the Civil War.

The trauma of that war leaves much for all Americans to contemplate, but especially evangelical Protestants. In its wake, and in large measure as a result of the energies that had led to the war, evangelicals were not only sundered North and South but also pathetically weakened as a spiritual force in both regions. In the North, varieties of formalist evangelicalism soon fell apart into quarreling factions of fundamentalists and modernists, both of which regained only portions of earlier evangelical vigor. In the South, with largely antiformalist types of evangelicalism prevailing, there was no inner motivation to confront the sin of racism until its proponents were forced to do so by a singular combination of African-American evangelical prophecy and Big Government national intervention. In other words, the evangelical energies that led, again in Richard Carwardine's words, to "the cultivation of regional demonologies," were energies that in the end severely compromised the character of evangelicalism itself.[35] A better grasp of history would help modern evangelical conservative Protestants realize that their predecessors met the challenge of the founders' political guidelines so well that, as a result of fifty years of political action climaxing in the 1860s, evangelicals came close to winning all of America, but only at the cost of nearly losing their own souls.

Finally, for analysis of the political situation more generally, better history shows how thoroughly evangelical political mobilization has been embedded in the founders' solution for religion and politics. In particular, the burden of evangelical politics is to recall, in their own terms to be sure, the moral calculations of the founders. Evangelical conservative Protestants have played fast and loose with the historical record, but they have gotten one thing right. Even if the founders did not operate from the evangelical assumptions they embrace, the founders did indeed rest their hopes for the future of the United States on the proper functioning of the republican moral calculus. In those terms, evangelical political mobilization today poses a challenge to all Americans that is, in fact, well rooted in what actually took place. Evangelical conservative Protestants often frame political issues bumptuously, but some of their questions are well grounded in the true history of the American founding. For example, can a republic survive where the virtue of its citizens is no longer a widespread concern? Or, is there any agency that has ever proven more effective than the churches at promoting the virtue of citizens? It is clear that evangelicals make a mistake in claiming the founders as their own. It is not clear that they make a mistake in thinking that abandoning the founders' formula for the well-being of a republic would bring the American nation into serious peril.

NOTES

1. *Notes of Debates in the Federal Convention of 1787 Reported by James Madison,* Bicentennial Edition (New York: Norton, 1987 [orig. 1966]), pp. 209–210.

2. Christopher Collier, *Roger Sherman's Connecticut: Yankee Politics and the American Revolution* (Middletown, Conn.: Wesleyan University Press, 1971), p. 327.

3. Marshall and Manuel, with Anna Wilson Fishel, *From Sea to Shining Sea for Children* (Grand Rapids, Mich.: Fleming H. Revell, 1993), pp. 18–19; Marshall and Manuel, with Anna Wilson Fishel, *The Light and the Glory for Children* (Tarrytown, N.Y.: Fleming H. Revell, 1992), p. 156.

4. Franklin to Stiles, 9 March 1790, *Benjamin Franklin: Representative Selections,* ed. Chester E. Jorgenson and Frank Luther Mott, rev. ed. (New York: Hill & Wang, 1962), p. 508.

5. For the first printing of the story, see *The Records of the Federal Convention of 1787,* ed. Max Farrand, 3 vols. (New Haven: Yale University Press, 1911), vol. 3, p. 471; and for the disavowals, Madison to Jared Sparks, 8 April 1831, and Madison to Thomas S. Grimké, 6 Jan. 1834, in ibid., pp. 499–500, 531.

6. David W. Bebbington, *Evangelicalism in Modern Britain: A History from the 1730s to the 1980s* (London: Unwin Hyman, 1989), pp. 2–17.

7. I am indebted to my Wheaton College colleague, political scientist Lyman Kellstedt, for assistance in analyzing the results of this survey.

8. For example, in Green, Guth, Kellstedt, and Smidt, *Religion and the Culture Wars* (Lanham, Md.: Rowman & Littlefield, 1996).

9. Most of the denominations in each of these first three categories are descended historically from the evangelicalism of the eighteenth century.

10. I have borrowed these categories from Lyman Kellstedt and his colleagues.

11. To further complicate the question of definition, a younger group of sociologists has recently published provocative studies focusing on just those Americans who *call themselves* evangelicals. This procedure leads to a smaller, but much more cohesive, subgroup of Americans. See, for example, Christian Smith (with Michael Emerson, Sally Gallagher, Paul Kennedy, and David Sikkink), *American Evangelicalism: Embattled and Thriving* (Chicago: University of Chicago Press, 1998).

12. I owe this information to a dissertation in progress at the University of Chicago Divinity School by Kristen Burroughs Kraakevik.

13. See, most recently, Billy Graham, *Just as I Am: The Autobiography of Billy Graham* (San Francisco: HarperCollins, 1997), chaps. 22 and 24.

14. For a splendid new account, see Joel A. Carpenter, *Revive Us Again: The Reawakening of American Fundamentalism* (New York: Oxford University Press, 1997).

15. Steve Bruce, *The Rise and Fall of the New Christian Right: Conservative Protestant Politics in America, 1978–1988* (Oxford: Clarendon Press, 1988), p. 30.

16. Robert Wuthnow, *The Restructuring of American Religion: Society and Faith Since World War II* (Princeton: Princeton University Press, 1988).

17. For example, David Barton, *Spirit of the American Revolution* (Aledo, Tex.: Wallbuilders, 1994), and *Original Intent in the Courts, the Constitution and Religion* (Aledo, Tex.: Wallbuilders); Tim F. LaHaye, *The Battle for the Mind* (Old Tappan, N.J.: Revell, 1980), and *The Battle for the Family* (Old Tappan, N.J.: Revell, 1982); Francis A. Schaeffer, *A Christian Manifesto* (Westchester, Ill.: Crossway, 1981); and John Whitehead, *The Second American Revolution* (Elgin, Ill.: David C. Cook, 1982).

18. Moore and Kramnick, *The Godless Constitution: The Case Against Religious Correctness* (New York: Norton, 1996), is the work of sophisticated scholars but displays so much exasperation at the populist historical simplicities of evangelical Protestant authors as to commit their own simplicities of liberal individualism in rebuttal.

19. John M. Murrin, "Religion and Politics in America from the First Settlements to the Civil War," in *Religion and American Politics*, ed. Mark A. Noll (New York: Oxford University Press, 1990), p. 31.

20. Capsule biographies, with denominational affiliations, are found in M. E. Bradford, *A Worthy Company: The Dramatic Story of the Men Who Founded Our Country* (Westchester, Ill.: Crossway, 1988).

21. The strongest argument for a Protestant presence are Alan Heimert, *Religion and the American Mind from the Great Awakening to the Revolution* (Cambridge: Harvard University Press, 1966), and Barry Alan Shain, *The Myth of American Individualism: The Protestant Origins of American Political Thought* (Princeton: Princeton University Press, 1994), but both Heimert and Shain recognize other influences as well. Solid treatments suggesting even more intermingling of sacred and secular categories are Nathan O. Hatch, *The Sacred Cause of Liberty: Republican Thought and the Millennium in Revolutionary New England* (New Haven: Yale University Press, 1977); Patricia U. Bonomi, *Under the Cope of Heaven: Religion, Society, and Politics in Colonial America* (New York: Oxford University Press, 1986); Ellis Sandoz, *A Gov-*

ernment of Laws: Political Theory, Religion, and the American Founding (Baton Rouge: Louisiana State University Press, 1990); Ronald J. Hoffman and Peter J. Albert, eds., *Religion in a Revolutionary Age* (Charlottesville: University Press of Virginia, 1994); and Dale S. Kuehne, *The Design of Heaven; Massachusetts Congregationalist Political Thought, 1760–1790* (Columbia: University of Missouri Press, 1996). For a popular text arguing for much more explicitly Christian influence on the founding documents, see Gary Amos and Richard Gardiner, *Never before in History: America's Inspired Birth* (Dallas, Tex.: Haughton, 1998).

22. Bernard Bailyn, ed., *The Debate on the Constitution*, 2 vols. (New York: Library of America, 1993).

23. Roger Finke and Rodney Start, "How the Upstart Sects Won America, 1776–1850," *Journal for the Scientific Study of Religion* 18 (1989): 27–44.

24. Stephen Marini, "The Government of God: Religion in Revolutionary America," unpublished ms.; Russell E. Richey, Kenneth E. Rowe, and Jean Miller Schmidt, eds., *Perspectives on American Methodism* (Nashville: Kingswood, 1993), section 1, "The Founding Period."

25. Nathan O. Hatch, *The Democratization of American Christianity* (New Haven: Yale University Press, 1989); Russell E. Richey, *Early American Methodism* (Bloomington: Indiana University Press, 1991).

26. For a survey, see Sydney E. Ahlstrom, *A Religious History of the American People* (New Haven: Yale University Press, 1972), Part IV, "The Golden Day of Democratic Evangelicalism."

27. West, *The Politics of Revelation and Reason: Religion and Civic Life in the New Nation* (Lawrence: University Press of Kansas, 1996). West expands upon solid accounts by, among others, Thomas J. Curry, *The First Freedoms: Church and State in America to the Passage of the First Amendment* (New York: Oxford University Press, 1986), pp. 193–222; and John F. Wilson, "Religion, Government, and Power in the New American Nation," in *Religion and American Politics*, pp. 77–91.

28. See Mark A. Noll, *One Nation Under God? Christian Faith and Political Action in America* (San Francisco: Harper & Row, 1988), chap. 5, "The Campaign of 1800: Fire Without Light."

29. See Richard R. John, *Spreading the News: The American Postal System from Franklin to Morse* (Cambridge: Harvard University Press, 1995), pp. 169–205; William G. McLoughlin, *Cherokees and Missionaries, 1789–1839* (New Haven: Yale University Press, 1984).

30. Carwardine, *Evangelicals and Politics in Antebellum America* (New Haven: Yale University Press, 1993).

31. Curtis D. Johnson, *Redeeming America: Evangelicals and the Road to Civil War* (Chicago: Ivan R. Dee, 1993).

32. See Kathryn, Teresa Long, *The Revival of 1857–58: Interpreting an American Religious Awakening* (New York: Oxford University Press, 1998).

33. The key account of antiformalist religion in the early United States is Nathan O. Hatch, *The Democratization of American Christianity* (New Haven: Yale University Press, 1989).

34. Carwardine, *Evangelicals and Politics in Antebellum America*, p. 322.

35. Ibid., p. 452.

6

The Influence of Judaism and Christianity on the American Founding

Michael Novak

Dare I open this part of the symposium with a provocation? Can an atheist be a good American? That has been done, many times. Can American liberties survive if most of our nation is atheist? The most common, almost universal, judgment of the founders was that it could not. The aim of this chapter, provocatively put, is to explore the reasoning of the founders on this question.

Put more moderately, the aim of this chapter is to lift into view the convergence of Whig and Jewish-Christian[1] theories of liberty in the Revolutionary era. It highlights "the logic of liberty" at work in the arguments of the founders, which linked liberty to reliable moral habits (virtues), and virtue to religion, and issued urgent warnings about the cultural precariousness of all three. Few historians or political philosophers are both trained in theology and familiar with the traditions of religious reflection on liberty, and so this modest effort may shed some light on connections no longer remembered without effort.

CHRISTIANS AND WHIGS

President Jefferson was on his way to church of a Sunday morning with his large red prayer book under his arm when a friend querying him after their mutual good morning said which way are you walking Mr. Jefferson. To which he replied to Church Sir. You going to church Mr. J. You do not believe a word in it. Sir said Mr. J. No nation has ever yet existed or been governed without religion. Nor can be. The Christian religion is the best religion that has ever been given to man and I as chief Magistrate of this nation am bound to give it the sanction of my example. Good morning Sir.

—The Rev. Ethan Allen[2]

In a famous essay, "Why I am Not a Conservative," F. A. Hayek argued that the proper name for a partisan of liberty, political and economic, is "Whig."[3] A partisan of liberty can scarcely be considered conservative, for liberty is a dynamic force that introduces surprising changes. In the middle of the twentieth century, neither could a partisan of liberty be called a progressive, for this term had been captured by socialists, social democrats, and other partisans of big government. Partly by a process of elimination, then, Hayek fell back on Whig. But he had another reason, too.

Hayek believed there is a tradition of *ideas* that can properly be called Whig. Following the lead of the historian of liberty, Lord Acton, Hayek further agreed that St. Thomas Aquinas (1224–1274) is properly called "the first Whig." There are three reasons for this: the argument of Aquinas that the first locus of political power lies in the consent of the people; his argument that the human person is born to be free and provident over his own destiny (*imago Dei*); and his argument that civilization is constituted, not by force, but by conversation—the rational persuasion of one person by another. These three arguments, crystallized by Aquinas, are three pillars of a free and civil society.[4]

Before linking them to Britain, Acton summarizes these views of Aquinas as follows:

> A king who is unfaithful to his duty forfeits his claim to obedience. It is not rebellion to depose him, for he is himself a rebel whom the nation has a right to put down. But it is better to abridge his power, that he may be unable to use it. For this purpose, the whole nation ought to have a share in governing itself; the Constitution ought to combine a limited and elective monarchy, with an aristocracy of merit, and such an admixture as shall admit all classes to office, by popular election. No government has a right to levy taxes beyond the limit determined by the people. All political authority is derived from popular suffrage, and all laws must be made by the people or their representatives. There is no security for us as long as we depend on the will of another man.[5]

When at the end of World War II Hayek helped to organize a society committed to rebuilding Europe as a free society, he recalled such Whig principles, and at first proposed calling his group the Acton-Tocqueville society, to indicate the tradition of ideas he had in mind.[6]

It was, of course, a commonplace for Thomas Jefferson and others among the American founders to say that "there was but one opinion on this side of the water. All American Whigs thought alike on these subjects."[7] Compared to Hayek's usage, however, what the Americans had in mind was a different meaning of Whig, at least on the surface. Its more immediate roots were Protestant, deeply steeped in the antipathy for the Stuarts manifested in the Revolution of 1688. Its more ancient roots, however, antedated Christianity altogether—they went back to the German (Saxon) tribes that migrated to

Britain in its pre-Christian era. According to the historians of English liberty favored by Jefferson and his peers, these ancient Germanic tribes had institutionalized the three principles listed previously long before Aquinas articulated them.[8] All tribal power, these historians maintained, was vested in the people, and their consent was expressed in large councils called together at least annually. In these, after argument and deliberation, the consent of all was secured for the ratification of significant decisions.[9]

The freedoms implicit in these arrangements, including the recognition of the private property rights of all freemen, came in British speech to be recognized as "the basic rights of Englishmen." These rights were rooted in tradition, not abstraction. They had been real and practiced for centuries, even though they were often infringed upon and, for a time, taken away. The great act of despoliation, beloved of tories (such as David Hume in his *History of England*), came with the feudal aristocracy, feudal privileges, and feudal landholding arrangements imported by the Normans after 1066.[10] This despoliation was renewed by the impositions of the hated Catholic Stuarts.

In Britain and America, the party of liberty was the Whigs, a party committed to the ancient traditions of their people, who pictured their foes as tyrants, usurpers, and violators of ancient—even natural—rights For the Whigs, "natural" was linked to "ancient" and "traditional," not to theory and abstraction, not to a utopian future. Their hope for a renewal of "ancient traditions of natural rights" was tempered by centuries of memories about how frequently and how easily these rights had been lost. Holding on to them, the American founders knew, is a precarious task.

In its modern period in Britain, as its historian Herbert Butterfield has emphasized, the Whig party was also the Christian party—emphatically Protestant and radically opposed to the Catholic Stuarts and all that they were supposed to represent.[11] The most interesting feature of the Whig tradition is how deeply it drew upon both natural reason and the Jewish-Christian Bible for its arguments on behalf of liberty. In America, these arguments from the Bible were especially important, because so many Americans took religion seriously, and because no other national institution was so deeply involved in the moral and civil education of the young. Moreover, ministers of the Gospel were the major speakers on regular occasions before the legislatures and public officials of the states, at annual civic festivals, and on patriotic holidays. American oratory, political and otherwise, was shaped by the rhetorical strategies, learning, passion, cadence, and even sounds of the Protestant pulpit. (What speaker in our day can fail to hear in his inner ear the voice of Martin Luther King, Jr.?) From the days of John Winthrop's discourse on the *Arbella* envisaging "the city on a hill," American religion had a *worldly* character. And right from the start the American *world* had a religious character.

Thus, the Americans of 1776 identified themselves with the Whigs, who wrested respect for Parliament from King John in the Magna Carta in 1215 and who deposed Charles II in the Glorious Revolution of 1688. They not only thought of themselves as traditionalists, they thought that it was King George III who was guilty of introducing novelties and abuses—a long train of abuses—and thus abrogating ancient rights and trampling upon sacred traditions. Against him they argued tradition; and they accused him of being the revolutionary who was overthrowing the ancient just order.

In their intentions and their presuppositions, the Americans were nearly the opposite of the French Revolutionaries of 1789–1791. The Americans saw themselves as restoring an ancient regime (the ancient Saxon liberties), the French as destroying one (that of the Bourbons). The Americans cited natural rights and reason in the same breath with tradition, the French cited abstract Reason, spelled with a capital "R," as an Ockham's razor taken to tradition. The Americans took care to adopt their Constitution through a long process of debate, deliberation, and consent from below, state by state. In the name of the General Will, the French turned to the swifter, cleaner logic of the guillotine. The Americans were Whigs, the French Jacobins.[12]

In another way, too, the Americans were unlike the French revolutionaries. While it may be said that both revolutions were fruits of the Enlightenment, it cannot be said in the same sense of each. For the French revolutionaries, the Enlightenment was against religion as light is opposed to darkness; they wished to *"écraser l'infâme."* For the Americans, religion—the Christian Bible, the Protestant churches—were sources of the revolution, and the cause of liberty was passionately embraced by the churches. In America, the fires of revolution were lit by the Puritan preachers of New England and their counterparts throughout the thirteen colonies. By contrast, the fury of the revolution in France was directed *against* church and synagogue, and in Paris the revolutionaries installed a prostitute upon the altar of Notre Dame cathedral. (For a vivid account of how contemporary Americans took the news, see the discourse of John Thayer in Boston in 1798.)[13]

The religiousness of the American Revolution, then, was utterly unlike the atheism of the French Revolution. When news reached the Continental Congress of the shelling of Boston in early September 1774, it voted that a distinguished preacher, "who loves his country," be asked to begin the next day's session with a prayer. And when upon the morrow the white-haired chaplain so did, praying from the Thirty-Fifth Psalm, he left not a dry eye in the chamber.[14] George Washington, too, in one of his first official acts as Commander of the army, asked all his men to pray, and many times in later years gave thanks to Divine Providence for its many and signal interventions on behalf of the cause of liberty. In his first Inaugural Address, Washington observed that "Every step by which [the American people] have advanced to the character of an independent nation seems to have been distinguished by some token of providential agency."[15]

During the past fifty years, markedly so among political philosophers concerned with the founding of the American Republic, it has become the convention so to stress the Enlightenment that the religious sources of American habits and institutions are abruptly dismissed.[16] Excessive credit is given to Locke (much is due him, but not all), and Locke is interpreted in a thoroughly secular way. Some authors have even written that the founders intended to confine religion to the narrow sphere of private conscience, thus to set it on the path to extinction.[17] Today, in dramatic contrast to the view of religion emphasized by the founders, one certainly gains the impression from the law schools and the nation's courts that large parts of the legal profession have come to regard religion as a force inimical to democracy. Unlike the founders, today's judges describe its influence on history as baleful, divisive, conducive to warfare and to hate, and in need of quarantining, like a disease.[18] In this respect, important elites in American life seem to have more in common with the French understanding of the antagonism between the Enlightenment and religion than with the understanding of the founders. It is not too much, I think, to call this tendency the Europeanizing of the American founding. Even Tocqueville noticed the difference:

> There is no country in the world in which the boldest political theories of the eighteenth-century philosophers are put so effectively into practice as in America. Only their anti-religious doctrines have never made any headway in that country.[19]

This Europeanization of the American founding has three main parts. First, it holds reason to be adversarial to revelation—the Enlightenment to religion. Second, it holds that a morality based upon reason alone is superior to Christian morality, indeed, that Christianity is a threat to republican institutions. Third, it holds that the extinction of religion, in the public sphere at least, would bring the public into greater conformity with republican principles. By contrast, the American founders held that the extinction of Christianity would cause the nets of the Constitution to burst asunder in disintegration.

Quite contrary to these three principles of the European Enlightenment is the Third Article of the Constitution of the Commonwealth of Massachusetts, ratified in 1780:

> Art. III. As the happiness of a people and the good order and preservation of civil government essentially depend upon piety, religion, and morality, and as these cannot be generally diffused through a community but by the institution of the public worship of God and of public instructions in piety, religion, and morality: Therefore, To promote their happiness and to secure the good order and preservation of their government, the people of this commonwealth have a

right to invest their legislature with power to authorize and require, and the legislature shall, from time to time, authorize and require, the several towns, parishes, precincts, and other bodies-politic or religious societies to make suitable provision, at their own expense, for the institution of the public worship of God and for the support and maintenance of public Protestant teachers of piety, religion, and morality in all cases where such provision shall not be made voluntarily.[20]

Earlier, John Adams had exhorted clergymen to lead the way toward freedom. "Let the pulpit resound with the doctrine and sentiments of religious liberty," he said. "Let us hear of the dignity of man's nature, and the noble rank he holds among the works of God. . . . Let it be known that British liberties are not the grants of princes and parliaments." The clergy more than answered his call. In 1775, Adams bragged that the Philadelphia ministers "thunder and lighten every Sabbath" against George III's despotism, and Jefferson noted that in Virginia "pulpit oratory ran like a shock of electricity through the whole colony." John Wingate Thornton concluded that "To the Pulpit, the Puritan Pulpit, we owe the moral force which won our independence."[21] In America, religion favored the cause of liberty, and political statesmen favored religion. No other institution in America was so responsible for inspiring and motivating the American War of Independence as the Protestant churches—and the few thousand Catholics of the land along with them.

But this is not all. Beyond guidance on the question of independence, the people also needed public instruction in the philosophy of freedom, the political philosophy of republican government, and the doctrine of natural rights; and this education was also, for the most part, carried out by the churches. This record supplied evidence to the founders of the American Republic that of all philosophies and religions, Protestant Christianity is the best foundation for republican institutions. Here are but a few texts, to whose number scores of others could be added:

- James Madison: "The belief in a God All Powerful wise and good, is so essential to the moral order of the world and to the happiness of man, that arguments which enforce it cannot be drawn from too many sources nor adapted with too much solicitude to the different characters and capacities impressed with it."[22]
- Thomas Jefferson: "And can the liberties of a nation be thought secure when we have removed their only firm basis, a conviction in the minds of the people that these liberties are of the gift of God? That they are not violated but with his wrath?"[23]
- Joseph Story: "The promulgation of the great doctrines of religion, the being, and attributes, and providence of one Almighty God: the responsibility to him for all our actions, founded upon moral freedom and accountability; a future state of rewards and punishments; the cultiva-

tion of all the personal, social, and benevolent virtues—these can never be matters of indifference in any well-ordered community. It is, indeed, difficult to conceive how any civilized society can exist without them."[24]

- The preamble of the Constitution of North Carolina: "We, the people of the State of North Carolina, grateful to Almighty God, the Sovereign Ruler of Nations, for the preservation of the American Union and the existence of our civil, political, and religious liberties, and acknowledging our dependence upon Him for the continuance of those blessings to us and our posterity, do, for the more certain security thereof and for the better government of this State, ordain and establish this Constitution."[25]

THE LOGIC OF LIBERTY

The logic of the founders moves forward in five steps, through five interconnected insights. First, the founders saw in two human capacities— reflection and choice—the key to their concept of liberty. Second, from this, they developed an original, highly moral concept of the natural right to liberty, drawing both upon revelation and reason. Third, they experienced revelation and reason, at least in respect to liberty, as friends and correlates, not foes. Fourth, they learned from experience that in a republic liberty is not practicable without virtue, nor virtue without religion. This insight has a corollary: that the free society is necessarily precarious, given the changeability of human morals over time, and their persistent tendency to decline. Finally, they learned by trial and error that the advantages of liberty and the virtues it inculcates can be better secured when religion is not established. These five insights are tightly connected, one to another. Disentangling them requires some patience.

Why did the American founders believe that religion is a sound foundation for a republic, when Europeans of the Enlightenment held precisely the opposite? The Americans reached their own distinctive concept of natural rights by two different paths, one religious and one philosophical, and these two chains of argument reinforced each other in their minds. As the founders understood them, both reason and revelation showed the natural right to liberty to be a *moral* concept imposing moral obligations upon citizens, and located the very evidence for the existence of this natural right in man's moral nature.

This distinctive American understanding of natural rights is implicit, for example, in the opening lines of *The Federalist,* No. 1. Indeed, it is a precondition of the entire process of ratifying the proposed new Constitution of the United States. Here are the crucial words:

> it seems to have been reserved to the people of this country, to decide the important question, whether societies of men are really capable or not, of establishing good government from *reflection* and *choice*, or whether they are forever destined to depend, for their political constitutions, on accident and force.[26]

The question is not whether humans have these two capacities, "reflection" and "choice." If they didn't, there would be no point in proceeding with public debates, written arguments, and deliberative votes. The question is whether these observed capacities are strong enough for the great social task of forming governments.

Since no creature but human beings acts from these two capacities, reflection and choice are nature's testimony to human destiny. To live according to reflection and choice is both the law of nature and the law of God. Since both nature and God impel humans to exercise their liberty, it follows that humans must have a natural right to liberty. Without such a right, they could not obey either the law of their own nature or the law of God. Further, since to be free is to incur responsibility for one's own deliberate choices, no one can hand off his liberty to others; liberty is not alienable.

To violate a person's natural liberty is, therefore, to deface, deform, and frustrate the laws of nature and nature's God. It is both a sin against justice that cries out to heaven and a crime indictable before the tribunal of humankind. In religious terms generic enough not to be limited to Christians solely, Jefferson wrote: "The God who gave us life gave us liberty at the same time."[27] It is a self-evident step from this conviction to the phrase of the Declaration, "endowed by their Creator with certain inalienable rights."

Skills in constitution writing, however, are not the same as skills in metaphysics. The founders were not primarily metaphysicians, they were nation builders. They were less concerned to publish precise disquisitions on liberty than to contrive institutions of liberty that would work among people as they were. This point was emphasized on the eve of the constitutional convention by John Adams in his *A Defence of the Constitutions of Governments of the United States,* with a sharp elbow in John Locke's eye:

> A philosopher may be a perfect master of Descartes and Leibniz, may pursue his own metaphysical inquiries to any length, may enter into the innermost recesses of the human mind, and make the noblest discoveries for the benefit of his species; nay, he may defend the principles of liberty and the rights of mankind with great abilities and success; and, after all, when called upon to produce a plan of legislation, he may astonish the world with a signal absurdity. Mr. Locke, in 1663, was employed to trace out a plan of legislation for Carolina; and he gave the whole authority, executive and legislative, to the eight proprietors, the Lords Berkley, Clarendon, Albemarle, Craven, and Ashley; and Messieurs Carteret, Berkley, and Colleton, and their heirs. This new oligarchical sovereignty created at least three orders of nobility . . . Who did this legislator think would live under his government? He should have first created a new species of beings to govern, before he instituted such a government.[28]

The American founders, evidently, were quite clear about who would live under their own new government. They wanted an independent republic and a constitution that would work in America—that is, would both endure among Americans and be worthy of American hopes? Through and through, such a project had to exhibit reflection and choice at work, in order to meet the standards of the natural right to liberty for which it was designed. Such a requirement endowed the building of the republic with substantive moral purpose. An entire citizenry had to be taught how to pursue the public business—and conduct their private lives—in ways compatible with sober reflection and reasoned choice.[29]

For it is soon a matter of immediate experience, if not of self-evidence, that not every human all the time is in the frame of mind required for reflection and deliberate choice. Passion, ignorance, bias, interest, fear—all these are common motives and conventional means for cutting reflection short and acting in ways contrary to dispassionate choice. The free citizen must be able to summon up at will a capacity for sober reflection and duly measured choice, such as the authors of *The Federalist* properly demanded of them. Thus, citizens who depend upon reflection and choice will necessarily depend upon an array of inclinations, dispositions and habits that, when duty calls, clear their souls of passion, ignorance, bias, interest, and fear.

George Washington, in particular, grasped the inner dependence of the republican experiment upon the sound habits of its citizens. For this reason alone, at full risk to his own reputation (with everything to lose, nothing to gain), he could not refuse to come out of retirement to guide the first generation of citizens of the new republic through its first foundational years. His principle was this: A nation, like a child, forms its character around its earliest transactions. Therefore, Washington determined to lead the nation at large through the ways in which a citizenry called to self-government must comport itself. The people themselves must become an example to the world of reflection and deliberate choice, and the enabling and supportive virtues on which these capacities depend.[30]

This distinctive concept of natural rights embodied, therefore, a national moral project. This project may be expressed through the two-sided meaning of the term *self-government*. A republican experiment is an experiment in public self-government through public institutions on the part of the whole people. At the same time, such public self-government can only succeed if its citizens also practice self-government in their personal lives. That is, the citizens must comport themselves with capacities for sober reflection and deliberate choice at the ready. It is not necessary for all or even most to be saints. Nonetheless, to suppose that a republican government could succeed without at least a modicum of virtue in its citizens would be a pipe dream.[31]

Further, it is the great merit of the Protestant Christian religion (which in this is remarkably close to Orthodox Judaism) that it emphasizes both personal responsibility and self-mastery. It emphasizes these virtues for reasons both religious and prudent in the ways of the world. It sees them as commanded equally by the laws of nature and nature's God.

On these points, Madison, Washington, Jefferson, Adams, and the others were as one.

THE CONVERGENCE OF REVELATION AND REASON

Upon these two foundations, the law of nature and the law of revelation, depend all human laws; that is to say, no human law should be suffered to contradict these.—Blackstone[32]

If ever on a hot and muggy day in July, when you were young, you dove into the clear cool water of a mountain lake, you know the shock that greets you when you dive from the intellectual world of modern secular scholarship into a leisurely reading of the papers of the founding fathers. The latter were so plainly religious, compared to intellectuals of today, and not merely religious, but pious—moved by sentiments of whose warmth and tenderness there can be no doubt.

For the founders, reason and revelation are not in fundamental opposition. Rather, regarding the character and centrality of liberty, they converge. In their view, the ideas and practice of Judaism and Christianity are the best foundation for republican government. This point of view is the decisive stumbling block for many contemporary scholars, who are accustomed to thinking of Judaism and Christianity as threats to the free society. Such scholars hold that reason and revelation are radically opposed to each other.

Yet the founders drew much inner strength from several texts. One supposed skeptic among the founders, Benjamin Franklin, proposed as a motto for the seal of the United States a powerful religious maxim of long standing: "Rebellion to tyrants is obedience to God."[33] To oppose George III, and to commit one's life and honor to liberty, not only was there no need to renounce Christian faith; that faith itself was fertile with motives.

The wise and much-revered Dr. Benjamin Rush of Philadelphia anchored the republican form of government in religion: "The only foundation for a useful education in a republic is to be laid in religion. Without this there can be no virtue, and without virtue there can be no liberty, and liberty is the object and life of all republican governments."[34] This text expresses the essential core of the logic of the founders: A Republic means liberty. Liberty needs virtue. Virtue among the people is impossible without religion. Therefore, there must be education in religion. Otherwise, there will sooner or later be moral weakness, from which will follow obsequious obedience to tyrants. Many distinguished lawyers and scholars today, atheists and secularists in particular, do not believe these things.

Rush feels so strongly about this that he would sooner see the teachings of Confucius or Mahomet taught in American schools than "see them grow up wholly devoid of a system of religious principles." Unmistakably, however, he points out that the religion *he* means is "that of the New Testament." (Almost all his references, however, are to the Jewish testament.) "It is foreign to my purpose," Rush continues, "to hint at the arguments which establish the truth of Christian doctrine." (He holds, with the Christian university tradition in which nearly all the founders shared, that there *are* such arguments, even though voicing them is not his present purpose.) "My only business is to declare, that all its doctrines and precepts are calculated to promote the happiness of society, and the safety and well-being of civil government." Rush then utters a sentence that he will repeat three times, and so I add emphasis to it: *"A Christian cannot fail of being a Republican."* Rush has three arguments for this point, and that is why he repeats it thrice.

His first argument is that "the history of the creation of man, and of the relation of our species to each other by birth, which is recorded in the Old Testament, is the best refutation that can be given to the divine right of kings, and the strongest argument that can be used in favor of the original and natural equality of all mankind."

In other words, one does not need Locke to come to natural rights. Locke rendered valuable service in bringing arguments from reason to this same conclusion. But the basic point is available to any coppersmith or carpenter who reads his Bible closely. Each citizen, no matter how humble, knows that God knew his name before the ages, that all are equal in his sight, and that the mighty will be brought low and the lowly exalted.

Then comes Rush's second argument: "A Christian, I say again, cannot fail of being a republican, for every precept of the Gospel inculcates those degrees of humility, self-denial, and brotherly kindness, which are directly opposed to the pride of monarchy and the pageantry of a court."

Here an objection may as well be faced: Rush's presentation, emphasizing kindness, indicates how much the Christian teaching seems to differ from Locke's "state of nature," in which men are certainly not social, civil or brotherly.

But is there really a contradiction? Man in the state of nature is by definition outside Christianity, outside any religion. This does not contradict, it reinforces, what Rush holds, viz., that without religion virtue is impossible. What Christians mean by "original sin"—the inherited disorder of man's nature in which each of us is born—is not exactly what Locke intends by "state of nature." But both concepts, "original sin" and "state of nature," put the brakes on utopian hopes about the moral potency of human nature, left to itself. Even the great John Witherspoon, president of Princeton, signer of the Declaration of Independence, teacher of James Madison, three Supreme Court Justices, 21 senators, 29 congressmen, and 30 lower court judges—

even John Witherspoon used the term "state of nature" to describe humans in the state of original sin, outside God's grace.[35]

In fact, by one gauge, Christians may be more pessimistic than Locke. Locke places considerable hope in civil society, but the American founders believed that even a good social contract and a well-intentioned civil society will in time disintegrate, unless fortified by virtue, itself reinforced by religion. They tended to go beyond Hobbes and Locke in tying natural rights to the "eternal and immutable law" of God, which they called "the law of nature."[36]

To generalize this point: When the founders use the terminology and arguments of Locke, as they often do, they are neither denying nor qualifying their Christian beliefs. They do not advance academic arguments; they do not explore crucial differences between Locke and Sidney.[37] They are not acting as philosophers but as nation builders among a particular—and religious—people.

Some followers of Leo Strauss today are said to argue that Locke used conventional Christian language in order to subvert it. (Locke never asserts such an intention.) But it is equally possible that, in good faith, Locke's philosophical equipment was not subtle enough to make all the distinctions his argument needed. One does not suppose that those whose moves in chess end in disaster intended what they did not have the wit to foresee. Just so, one ought not to take as willful the unforeseen logical consequences of moves taken in the heat of play even by philosophers. On the borderline between philosophy and religion, it is a common occurrence that thinkers are inadvertently led into trains of logic that were no part of their intention.

Besides, if it is legitimate to argue that Locke used Christian terms to subvert Christian premises, it is equally legitimate to hypothesize that many in the founding generation used Lockean terms to subvert Lockean premises, by using them to Christian purposes. It is true that "natural rights" are not mentioned in the Bible *in ipsis verbis* (but then neither is the "trinity"), and that Locke supplied the term. Yet the content the founders give to the term had more to do with what they learned from the Bible than with the content Locke gave to it.

"And lastly," Benjamin Rush writes in offering his third reason why a Christian cannot fail of being a republican, "his religion teacheth him, in all things to do to others what he would wish, in like circumstances, they should do to him."[38] This is a good teaching for a society that wishes to be civil and brotherly and whose desperate struggle is to maintain the union.

The physician of Philadelphia is not the only one to hold that biblical religion is particularly linked to republican government. John Adams himself wrote to Rush in 1807: "The Bible contains the most profound philosophy, the most perfect morality, and the most refined policy, that ever was conceived upon earth. It is the most republican book in the world."[39]

Noah Webster repeated this theme in 1834, eight years after the death of Jefferson and Adams: "the Christian religion ought to be received, and maintained with firm and cordial support. *It is the real source of all genuine republican principles.* It teaches the equality of men as to rights and duties; and while it forbids all oppression, it commands due subordination to law and rulers. It requires the young to yield obedience to their parents, and enjoins upon men the duty of selecting their rulers from their fellow citizens of mature age, sound wisdom, and real religion."[40]

Lest this admonition sound merely theoretical, Webster, as becomes the author of a dictionary, uses words limpidly: "Never cease then to give to religion, to its institutions, and to its ministers, your strenuous support. . . . Those who destroy the influence and authority of the Christian religion, sap the foundations of public order, of liberty, and of republican government."

Because the principle we are tracking seems so strange to contemporary secular scholars, it is no doubt useful to provide two more texts, the more precisely to stress the convergence in question. A native of Scotland and later a justice on the Supreme Court, Pennsylvania's James Wilson wrote in "The Laws of Nature" in 1790:

> How shall we, in particular cases, discover the will of God? We discover it by our conscience, our reason, and by the Holy Scriptures. The law of nature and the law of revelation are both divine; they flow, though in different channels, from the same adorable source. It is, indeed, preposterous to separate them from each other. The object of both is—to discover the will of God—and both are necessary for the accomplishment of that end.[41]

A second example of that confidence in the convergence of reason and revelation appears in a passage from a New England divine, Samuel Cooper, D.D., preached before Governor John Hancock and the Senate and the House of Representatives of Massachusetts on October 25, 1780, on the day of the Commencement of the Constitution of Massachusetts and the Inauguration of the New Government. Cooper had received his doctorate at Edinburgh after graduation from Harvard, served as member of the Harvard Corporation, and turned down the presidency of Harvard. His sermon, anthologized even in Holland, is often taken as the model American patriotic sermon.

Cooper began his sermon that October day with an extended parallel between the people of Israel and "our own circumstances" of the present day. His text for the day was the thirtieth chapter of Jeremiah, and he dwelled on the groaning of the Israelites in captivity, desolation, and conquest. He did not hesitate to link George III to Nebuchadnezzar. Recognizing that the Hebrew government, "tho' a theocracy, was yet as to the outward part of it, a free republic, and that the sovereignty resided in the people," he spelled out his meaning from vivid examples. In this argument, he follows Algernon Sidney in setting forth a theory of civil government and republican liberty that emphasized their reliance on virtue and religion. "Such a constitution," he proceeded, "twice established by the hand of heaven in that nation, so far as it respects civil and religious liberty in general, ought to be regarded as a solemn recognition from the Supreme Ruler himself of the rights of human nature." Abstract the key points of that constitution from circumstances peculiar to the situation of the Jews at that time, he adds, and you may discern "in general what kind of government infinite wisdom and goodness would establish among mankind."

Then comes a passage directly germane to our present concern, the convergence of revelation and reason:

> We want not, indeed, a special revelation from heaven to teach us that men are born equal and free; that no man has a natural claim of dominion over his neighbours, nor one nation any such claim upon another; and that as government is only the administration of affairs of a number of men combined for their own security and happiness, such a society have a right freely to determine by whom and in what manner their own affairs shall be administered. These are the plain dictates of that reason and common sense with which the common parent of men has informed the human bosom. It is, however, a satisfaction to observe such everlasting maxims of equity confirmed, and impressed upon the consciences of men, by the instructions, precepts, and examples given us in the sacred oracles.[42]

Having made the case for liberty, independence, and republican government from revelation, Dr. Cooper raises again the question of virtue, from reason's point of view.

> As piety and virtue support the honour and happiness of every community, they are peculiarly required in a free government. Virtue is the spirit of a republic; for where all power is derived from the people, all depends on their good disposition. If they are impious, factious and selfish; if they are abandoned to idleness, dissipation, luxury, and extravagance; if they are lost to the fear of God, and the love of their country, all is lost.

If the whole of Dr. Cooper's sermon was actually read that day, that was a long and learned discourse they heard at Harvard in October 1780. The new House and Senate of Massachusetts, in the middle of a dangerous war, had reason to feel much strengthened by the artillery of philosophy and religion that was rolled up to their support.

What faith taught them, reason supported. What reason taught them, revelation reinforced.

FOUNDATION, YES; ESTABLISHMENT, NO

The first ground for the American belief that religion is a friend, not a foe, to republican government, then, lay in the distinctively moral idea of natural rights cherished by the American founders, and in their familiar ease in relating reason to revelation, and revelation to reason, as two converging arguments on behalf of human liberty. The second ground lies in an original approach to religion, public and private, as the "foundation" of republican virtue. The Americans developed an original conception of "foundations." In Europe, to found a system of government upon religion meant to build upon an established church with prescribed doctrines and rituals, so as to secure a unified public ethos. In America, it became clear by trial and error that that traditional method had destructive consequences both for the church and for the state.

Uneasily at first, for want of knowledge about how to do things any better, these European traditions of church and state had been carried over into America. Catholic Maryland, having learned a salutary lesson from the sad experience of Catholic states in Europe, had launched an early and tentative experiment in religious liberty; it did not last long. Pennsylvania, under the Quakers, did better. Virtually all the other states had established churches, many of them continuing to retain these establishments for at least two generations after independence. These arrangements awakened much objection, not least from dissenting churches such as the Baptists and other evangelicals. (What today would be called the "religious right" was then the "religious left.")

In sum, the traditional alliance of throne and altar saddled the *state* with tasks for which it had little or no competence, and bred hostility and resentment among religious dissenters and nonbelievers. This traditional arrangement also saddled the *church* with practices that, however common they had been in the past, had come to seem from painful experiences inimical to Christian ideals and aspirations—the use of the state to punish or to banish heretics, for instance, as had happened in Massachusetts with respect to Roger Williams.

Therefore, in order to strengthen both the church and the republican state, the founding generation decided not to establish a national church. These almost unanimously Protestant leaders elected, instead, to build the foundation of the republic elsewhere.[43]

Where, then? They chose the open exercise of everyday religious life in every locality and state. In other words, through the open, visible, and often publicly encouraged practice of a vigorous religious life, in free and mutually respectful amity, the American people would form and publicly exhibit those religious habits of the heart necessary for the proper working of republican institutions. And these religious habits of the heart, demonstrated daily in private and in public behavior, would be the moral foundation of the republic. Thus, when Madison wrote that our rights are not protected by "parchment barriers," but by the habits and institutions of the American people,[44] this was the strong foundation on which he relied.

It is important to pause for a moment to see how original this solution was. Most scholars and lawyers appear to consider it from the point of view of the state. But its most striking originality is evident in the advance it represents for religious bodies in general and Christianity in particular. Before the founding of America, the injunction of the Lord "Give unto Caesar that which is Caesar's, and unto God that which is God's" (Matthew 22:21) had always run headlong into a contradiction. All power, even Caesar's, comes from God, and thus does not even Caesar owe public homage to God? But if Caesar does what is in him to give God His due, then Caesar's choice of worship seems to prevail, at least in public, over that of the dissenting individual. How can the individual give to God what is God's, if he is first compelled by Caesar's religion?

The American solution was a self-denying ordinance on the part of the federal government: "Congress shall make no law respecting an establishment of religion . . . " That is, in matters pertaining to God, the federal government openly declares its own incompetence. Caesar withdraws his authority from the sphere of conscience. In this manner, the way is cleared as never before for the citizen to give to Caesar what is in the express competence of Caesar, and to give to God His full due. He may do so alone or with others, according to both personal and *social* conscience. (Not all believers imagine that individual conscience is isolated in solitariness; many understood themselves as participants in a historic community of belief, so that for many people, conscience in its depths is *social,* not merely atomic.) Thus, when believers engage in the "free exercise" of their religion, they may act openly in the public square, through a diversity of institutional forms, and not solely in private. They may even expect the recognition of religion by public agencies in many various and traditional ways. What is strictly forbidden, Madison explained to Congress, is the establishment of *a* religion by the federal Congress.[45]

If a fundamental Christian conception is that the dignity of the human person is rooted in the act of freedom by which each responds to the call of his Creator and Redeemer, that conception had never before been given such untrammeled (but not unambiguous) political expression. Under a regime in which government is limited, respectful of individual rights, and under the rule of law, moreover, government is not the only or even the chief actor in the public square. In a free society, there is plenty of room in the vast open spaces of civil society for the public exercise of religion. ("Public" is an equivocal term; when it is employed to mean the opposite of "private, internal," it does not solely apply to actions of the State. Many institutions, including the churches, are public actors.)

A crucial ambiguity in this arrangement remains. Has not Caesar, as well, a responsibility to pay public homage to God? Here the U.S. Constitution makes no public provision, even though traditional practices do. The Constitution expressly avoids the explicit confession of Christian faith found in the Constitutions of several of the states. On the other hand, the U.S. Congress works under the prayers and counseling of a salaried pastor. Presidents issue proclamations of Days of National Thanksgiving, and both Congress and presidents have declared national days of prayer and fasting in cases of urgent national need. The U.S. government pays for the installation of Stars of David and crosses on the graves of U.S. servicemen buried overseas. But federal homage to the Creator and source of our rights, Who is the Lawgiver, Governor, and Judge mentioned in the Declaration of Independence, is limited—more limited than homage openly paid by states and localities, visible in the practices of state establishments of religion at that time. In maintaining a sphere of reverential silence, however, in the place where its citizens give to the transcendent God the particular names they have learned from their families, the American Federal State may be paying the only form of homage becoming to a pluralistic people. It is not an achievement without ambiguity; but it is a great achievement.

Thus, what Madison wrote in *Federalist,* No. 14, about the body of the Constitution might with even greater force be said of the originality of the founders with respect to religious liberty.

> They accomplished a revolution which has no parallel in the annals of human society: They reared the fabrics of governments which have no model on the face of the globe.[46]

That it is original does not mean, of course, that it will endure forever. And that possibility, indeed probability, led to another step in the logic of the framers.

THE PRECARIOUSNESS OF LIBERTY

There is a danger in the American solution. That danger may be a greater threat to the state than it is to Judaism and Christianity. The danger is that a three-step process may ensue, undermining conscience and clearing the way for tyranny.

- The first step in the decay of the republican experiment would be to conceive of the human person as solitary and atomic, cut free from—liberated from, unbridled by—bonds and responsibilities to multiple communities (family first of all, covenantal communities, freely chosen associations, etc.). This step follows in the path of Locke, rather than in the way of the ancient Saxons and the early Whig tradition.
- The second step would be to imagine that such an individual is unable to discern by intellect any responsibilities or obligations except those whose origin lies in his own volition; that is, each merely chooses to create the laws, or lack of laws, under which he or she will live.

- The third step would be to empower the government to root out every vestige of religious expression from every aspect of public life; that is, to change the nonestablishment of religion into an erasure of religion (écrasez l'infâme).

A people that descended these three steps would put Judaism and Christianity on the road to extinction, not solely in the public square but in private life as well. Such steps would clear the path in America, as it did in France, for the inexorable logic of the Terror. Why? Because once these steps had been taken, the triumph of political orthodoxy and legal positivism would be assured. Against these, there would remain no principled intellectual defense. If legitimate authority wills to put something into law, and does so, citizens can no longer argue that that is unjust (says who?) or in violation of the laws of nature and nature's God (so what?).

To prevent the nation from taking such a self-destructive track, the founders often stressed the dependence of liberty on truth. They loved the text from St. John: "And ye shall know the truth, and the truth shall make you free" (John 8:32).[47] Accordingly, they believed that there are laws of nature and laws of God, whose truth is either self-evident or easily discovered by serious persons of goodwill and sound judgment. Anybody who wishes to preserve his freedom had better learn—and help others to learn—these truths. The founders took extraordinary care in recommending the study of those books in which such truths may be found.

No one can argue, then, that the founders did not foresee, and attempt to forestall, these dangers. Thomas Jefferson made George Washington's Farewell Address required reading at the University of Virginia, since in it Washington clearly describes the "pillars" of the free society and the dangers to which it is vulnerable. Washington does not call religion "optional." The word he uses is "indispensable."

> Of all the dispositions and habits which lead to political prosperity, Religion and morality are indispensable supports. In vain would that man claim the tribute of Patriotism, who should labour to subvert these great Pillars of human happiness, these firmest props of the duties of Men and citizens. The mere Politician, equally with the pious man ought to respect and cherish them. A volume could not trace all their connections with public and private felicity. Let it simply be asked where is the security for property, for reputation, for life, if the sense of religious obligation desert the oaths, which are the instruments of investigation in Courts of Justice? And let us with caution indulge the supposition, that morality can be maintained without religion. Whatever may be conceded to the influence of refined education on minds of peculiar structure, reason and experience both forbid us to expect that National morality can prevail in exclusion of religious principle.

'Tis substantially true, that virtue or morality is a necessary spring of popular government. The rule indeed extends with more or less force to every species of free Government. Who that is a sincere friend to it, can look with indifference upon attempts to shake the foundation of the fabric.[48]

John Adams was even clearer in his warning in 1798:

We have no government armed with power of contending with human passions unbridled by morality and religion. Avarice, ambition, revenge, or gallantry, would break the strongest cords of our Constitution as a whale goes through a net. Our Constitution is made only for a moral and religious people. It is wholly inadequate to the government of any other.[49]

So strongly did John Adams believe this that when he wrote to his cousin Zabdiel, a minister of the Christian gospel, two weeks before the adoption of the Declaration of Independence, he described his fears for the future, and urged upon him the importance of his work in religious ministry:

Statesmen my dear Sir, may plan and speculate for Liberty, but it is Religion and Morality alone, which can establish the Principles, upon which Freedom can securely stand.

Adams then wrote a shocking warning that the alternative to virtue in the people is tyranny.

The only foundation of a free Constitution is pure Virtue, and if this cannot be inspired into our People, in a greater Measure, than they have it now, They may change their Rulers, and the forms of Government, but they will not obtain a lasting Liberty.—They will only exchange Tyrants and Tyrannies.

After these heavy thoughts, Adams encouraged his cousin to continue with enthusiasm as a minister of God, for the good of the republic—"You cannot therefore be more pleasantly, or usefully employed than in the Way of your Profession, pulling down the Strong Holds of Satan."[50] Adams, like Franklin, feared for the future of the Republic.

"The only foundation of a free Constitution is pure Virtue." A way must be found to inspire virtue in our people, or independence is in vain. The foundation of the American republic is not an established church; it is the religious and moral habits of its people. This is a foundation deeper and stronger—and truer to Christianity—than an establishment of religion by Caesar. It is, however, a foundation that is subject to erosion over time. That erosion can be prevented only by eternal vigilance. This was a common sentiment—and a common concern—of the founding generation.

CONCLUSION

Judaism and Christianity provided a great deal more than meets the eye, then, to the American founding. They reinforced in men's minds the role of reason in human affairs; the idea of progress in history (as opposed to a wheel of endless rotation); the centrality of personal dignity and personal liberty in human destiny; and the idea of a cosmic process conceived, created, and governed (even in its tiniest details) by a benevolent Deity: Lawgiver, Governor, Judge, gentle and caring Providence. This Deity would one day ask of each human an accounting for his thoughts and deeds. In other words, liberty is no trifling matter. How humans use this liberty matters infinitely. Liberty, so to speak, is the purpose for which the sun and the stars are made. In that respect, America's experiment in liberty is especially dear to Providence. Looking down on it, God smiles. So, at least, the founders inscribed on the Seal of the United States:

ANNUIT COEPTIS

The other inscription they placed on the Seal, in its seventh and final draft, called attention to the originality of their new design:

NOVUS ORDO SECLORUM

In its place, for the first six drafts, they had originally had a single word:

VIRTUE

Given their understanding of liberty, calling attention to virtue must have seemed to them too obvious. What they needed to emphasize was the newness and daring of their experiment. For sometimes experiments go wrong. It is all too easy to see how this one might do so.

One thing our generation must not do is take our republic's longevity for granted.

NOTES

The author thanks Thomas Kilroy for distinguished research assistance.

1. Most of the materials in this chapter—and in the writings of the founding generation—are Christian, but most of the relevant points are shared alike by Jews and Christians and are, in fact owed by Christians to their Jewish inheritance. Thus, I say "Jewish-Christian" rather than mostly "Christian."

2. From Rev. Ethan Allen's handwritten history "Washington Parish, Washington City" in the Library of Congress MMC Collection, 1167, MSS, as quoted in James H. Hutson, *Religion and the Founding of the American Republic* (Washington, D.C.: Li-

brary of Congress, 1998), p. 96. According to the most sustained study of Jefferson's religious convictions, it is probably more accurate to say that Jefferson was a Unitarian rather than a Christian. He disbelieved in miracles and other evidences of the workings of grace beyond the natural order. But he did believe that Protestant Christianity—as distinct from "monkish superstition"—is crucial to the American Republic, and for this reason he kept his own heterodoxies private and gave biblical Christianity public support. His letters show that he also believed in a divine Judge and, provisionally, in eternal life. The chronicler of his religious journey concludes that:

Jefferson assumed an ordered, theocentric world; chaos was not king. He also affirmed that ours was and is a moral universe; unrestrained libertinism did not, must not, rule. In addition, he believed that free men and women could not find ultimate satisfaction in a religion devoid of Reason; phantoms and fanaticisms must not drive Reason from its proper place. And finally, Thomas Jefferson knew that he was not God. A large measure of perspective, a considerable degree of humility, arose from the keen sense that he, too, was only one of God's creatures. He, along with all other human beings, did not enter into the world booted and spurred, to mount the backs of those less fortunate. Rather, he, like all women and men, was bound in a bundle with the living, called and challenged to elevate, educate, liberate, and introduce lasting reforms in politics, morality, and religion.

Edwin S. Gaustad, *Sworn on the Altar of God: A Religious Biography of Thomas Jefferson* (Grand Rapids, Mich.: Eerdmans, 1996), p. 228.

3. *The Constitution of Liberty* (Chicago: University of Chicago Press, 1978), appendix.

4. The references in Aquinas for these three propositions are, successively: for the first, *Summa Theologica*, Ia–2ae.cv.1.; for the second, *Commentary*, II Sentences, XLIV.i.3, ad 1. and *Summa Theologica*, 2a–2ae.lxiv.2, ad 3; and for the third, *Commentary*, I *Politics*, lect. I. See also Thomas Gilby, O.P., *The Political Thought of Thomas Aquinas* (Chicago: University of Chicago Press, 1958), p. 290, and *Between Community and Society: A Philosophy and Theology of the State* (London: Longmans, 1953), pp. 93, 185.

5. After quoting this text, Lord Acton comments, "This language, which contains the earliest exposition of the Whig theory, is taken from the works of St. Thomas Aquinas, of whom Lord Bacon says that he had the largest heart of the school divines. And it is worthwhile to observe that he wrote at the very moment when Simon de Montfort summoned the Commons; and that the politics of the Neapolitan friar are centuries in advance of the English statesman's." From "The History of Freedom in Christianity," in *The History of Liberty*, ed. J. Rufus Fears (Indianapolis: Liberty Classics, 1985), p. 34.

6. F. A. Hayek, "Opening Address to a Conference at Mont Pelerin," in *New Studies in Philosophy, Politics, Economics and the History of Ideas* (Chicago: University of Chicago Press, 1978), p. 158.

7. A fuller portion of the letter is even clearer about the breadth of the Whig tradition:

But with respect to our rights, and the acts of the British government contravening those rights, there was but one opinion on this side of the water. All American whigs thought alike on these subjects. When forced, therefore, to resort to arms for redress, an appeal to the tribunal of the world was deemed proper for our justification. This was the object of the Declaration of Independence. Not to find out new principles, or new arguments, never before thought of, not merely to say things which had never been said before; but to place before mankind the common sense of the subject, in terms so plain and firm as to command their assent, and to justify ourselves in the independent stand we are compelled to take. Neither aiming at originality of principle or sentiment, nor yet copied from any particular and previous writing, it was intended to be an expression of the American mind, and to give to that expression the proper tone and spirit called for by the occasion. All its authority rests then on the harmonizing sentiments of the day, whether expressed in conversation, in letters, printed essays, or in the elementary books of public right, as Aristotle, Cicero, Locke, Sidney, etc. The historical documents which you mention as in your possession, ought all to be found, and I am persuaded you will find, to be corroborative of the facts and principles advanced in that Declaration.

Thomas Jefferson to Henry Lee, May 8, 1825, in Adrienne Koch and William Peden, eds., *The Life and Selected Writings of Thomas Jefferson* (New York: Modern Library, 1944), p. 719.

8. Trevor Colbourn, *The Lamp of Experience: Whig History and the Intellectual Origins of the American Revolution* (Indianapolis: Liberty, 1998). Colbourn describes Jefferson's readings in history, and especially his affection for Rapin's *History of England*, pp. 193–196.

9. As Colbourn recounts, these are the facts as the founding generation understood them. Recent scholarship has shown that the reality of Saxon life was considerably cruder, and that the founders were unwittingly influenced by an unrealistic picture of the past. Ibid., Appendix I, "The Saxon Myth Dies Hard."

10. Colbourn stresses the antagonism to Hume among the Whigs, Jefferson included. See ibid. pp. 216–220.

11. Herbert Butterfield, *The Whig Interpretation of History* (New York: AMS Press, 1978).

12. See, among others, Russell Kirk, *The Conservative Constitution* (Washington, D.C.: Regnery, 1990), especially chapters 2, 3, and 8, and Stanton Evans, *The Theme Is Freedom* (Washington, D.C.: Regnery, 1994), pp. 246–247.

13. For a dramatic account of the horror excited in Boston by the Terror in France, see the "Sermon of the Reverend John Thayer in 1798," in Ellis Sandoz, ed., *Political Sermons of the American Founding Era (1730–1805)* (Indianapolis: Liberty, 1991), pp. 1239–1261.

14. John Adams described that prayer in a letter to his wife, Abigail:

When the Congress met, Mr. Cushing made a motion that it should be opened with Prayer. It was opposed by Mr. Jay of New York, and Mr. Rutledge of South Carolina because we were so divided in religious sentiments, some Episcopalians, some Quakers, some Anabaptists, some Presbyterians, and some congregationalists, that we could not join in the same act of worship.

Mr. Samuel Adams arose and said that he was no bigot, and could hear a Prayer from any gentlemen of Piety and virtue, who was at the same time a friend to his Country. He was a stranger in Philadelphia, but had heard that Mr. Duché deserved that character and therefore he moved that Mr. Duché, an Episcopal clergyman, might be desired to read Prayers to Congress tomorrow morning. The motion was seconded, and passed in the affirmative. Mr. Randolph, our president, vailed on Mr. Duché, and received for answer, that if his health would permit, he certainly would.

Accordingly, next morning [the Rev. Mr. Duché] appeared with his clerk and in his pontificals, and read several prayers in the established form, and read the collect for the seventh day of September, which was the thirty-fifth Psalm. You must remember, this was the next morning after we heard the horrible rumor of the cannonade of Boston.

I never saw a greater effect upon an audience. It seem as if heaven had ordained that Psalm to be read on that morning. After this, Mr. Duché, unexpectedly to every body, struck out into an extemporary prayer, which filled the bosom of every man present. I must confess, I never heard a better prayer, or one so well pronounced.

Episcopalian as he is, Dr. Cooper himself [Adam's personal pastor] never prayed with such fervor, such ardor, such earnestness and pathos, and in language so elegant and sublime, for America, for the Congress, for the province of Massachusetts Bay, and especially the own of Boston. It has had an excellent effect upon everybody here. I must beg you to read that Psalm.

See William J. Federer, ed., *America's God and Country* (Coppell, Tex.: FAME Publishing, 1994), pp. 136–137.

15. George Washington, "First Inaugural Address," *Inaugural Addresses of the Presidents of the United States* (Washington, D.C.: U.S. Government Printing Office, 1965), p. 2.

16. See, for instance, the collection edited by Robert H. Horowitz, *The Moral Foundations of the American Republic* (Charlottesville: University Press of Virginia, 1986). Of fourteen essays in this collection, only two focus on religion. Walter Berns's essay "Religion and the Founding Principle" is one of those two; he treats religion as a subordinate institution: "The origin of free government in the modern sense coincides and can only coincide with the solution of the religious problem, and the solution of the religious problem consists in the subordination of religion" (p. 223). It would be equally true that the American system subordinates politics "under God" by declaring its own incompetence in the field of religion. To give Caesar what is Caesar's is not to subordinate religion. To give God what is God's is not to subordinate politics.

17. See the discussions of Straussian writers in Thomas G. West, "Religious Liberty: The View from the Founding," a lecture prepared for a Salvatori Center Conference on Modern Freedom, April 19, 1996. Unfortunately, the published version of this lecture, in Daniel C. Palm, ed., *On Faith and Free Government* (Lanham, Md.: Rowman & Littlefield, 1997), omits the relevant materials. For example, Strauss wrote that in Locke and in modernity "the individual, the ego, had become the center and origin of the moral world, since man—as distinguished from man's end—had become that center or origin." *Natural Right and History* (Chicago: University of Chicago, 1969), p. 248. Modern commentators claim that the founders were proponents of this Lockean hierarchy and intended to make the human will, not the will of God, sovereign.

18. Russell Hittinger, "The Supreme Court v. Religion: Judicial Perceptions of Belief," *Crisis* (May 1993). Hittinger writes:

According to the dicta of the majority in *Lee v. Weisman,* the picture of religion is easily summarized. Religion is a potentially dangerous and harmful phenomenon. It is apt to engender divisiveness, even homicidal urges, in the political community. It threatens the psychological health and development of children. It tends to subvert the ordinary meanings and values of life. It is not rational, but rather subjective and idiosyncratic. It is contrary to the institution of democracy.

19. Tocqueville introduced this quote with the following observation:

I have sometimes asked Americans whom I chanced to meet in their own country or in Europe whether in their opinion religion contributes to the stability of the State and the maintenance of law and order. They always answered, without a moment's hesitation, that a civilized community, especially one that enjoys the benefits of freedom, cannot exist without religion. In fact, an American sees in religion the surest guarantee of the stability of the State and the safety of individuals. This much is evident even to those least versed in political science.

The Old Regime and the French Revolution, trans. Stuart Gilbert (Garden City, N.J.: Anchor Books, 1955), p. 153.

20. *The Federal and State Constitutions, Colonial Charters, and Other Organic Laws of the United States,* Benjamin Perley Poore, ed. (Washington, D.C.: Government Printing Office, 1878), p. 957.

21. John Adams, as quoted in Stanton Evans, *The Theme Is Freedom* (Washington, D.C.: Regnery Pub., 1994), p. 239; Leonard J. Kramer, "Muskets in the Pulpits," *Journal of the Presbyterian Historical Society* 31 (December 1953): 29, as quoted in Hutson, *Religion and the Founding of the American Republic,* p. 42; *Political Sermons of the American Founding Era, 1730–1805,* Ellis Sandoz, ed. (Indianapolis: Liberty Fund, 1998), frontispiece.

22. James Madison, quoted in Hutson, *Religion and the Founding of the American Republic,* p. 96.

23. Thomas Jefferson, *Notes on the State of Virginia, Thomas Jefferson: Writings* (New York: The Library of America, 1984), Query XVIII, p. 289.

24. Joseph Story, *The Constitution of the United States* (Lake Bluff, Ill.: Regnery Gateway, 1986), pp. 314–315.

25. *The Federal and State Constitutions,* op. cit., p. 1409.

26. Emphasis added. James Madison, et al., *The Federalist Papers* (New York: Penguin Books, 1987), p. 87.

27. Thomas Jefferson, "Summary View of the Rights of British America," *Thomas Jefferson: Writings* (New York: The Library of America, 1984), p. 122.

28. Quoted in Russell Kirk, *The Conservative Constitution* (Washington, D.C.: Regnery, 1990), chap. 6, p. 81.

29. I am indebted to Matthew Spalding and Patrick J. Garrity for displaying the power of this theme in their splendid study of citizenship: *A Sacred Union of Citizens* (Lanham, Md.: Rowman & Littlefield, 1996).

30. Ibid., esp. chap. 1 "Remembering Washington's Legacy," pp. 3–4, and chap. 2, "Establishing the National Character," pp. 10–11.

31. James Madison, *Notes of Debates in the Federal Convention of 1787* (New York: W. W. Norton & Co., 1987), p. 209.

32. Sir William Blackstone, *Commentaries on the Laws of England,* quoted by Verna M. Hall, *Christian History of the Constitution* (San Francisco: Foundation for American Christian Education, 1962, 1979), pp. 140–146. Most of the American founders were lawyers, and many would have gotten their Locke through Blackstone and spent more time with Blackstone.

33. Common Revolutionary slogan and Ben Franklin's proposed motto for the dollar bill. William J. Bennett, ed., *Our Sacred Honor* (New York: Simon & Schuster,

1997), p. 412. We have taken as many citations as possible from the Bennett volume, an easily accessible compendium of texts from the founders.

34. Benjamin Rush, "Of the Mode of Education Proper to a Republic" in 1798. Bennett, *Our Sacred Honor*, p. 412.

35. From 1771 through part of 1772, the young James Madison stayed on at Princeton after his graduation for an extra year of study with Witherspoon in philosophy and Hebrew. Four years later, two weeks before the Declaration of Independence, one of Witherspoon's great sermons was published in Philadelphia, where it aroused great excitement and admiration. This was the first time in his life, Witherspoon said, that he had addressed a question of politics from his pulpit. But since the cause was liberty, and since the loss of civil rights always presaged the loss of religious liberties, he judged that in the face of imminent war he was right to speak to the religious necessities of the moment.

At one turn in his argument, Witherspoon further explained how all his experience of the world and his observation every day led him to see confirmed the evidentiary basis for what Christian doctrine termed "original sin," the ravages wreaked in previously tranquil communities by greed, lust, ambition, pride, selfishness, profligacy, luxury, sloth, and other sinful states of soul; how even brother sets upon brother, and neighbor upon neighbor, who in civil war burn down the very house in which they had once been happy guests. He referred to man's sinful condition as "the state of nature," including even the ordinary state of human beings without the grace that comes through Jesus Christ.

> I do not speak this only to the heaven, daring profligate, or grovelling sensualist, but to every insensible secure sinner; to all those, however decent and orderly in their civil deportment, who live to themselves and have their part and portion in this life; in fine to all who are yet in a state of nature, for "except a man be born again, he cannot see the kingdom of God." The fear of man may make you hide your profanity: prudence and experience may make you abhor intemperance and riot; as you advance in life, one vice may supplant another and hold its place; but nothing less than the sovereign grace of God can produce a saving change of heart and temper, or fit you for his immediate presence.

Sandoz, *Political Sermons of the American Founding Era*, pp. 532–546.

36. The difference between the founders and Hobbes (who stands behind Locke) is explicit in a passage from Alexander Hamilton:

> Moral obligation, according to him [Hobbes], is derived from the introduction of civil society; and there is no virtue but what is purely artificial, the mere contrivance of politicians, for the maintenance of social intercourse. But the reason he ran into this absurd and impious doctrine was that he disbelieved the existence of an intelligent superintending principle, who is the governor and will be the final judge of the universe. . . .
>
> To grant that there is a supreme intelligence who rules the world and has established laws to regulate the actions of his creatures; and still to assert that man, in a state of nature, may be considered as perfectly free from all restraints of law and government, appears to a common understanding altogether irreconcilable. Good and wise men, in all ages, have embraced a very dissimilar theory. They have supposed that the deity, from the relations we stand in to himself and to each other, has constituted an eternal and immutable law, which is indispensably obligatory upon all mankind, prior to any human institution whatever. This is what is called the law of nature. . . . Upon this law depend the natural rights of mankind.

"The Farmer Refuted" (1775), ed. Harold C. Syrett, *Papers* (New York: Columbia University Press, 1961), vol. 1, p. 87. Quoted by Thomas West, Salvatori lecture, op. cit.

37. In working out this argument, I have noted that when the founders cite authorities for their theories they often pair together Algernon Sidney and John Locke, although they more often cite Locke. It has struck me again and again, however, that Sidney is religiously more orthodox than Locke, and closer to the traditions of Aristotle and Cicero both in defining liberty and in linking it to certain indispensable virtues. The hypothesis has forced itself upon me that Sidney is a better guide to what the founders actually said and did on *these* matters (not all matters) than the works of Locke. Sidney gives a larger role to virtue in the definition of liberty; Locke tends to stress the natural equality of all and thus to see individuals as "equal," that is, denuded of the virtues that characterize them differentially. In this, Sidney is closer to the ancients, and Locke to the tendencies of modernity. See Thomas West, Introduction, *Discourses,* by Algernon Sidney (Liberty Fund: Indianapolis, 1997). Moreover, by interpreting the American constitutional tradition in a Lockean way, and thus detaching liberty from virtue, and virtue from religion, Lockean interpreters may have been nudging the country down the winding road to Gomorrah, into the decadence that has destroyed many nations. See Robert Bork's analysis of the three errors in liberal—i.e., Lockean—presuppositions, in *Slouching Toward Gomorrah,* pp. 53–54. But this is not the place for a long argument on the relative merits of Sidney and Locke. Both authors were, in their respective masterpieces, commenting on the same work of Filmer.

38. Bennett, *Our Sacred Honor,* p. 412.

39. John Adams to Benjamin Rush, February 2, 1807. Bennett, Our Sacred Honor, p. 408.

40. Emphasis added. Noah Webster, "Advice to the Young," from *Value of the Bible and the Excellence of the Christian Religion, 1834.* Bennett, *Our Sacred Honor,* p. 398.

41. James Wilson, "The Laws of Nature," 1790. Bennett, *Our Sacred Honor,* p. 406.

42. Sandoz, *Political Sermons of the American Founding Era,* p. 637.

43. The number one priority of the Catholic signer of the Declaration and participant in the Constitutional Convention, Maryland's Charles Carroll, friend of Washington, was no religious test for office. Nonestablishment—in advance, almost too much to hope for—greatly cheered the whole Catholic body. For evidence of the enthusiasm of Catholics for the founding, see the Thayer discourse, n. 12, supra.

44. Robert A. Goldwin, *From Parchment to Power: How James Madison Used the Bill of Rights to Save the Constitution* (Washington, D.C.: AEI Press, 1997), pp. 66–68.

45. When, at the Constitutional Congress, Peter Sylvester of New York objected to the provision that "no religion shall be established by law," because "it might be thought to have a tendency to abolish religion altogether," Madison replied that he understood the language to mean merely that "Congress should not establish *a* religion, and enforce the legal observation of it by law." *Annals of Congress,* 1:757 (August 15, 1789) as quoted in Walter Berns, "Religion and the Founding Principle," *The Moral Foundations of the American Republic,* ed. Robert H. Horwitz, p. 209.

46. *The Federalist Papers,* pp. 144–145.

47. Jefferson, e.g., declared that only one thing in the universe compels the free assent of man—compels it—and that is evidence. Jefferson, "Bill for Establishing Religious Freedom," in *Thomas Jefferson: Writings*, pp. 346–348.

48. George Washington, "Farewell Address," *George Washington: A Collection*, W. B. Allen, ed. (Indianapolis: Liberty Classics, 1988), pp. 521–522.

49. John Adams, "To the Officers of the First Brigade of the Third Division of the Militia of Massachusetts," October 11, 1798. Bennett, *Our Sacred Honor*, p. 370.

50. John Adams to Zabdiel Adams, June 21, 1776. Bennett, *Our Sacred Honor*, p. 371.

7

Why Revolutionary America Wasn't a "Christian Nation"

Jon Butler

When a historian of religion sets about to consider the question of eighteenth-century America as a Christian nation, it seems almost natural to locate a text in which to ground the discussion. One might think of a biblical text, as colonial clergymen did routinely when they preached. Or one might think of an "American" text that exemplifies some distinctive national feature of the question, as historians do customarily.

But what text? American historians inevitably gravitate to eighteenth-century possibilities. One obvious choice might be Hector St. John de Crèvecoeur's *Letters to an American Farmer*, published in 1782. Crèvecoeur discussed religion in his famous third letter, entitled "What Is an American?" But Crèvecoeur proved surprisingly problematic. As his letters proceeded, Crèvecoeur's view of the American character and future became darker and more angry; his understanding of colonial religion proved equally unsettling. Crèvecoeur pictured a society where "all sects are mixed," as did most eighteenth-century observers. But rather than underline the positive features of this pluralism, Crèvecoeur found that it underwrote a "religious indifference [that] is imperceptibly disseminated from one end of the continent to the other." Little wonder that his views have puzzled historians for generations, most of whom have preferred to skip Crèvecoeur's statements on religion altogether.[1]

One might turn to the charming work of the Anglican itinerant, Charles Woodmason. Woodmason plied the backcountry of the Carolinas and Virginia in the 1760s, and his piquant accounts of rural manners and spiritual liveliness have entertained historians ever since Richard J. Hooker first published the original manuscripts at the New York Historical Society in 1953. Woodmason decried dogs at backcountry worship—"Bring no Dogs with

You—they are very troublesome"—and bemoaned the denominational pluralism he found in the mid-eighteenth-century backcountry. Settlers "complain'd of being eaten up by Itinerant Teachers, Preachers, and Im-
posters . . . So that one day You might hear this System of Doctrine—the next
day another." The confusion seemed not to breed the "indifference" Crèvecoeur saw but a kind of spiritual paralysis. "By the Variety of Taylors who
would pretend to know the best fashion in which Christs Coat is to be worn[,]
none will put it on," Woodmason lamented. Still, however entertaining,
Woodmason's understanding has only weakly shaped the historical analysis
of religion in late-eighteenth-century America.[2]

Perhaps one might compromise on Jefferson's manuscripts, "The Philosophy of Jesus" and "The Life and Morals of Jesus." Jefferson's interest in the
figure of Jesus and especially his interest in what he called Jesus' "morals"
might seem a perfect reflection of a long-standing "American" repudiation of
denominational narrowness and doctrinal sectarianism. Jefferson seemed to
evince a distinctively "pragmatic American" interest in religion's fruits, its potential effects in encouraging men and women to treat each other well and
to raise a commonplace national interest to a transcendent one.

Yet it is not at all clear just how widely Americans really shared Jefferson's
sentiments. The master politician deftly kept his views to himself, an almost
unthinkable act of modesty in our own time. Moreover, Jefferson's emphasis
on morals and ethics seems to have run counter to public fascination with divine and miraculous intervention not only in the eighteenth and early nineteenth centuries but later, a fascination that Jefferson rejected. Both suggest
that Jefferson's own constricted understanding of "religion," limited largely
to matters of morals and ethics, was not widely shared by his fellow citizens.[3]

Rather than look for a text that solves the problem, I want to locate our discussion in a text that exemplifies the problem. That text is not difficult to
find. It is, of course, contained in the sixteen words that concern religion in
the First Amendment to the Federal Constitution of 1789: "Congress shall
make no law respecting an establishment of religion, or prohibiting the free
exercise thereof." I do not wish to debate the Amendment itself. It would be
presumptuous, if only given the hundreds of thousands of pages devoted to
this topic since the Amendment was ratified in 1791. Nor is the First Amendment the principal subject of our discussion. Yet any serious consideration of
the problem of later eighteenth-century America as a "Christian nation" must
grapple with its words. They do not in themselves answer our question. But
they signify the complexity of the question we seek to answer.

Obviously, the question of later eighteenth-century America as a Christian
nation is a compound one. And contemporary politics at least deepens its difficulty. Let's be blunt. It is no longer possible for historians generally, or for *a* historian—*this* historian—to pretend that any judgment about this question is

merely an exercise of abstract scholarship. The debates of the past three decades have inevitably politicized scholarship in this area. The result and reaction to Supreme Court decisions outlawing compulsory prayer and Bible reading in the public schools and the growth and frustration of movements to "restore" compulsory public school prayer and compulsory Bible reading since the 1960s have accelerated it. Now the phrase "Christian nation" is taken to mean or infer support for reintroducing collective Christian prayer, if not compulsory Bible reading, into the public schools and beyond. It symbolizes a panoply of efforts to reform America in the twilight of the twentieth century by looking back to the formation of the American nation for moral and spiritual guidance in the new millennium—Christian, of course, not merely "religious."

Only by acknowledging the sheer partisanship that now invades these matters can we go back to the eighteenth century with any sense of honesty. Perhaps, we ought to return to it with relief. For the moment, let us imbibe the sheer luxury of pure historical inquiry into the question of late eighteenth-century America as a Christian nation. Let us look at government, society, and people to recover what men and women of the time did and believed and to determine what we, as historians, might make of their judgment. In so doing, we might ask how the First Amendment enlarges or constricts our understanding. It will, I think, suggest the complicated, fascinating, and historically unique spiritual milieu in which the nation was born.

It also will, I think, demonstrate the remarkable risks taken by remarkable men and women in remarkable times. These risks and the achievements they generated challenge modern Americans who would pretend to exercise equal leadership on still difficult questions of religion, the state, conscience, and faith. If these questions are now the domain of the shrill and the strident, perhaps understanding the intricacies of the past might lead us out of the darkness and anger that engulfs this topic three centuries later.

Was America a "Christian nation" on the eve of the Revolution? Colonial law certainly would have made it appear so throughout most of the eighteenth century. Indeed, one of the great transformations of the eighteenth century centered on the renewal, not the decline, of the state church tradition in colonial America. Between 1690 and 1710 the colonial legislatures in South Carolina, North Carolina, Maryland, and New York effectively established the Church of England as the governmentally supported religion in their colonies, and the Virginia Burgesses thoroughly reworked the feeble Anglican establishment of the early seventeenth century. To the north, the old Puritan order in Massachusetts and Connecticut not only survived what contemporaries and historians have, rightly or wrongly, long described as "declension" or, put differently, the creation of a new, more diverse, more commercial, and more secular society. The state church apparatus found itself strengthened, not weakened. It became more elastic, and unlike the Anglican establishments to the south, it survived into the nineteenth century. In all, then, seven of the thirteen colonies gave legal support to a single expression of Protestant Christianity for 60 to 150 years before the Revolution.

Even where the law did not establish a single church, it usually upheld Protestant Christianity. Above all, the law punished. In colonies with church establishments, the law may have tolerated religious activity by dissenters, but it did not always do so, and it sometimes made that activity difficult. In colonies without establishments, the law customarily penalized a wide variety of settlers who may not have upheld Protestant Christianity in at least some perfunctory fashion. It openly discriminated against Catholics and Jews, denying them the right to own property or to vote, sometimes both, in different colonies. The law penalized blasphemers who spoke ill of Protestant Christianity. Long after the Salem witch trials of 1692 the law outlawed magic and witchcraft. Perhaps the situation in Pennsylvania, usually regarded as the most tolerant of all the colonies, expressed the legal situation well. Throughout the pre-Revolutionary period, Pennsylvania forced officeholders to swear to their belief in the divinity of Jesus, banned blasphemy, forbade Sunday labor, and urged all settlers to attend Christian services on the Sabbath so "looseness, irreligion, and Atheism may not creep in under the pretense of conscience."[4]

The eighteenth century also witnessed an explosion of congregational expansion that substantially increased church participation and membership in ways that might give life to the laws' strictures. Fully 85 percent of the colonial congregations that existed at the beginning of the American Revolution had been formed after 1700 and no less than 60 percent of these congregations had been formed after 1740. This expansion occurred in two waves, the first between 1680 and 1710, and the second between 1740 and 1770. The expansion came primarily from two causes. The first was revivalism, meaning the growth of evangelical, born-again Christianity in its rudimentary modern sense. The second was denominational expansion, meaning the systematic provision of leadership and ministry by ever more religious organizations, often headquartered in Philadelphia (not Boston), including Quakers, Presbyterians, Baptists, German Lutheran, and German Reformed, among others.

Thus, where we think of the early seventeenth century, and especially early New England, as the preeminent period of religious activity in colonial America, the eighteenth century dwarfed that activity and expansion many times over. It contributed crucial new forms of ministry, especially revivalism, and it bolstered new models of denominational leadership central to American religion in the next two centuries.[5]

Were we to stop here, perhaps the answer to our question "Was late eighteenth-century America a Christian nation" might be yes. But as lawyers and mathematicians know, if the law and statistics are not funny things, they are at least arguable. This is particularly true when the facts turn out to be more complicated than they seem, not merely in the courtroom but in life, and when these complications occurred long before the relationship between religion and government changed after American independence.

One complication centered on the people. Put simply, whatever the law required or demanded, and however much congregational expansion skyrocketed in the eighteenth century, the people by no means either responded or followed. Though historians do indeed argue about these things, it is all but impossible to calculate church membership at more than 20 percent of colonial adults before the American Revolution, a figure that would only decline further when the enslaved population is added, given the overwhelming failure of Christian proselytizing among the half-million Africans forcibly transported to the mainland colonies after 1680. In short, surprising as it may seem, church membership was far lower on the eve of independence—about 80 percent of adults did not belong—than it is at the end of the twentieth century, when it runs about 60 percent of adults.[6]

Nor does computing attendance improve the situation. In fact, very few congregations recorded attendance, and when clergymen bragged about it, as Anglican ministers did in reports to the Bishop of London in 1724, their facts often seemed contradictory, to put it generously. Something seems suspicious when, for example, the minister in Virginia's Henrico Parish reported "sometimes 100 or 200 attend" but "20 is the greatest number that do [take communion] at one time," or when the minister of St. Paul's church in Narragansett, Rhode Island, reported congregations of 150 to 270 on Sundays but only 17 communicants. If these figures are accurate, these allegedly numerous listeners evinced a spiritual shyness that could have made even Puritans blush.[7]

In this light, we might rethink the eighteenth-century colonial congregational expansion. Rather than seal the identity of the colonies as "Christian," congregational growth mainly helped to keep Christianity's head above the waters of the public indifference to Christian practice and belief that concerned Crèvecoeur and Woodmason. This in itself was no mean accomplishment, and it bore immense significance for Christianity's fate during and after the Revolution and for Christianity's expansion in the early national and antebellum periods, when techniques devised in the pre-Revolutionary era made powerful contributions to religious and social reform before the Civil War.[8]

Ironically, perhaps, both the revivalism and proliferation of institutional formation and leadership that escalated congregational growth in the four score years before the Revolution cast the "Christian nation" question into doubt. Perhaps an oxymoron will help. We might say that, on the surface, the pre-Revolutionary "colonial nation" was nominally or even formally Christian. The law demanded adherence to a rudimentary Christianity and seven colonies established state churches. But these laws made sense precisely because actual Christian adherence in the population was relatively weak—perhaps no more so than it was in contemporary Europe, including Britain—not because attachment to Christianity was strong and overwhelming. In short, the law existed to compel Christian attachment. The law did not measure the Christian commitment of the people.

The proliferation of congregations, combined with Enlightenment doubts about coercion in religion generally, threw into doubt even the old minimal or formal pattern of Christian church establishment. In the aftermath of the Revolution, this led most states to withdraw from or greatly reduce government involvement with religion and culminated in the First Amendment to the Federal Constitution.

The remarkable proliferation of congregations between 1680 and 1770 led settlers in many places to ask the question that Charles Woodmason heard in the Carolina backcountry in the 1760s: "Whose Christianity?" The post-1680 congregational growth was not monochromatic. Instead, it introduced a religious pluralism unprecedented in Western society. Numbers alone tell part of the story. [See table 7.1.] About 75 percent of all seventeenth-century churches were Congregational (in New England) or Anglican (Church of England and largely in Virginia). By the Revolution, however, Congregational and Anglican churches formed only about 35 percent of all colonial congregations. Now, 65 percent of the congregations were Presbyterian, Baptist, Quaker, German Reformed, Lutheran, Dutch Reformed, Methodist, Catholic, Moravian, Separatist-Congregational, German Baptist, Mennonite, French Protestant, Sandemanian, Jewish, and Rogerene, many of which had only been thinly visible or could not even be found in the colonies as late as 1700.[9]

Table 7.1 Congregations in 1776

Congregational	668 (21%)
Presbyterian	588 (17%)
Anglican	495 (15%)
Baptist	494 (15%)
Friends	310 (10%)
German Reformed	159 (5%)
Lutheran	150 (5%)
Dutch Reformed	120 (4%)
Methodist	65 (2%)
Catholics	56 (2%)
Moravian	31 (1%)
Congregational—Separatist	27 (1%)
Dunker	24 (1%)
Mennonite	16 (.5%)
French Protestant	7 (.2%)
Sandemanian	6 (.2%)
Jewish	5 (.2%)
Rogerene	3 (.1%)
Total	3224

Source: Charles O. Paullin, *Atlas of the Historical Geography of the United States* (Washington, D.C., 1932), p. 50.

This vigorous pluralism never produced the religious antagonism and violence that characterized nineteenth- and twentieth-century America, to say nothing of the world in the 1990s. But it produced substantial tensions and arguments that unsettled familiar patterns of government aid to Christianity. In New England, the arguments prospered during a revivalism of the 1740s and 1750s among both Congregationalists and Baptists that produced so-called "separatist" congregations of "born-again" or "revived" believers. Many arguments centered on theology, and some were inevitably personal. But many others focused on the spoils of government support for local religion or involved new government activity in religion. When a congregation split between "Old Lights" and "New Lights," who retained monies levied for Christianity's support in the town?

The arguments among the disputing Congregationalists joined those of Baptists, who generally objected to paying levies for religion at all. In turn, traditional Congregationalists turned up coercive legislation surrounding religion. In 1742, for example, the Connecticut assembly passed an "Act for Regulating Abuses and Correcting Disorders in Ecclesiastical Affairs," clearly directed against Congregational and Baptist revivalists. The act effectively banned unapproved itinerant preaching, ordered ministerial associations not to "meddle" in affairs outside their own jurisdiction, and allowed magistrates to eject nonresidents from the colony if they preached without the permission of the local clergymen and a majority of his congregation.[10]

In Virginia, Anglicans, Presbyterians, and Baptists quickly fell out into disputes about the liberty of dissenters to preach and thereby contest the Anglicans' domination of Virginia's public religious life. As Thomas Jefferson rightly remembered the situation, the Anglican attack on Presbyterians and Baptists in the 1750s and 1760s had been preceded by efforts to curtail Quakers in the seventeenth century, "driving them from the colony by the severest penalties." (In fact, Virginia also chased Puritans from Nansemond County to Maryland in 1647–1648, which Jefferson did not know about.) In the late 1740s Virginia officials sought to inhibit the Presbyterian leader, Samuel Davies, by denying him a license to preach beyond his congregation. The Board of Trade in London, not American politicians, settled the matter, reminding Virginia's government in 1751 that "Toleration and a Free Exercise of Religion . . . should ever be held sacred in His Majesties Colonies."[11]

Baptists received even rougher treatment because their preaching combined social, legal, and theological challenges to the Anglicans' status in Virginia. John Williams described the physical attack on "Brother Waller," a Caroline County Baptist preacher, in 1771, only five years before the Revolution. Coercion here was not mild or merely irritating but physical and violent.

The Parson of the Parish would keep running the end of his horsewhip in [Waller's] mouth, laying his whip across the hymn book, etc. When done singing, [Waller] proceeded to prayer. In it he was violently jerked off the stage; [the parson and sheriff] caught him by the back part of his neck, beat his head against the ground, sometimes up, sometimes down, they carried him through a gate that stood some considerable distance, where a gentleman gave him . . . twenty lashes with his horsewhip.[12]

Certainly, Anglicans had much to defend, from their social status to the political power held by their members, to their control of local and provincial government, to their power to tax, and to their church buildings, which represented the finest widespread domestic public architecture in the colony and, perhaps, in the colonies generally.[13]

Even in places where there was no establishment, as in Pennsylvania, or where the establishment was weak, as in New York, eighteenth-century pluralism and revivalism brought difficulty rather than repose. Presbyterians who had fought Anglicans in Virginia had been well trained by their own internal disputing in the middle colonies. The arguments over revivalism produced innumerable personal confrontations in the 1740s and a fifteen-year schism in the Synod of Philadelphia from 1743 to 1758. George Whitefield caused dissension up and down the colonies as he drew listeners from clergymen jealous of his charismatic preaching. The combination of pluralism, lack of coercion, and lethargic ministerial leadership induced nominally German Lutheran and Reformed immigrants to Pennsylvania into utter spiritual indifference, the kind about which Crèvecoeur complained. Taken together, then, the specter of religious turmoil caused by pluralism, revivalism, and the bitterness engendered by government partiality in religion left the question of a colonial "Christian nation" increasingly open as the Revolution began.[14]

A question not left open was that of church establishment. The experience of colonial religious diversity, the failures of the old religious establishments, the association of the Church of England with king and parliament, and the principles of the Declaration of Independence all encouraged many Americans to rethink the relationship between government and religion as the Revolution proceeded. The old Church of England lost most in this reevaluation. Between 1776 and 1785 the legal establishments that the Church of England had won eighty years earlier collapsed everywhere from New York to South Carolina. As this occurred, even Connecticut relieved "separates," including Episcopalians, Baptists, Quakers, "or any other Denomination," from church taxes. Only Massachusetts held out firmly, continuing to collect taxes for the local ministry. Although the new state distributed the church funds by local vote, this was majoritarianism, not democracy; it effectively funneled aid only to traditional Congregational churches except in a few towns.[15]

The most important contest over religious identity and government occurred in Virginia. It merged growing colonial doubt about the wisdom of government involvement in religion with the narrower question of a single church establishment. The result proved dramatic. The Virginia debate stimulated a remarkable movement away from any substantial government aid for religious activity and directly shaped the religion clause in the First Amendment.

The Virginia debate, which occurred between 1779 and 1785, centered on two issues—general support for religion by aiding numerous Christian denominations and complete disestablishment. Proponents of aid to many denominations, including some Presbyterians and Patrick Henry, backed freedom of worship for all religious groups but advocated government support and tax funds for several if not all Protestant groups. In contrast, Thomas Jefferson, later supported by James Madison, offered a bill "for Establishing Religious Freedom." It prohibited tax levies for "any religious worship, place, or ministry whatsoever" and also upheld freedom of worship for all religious groups. Both sides struggled over these issues from 1779 to 1785 without any resolution.

A crucial debate during elections for the Virginia Burgesses in 1785 completely altered public opinion on the religion question. George Washington's turnaround symbolized the process. At first, Washington supported multiple establishment; he thought it was a fine idea to give government aid to several Protestant groups. But as the debate proceeded and stimulated increasing rancor, Washington turned against the proposal. Multiple establishment, Washington commented, seemed innocuous and natural, but it clearly would "rankle, and perhaps convulse the state."[16]

As a result, in 1786 the Virginia legislature turned down Patrick Henry's bill for multiple establishment. Overwhelming opposition to it came from Baptists, Methodists, Episcopalians, and some Presbyterians. The legislature then approved by a vote of 74 to 20 Thomas Jefferson's bill "for Establishing Religious Freedom." It outlawed government aid to religion and guaranteed freedom of worship to all religions in the state, not just Protestants or even merely to Christians.[17]

The Virginia debate renewed discussions in other states, and then with regard to the new federal government, about the relationship between America's religious identity and its relationship to government. In the states, it produced a rush of sentiment against a single establishment and against government aid to denominations generally. South Carolina's 1778 constitution had authorized government aid to several Protestant groups. But its 1790 constitution abandoned multiple establishment and guaranteed a broad freedom of worship. Multiple establishment bills failed in Georgia in 1782 and 1784, and in 1789 a new Georgia constitution eliminated multiple religious establishment entirely. The post-Revolutionary Maryland constitution permitted multiple establishment. But the Maryland assembly rejected funding for several Protestant groups by a two-to-one margin in 1785, and in 1810 a constitutional amendment eliminated multiple establishment in Maryland.[18]

In New Hampshire, government aid to local Protestant congregations slowly collapsed, and in 1819 the legislature repealed the statute permitting the collection of local church taxes. Only Connecticut and Massachusetts held out, Connecticut until 1818 and Massachusetts until 1833; tellingly, these establishments fell in large measure because citizens of both states tired of the incessant bickering about church taxes, especially as they watched tax-supported congregations split over the doctrine of Unitarianism and lawsuits over the tax revenues belonging to the now divided congregations increase.[19]

The First Amendment to the Federal Constitution passed in 1791 reflected this dual trend of eschewing a single church establishment and of prohibiting governmental activity in religion generally. The First Amendment prohibited a federal "establishment of religion," not merely of churches. Many commentators routinely describe the First Amendment as being about "church and state," following Jefferson in his famous 1802 letter to the Danbury Baptist Association where he backed a "wall of separation between church and state" in America. But the First Amendment banned government activity in religion generally and did not mention the narrower issue of church.

In its breadth, the First Amendment confirmed the eighteenth-century colonial American experience that religion increasingly took many forms, and complex ones, in this extraordinarily compound society. In this multifarious society, government should refrain from activity in religion. Congress specifically rejected wording that would have limited the First Amendment to narrower issues, such as prohibiting government support for a specific "religious doctrine," for "articles of faith or modes of worship," to protect only the "rights of conscience," to prohibit aid to "one religious sect or society in preference to others," or to establish a national church. All this language was deemed too narrow.[20]

The amplitude of the First Amendment and the debates surrounding its wording help answer our question about late eighteenth-century America as a "Christian nation." It is surprising—or perhaps it is not surprising at all—how seldom, if ever, men and women referred to America as a "Christian nation" between 1760 and 1790. Indeed, such a phrase would have puzzled or even alarmed advocates of church establishment, whether traditional single establishments or more general government aid to religion or multiple denominations. When Yale president Ezra Stiles supported the continuation of Connecticut's Congregational establishment in 1783, he did so precisely because he believed Connecticut—indeed, America—was not a Christian nation. Too much atheism, too much indifference, too much heterodoxy, and too much immorality made that phrase meaningless. Indeed, for Stiles, Connecticut's church establishment had a simple attraction: it coerced men and women to support Christianity in at least some rudimentary fashion when they would otherwise ignore it. Government tax revenues could guarantee the modicum of "religion" that might keep a sinful, spiritually indifferent society afloat.[21]

The Virginia Baptist John Leland agreed with Stiles's diagnosis of America's spiritual malaise but disputed Stiles's prescription. Leland likewise ridiculed the notion that a "Christian commonwealth" could or did exist in either Virginia or even the nation. Virginia and the nation needed saving, not praising. But unlike Stiles, Leland denied the government's right to engage the religious enterprise, and he did so on religious grounds, indeed, on specifically Christian grounds. As other Virginia opponents of general aid to religion put it in 1785, Christ "not only maintained and supported his gospel in the world for several hundred years without the aid of civil power, but against all the powers of the earth." To Leland, if not to Stiles, the contrast between early Christian practice and modern governmental aid to religion was stark and negative. If Christ did not use or want government aid, why did modern Christians?[22]

The debate about America's religious identity and about government involvement with religion changed after passage of the Bill of Rights and the First Amendment in 1791 and especially after the 1810s. America's attraction as a field for Christian proselytizing only increased as American power and vibrancy became more obvious. The lure of the new public schools as a vehicle for Christian, or at least Protestant, instruction proved irresistible. Protestants increasingly attached providence to American purposes, especially in foreign affairs. Few heeded Lincoln's caution when, after ministers assured him that God was on the North's side in the Civil War, he replied that he was more concerned that the North was on God's side. Fewer still observed even the least caution when the federal government began to mold American Indians into "Christian nations" in the 1870s and when, to aid the effort, the War Department assigned reservations to specific denominations—Presbyterian, Methodist, Episcopal, Catholic, and even Quaker. These denominations then excluded competing missionaries, sometimes by force. They taught Christian doctrine in government-funded schools. They openly, vigorously, and sometimes violently suppressed traditional Indian religion and ceremonies, including most notoriously the Ghost Dance, a campaign capped but not ended by the massacre at Wounded Knee in South Dakota in December 1890. And they did so unashamedly for over sixty years with the support of many religious groups and Indian "reformers" from the advent of President Grant's ill-named "Peace Policy" in 1869 until 1933, when the New Deal Indian commissioner John Collier abolished these policies.[23]

This struggle to shape America as a Christian nation after 1790 also frequently used "history" as a proselytizing instrument. Backers of such efforts rewrote a complex and often ambiguous eighteenth-century past to recast Revolutionary America as a "Christian nation," a phraseology that has appeared episodically in American history at crucial intervals down to the present.

Yet however politically useful in either the nineteenth century or in our own times, the concept of the "Christian nation" does not resonate well with the facts of eighteenth-century colonial and American history. Both before and after the American Revolution most, if not all, observers understood America as a society where Christianity was important yet not ubiquitous. In it, a partially Christian people imbibed multifarious religions—innumerable versions of Christianity plus Judaism, traditional African religious expression, native American religions, even notions of magic and occultism (to the chagrin of many). The capacity of all these religions to uplift and inspire was tempered by an often equally strong propensity to divide, anger, and demean. In the 1780s this complexity and energy increasingly prompted Americans to distrust governmental involvement in religion. At the founding of the republic they moved to protect the civil peace and spiritual renewal simultaneously by withdrawing from specific and general establishments of Christianity everywhere except Connecticut and Massachusetts, by prohibiting the federal government from "an establishment of religion," not merely an establishment of Christianity, and by requiring that the federal government never breach the "free exercise of religion." In short, although the people should or might become "Christian," such a national identity would best remain a matter of practice, not law or governmental encouragement.

This was not a unanimous construction, though unwittingly it might have been elegant. Certainly it was not easy. But it was the unique late-eighteenth-century construction that made the relationship between religion and the formation of the American republic so remarkable, so compelling, and so important. No other Western society knew it. And no other Western society ever wrote so bold, so novel, and so successful a prescription for religion's role in a nation's destiny.[24]

NOTES

1. Hector St. John de Crèvecoeur, *Letters from an American Farmer and Sketches of Eighteenth-Century America*, edited by Albert E. Stone (New York: Penguin Books, 1981), p. 76; Crèvecoeur's general comments are preceded by several long paragraphs on specific religious groups. On the difficulties of interpreting Crèvecoeur, see Jeffrey H. Richards, "Revolution, Domestic Life, and the End of 'Common Mercy' in Crèvecoeur's "Landscapes," *William and Mary Quarterly*, 3d ser., 55 (1998): 281–296, and Edmund S. Morgan, "More Letters from the American Frontier: An Edition of the Essays in English Left Unpublished," *New Republic* (July 10, 1995): 36–38.

One answer to the question of America as a "Christian nation" was provided in Mark A. Noll, Nathan Hatch, and George Marsden, *The Search for Christian America* (Westchester, Ill.: Crossway Books, 1983). Noll and his colleagues concentrated on the problem of America's "Puritan" origins and on the possible influence of eighteenth-century revivals as creators of a "Christian America." I have employed a different approach to the problem.

2. Richard J. Hooker, ed., *The Carolina Backcountry on the Eve of the American Revolution: The Journal and Other Writings of Charles Woodmason, Anglican Itinerant* (Chapel Hill: University of North Carolina Press, 1953), pp. 13 and 88; on the lack of Bibles, see pp. 16, 22, and 23.

3. Thomas Jefferson, *Philosophy of Jesus of Nazareth: Jefferson's Extracts from the Gospels: "The Philosophy of Jesus" and "The Life and Morals of Jesus,"* edited by Dickinson W. Adams and Ruth W. Lester (Princeton, N.J.: Princeton University Press, 1983). Charles Brockden Brown's 1798 novel *Wieland; or, the Transformation* centered on the story of divine intervention and its disastrous consequences and was an implicit criticism of groups like the Shakers, which the prophet Ann Lee was building in New England in the 1790s. See Stephen J. Stein, *The Shaker Experience in America: A History of the United Society of Believers* (New Haven, Conn.: Yale University Press, 1992).

4. Anson Phelps Stokes, *Church and State in the United States,* 3 vols. (New York: Harper and Brothers, 1950), vol. 1, pp. 191–192; Nicholas Trott, *The Laws of the British Plantations in America Relating to the Church and to the Clergy* (London: John Clark, 1721), pp. 74–76, 211–215, 231–232, 242–243, 255–256, 268–269, 288–290, 297, 303, 324–326, 337, 345; Carl Zollman, *American Church Law* (St. Paul: West Publishing Co., 1933), pp. 2–6.

5. Jon Butler, "Church Formation in Colonial America: Era of Expansion, 1680–1770," in *Mapping America's Past: A Historical Atlas,* ed. Mark C. Carnes and John A. Garraty (New York: Henry Holt, 1996), pp. 46–47. In general, also see Charles O. Paullin, *Atlas of the Historical Geography of the United States* (Washington, D.C.: Carnegie Institution, 1932), for a surprisingly perceptive analysis of colonial American church growth, as well as Roger Finke and Rodney Stark, *The Churching of America, 1776–1980: Winners and Losers in our Religious Economy* (New Brunswick, N.J.: Rutgers University Press, 1992), for interesting statistics and an unpersuasive explanation.

6. Butler, "Church Membership: Less than God-Fearing," in *Mapping America's Past: A Historical Atlas,* ed. Mark C. Carnes and John A. Garraty (New York: Henry Holt, 1996), pp. 50–51; Rodney Stark and Roger Finke, "American Religion in 1776: A Statistical Portrait," *Sociological Analysis* 49 (1988): 39–51.

7. Patricia U. Bonomi and Peter Eisenstadt, "Church Adherence in the Eighteenth-Century British American Colonies," *William and Mary Quarterly,* 3d ser., 39 (1982): 245–286.

8. On the subsequent rise of Christianity in the early national and antebellum eras, see Nathan O. Hatch, *The Democratization of American Christianity* (New Haven, Conn.: Yale University Press, 1989).

9. Charles O. Paullin, *Atlas of the Historical Geography of the United States,* p. 50. The background for Paullin's work is explained in Rodney Stark and Roger Finke, "American Religion in 1776: A Statistical Portrait," *Sociological Analysis* 49 (1988): 40–41; for unknown reasons, Stark and Finke, who base their own figures on Paullin's, count 497 Baptist congregations, whereas Paullin counted 494. To say the least, counting congregations at the time of the Revolution is a more difficult matter than might seem possible. Many vagaries exist in the "statistics" of the time and the mere existence of many congregations is not easy to establish. To an extent, then, these figures probably somewhat exaggerate the number of functioning congregations. Despite the age of Paullin's work, it seems reasonably accurate, if not so much in its exact count as in its assessment of the rough percentages that should be assigned to each denomination. More modern counts are to be obtained in Edwin Gaustad, *Historical Atlas of Religion in America,* rev. ed. (New York: Harper and Row, 1976), but this lacks the totals that Paullin provided; I have

not been able to examine the latest revision of Gaustad's work, which is to be published sometime in 2000.

10. The best detailed description of this difficulty in New England remains C. C. Goen, *Revivalism and Separatism in New England, 1740–1800: Strict Congregationalists and Separate Baptists in the Great Awakening* (New Haven, Conn.: Yale University Press, 1962), esp. pp. 58–67. Of course, the law had been used against "dissenters" earlier. In New York in 1707 Lord Cornbury denied a preaching license to the Presbyterian Francis Makemie, then held Makemie in jail for forty-six days. A jury found Makemie not guilty of violating the law against preaching without a license but charged him with all trial costs, a vindictive act that prompted the New York Assembly to outlaw the imposition of trial costs upon the innocent in 1708. See Michael Kammen, *Colonial New York: A History* (New York: Scribner, 1975), pp. 157–158; Thomas J. Curry, *The First Freedoms: Church and State in America to the Passage of the First Amendment* (New York: Oxford University Press, 1986), pp. 69–70

11. Thomas Jefferson, *The Life and Selected Writings of Thomas Jefferson*, ed. Adrienne Koch and William Peden (New York: Modern Library, 1944), p. 40, for Jefferson's understanding of the history of religious liberty or persecution in Virginia, and Jon Butler, "Two 1642 Letters from Virginia Puritans," *Proceedings of the Massachusetts Historical Society* 84 (1972): 99–112, for the harassment of "Puritans" in seventeenth-century Virginia. Board of Trade quoted in Curry, *The First Freedoms*, p. 100.

12. Quotation from John Williams's diary, 1771, in Rhys Isaac, "Evangelical Revolt: The Nature of the Baptists' Challenge to the Traditional Order in Virginia, 1765 to 1775," *William and Mary Quarterly*, 3d ser., 31 (1974): 347

13. On the Anglican hierarchy in Virginia see Rhys Isaac, "Religion and Authority: Problems of the Anglican Establishment in Virginia in the Era of the Great Awakening and the Parsons' Cause," *William and Mary Quarterly*, 3d ser., 30 (1973): 3–36, and Isaac, *The Transformation of Virginia, 1740–1790* (Chapel Hill: University of North Carolina Press, 1982). Isaac may, indeed, exaggerate the "high church" character of Virginia Anglicanism, but he does not exaggerate the status and power of the Anglican elite there, whatever its theological inclinations.

14. Charles H. Maxson, *The Great Awakening in the Middle Colonies* (Chicago: University of Chicago Press, 1920); Harry S. Stout, *The Divine Dramatist: George Whitefield and the Rise of Modern Evangelicalism* (Grand Rapids, Mich.: W. B. Erdmans, 1991). The question of the German immigrant experience, which begs for additional study, is briefly discussed in Stephanie Grauman Wolf, *Urban Village: Population, Community, and Family Structure in Germantown, Pennsylvania, 1683–1800* (Princeton: Princeton University Press, 1976), pp. 214–216.

15. Curry, *The First Freedoms*, pp. 134–192.

16. Ibid., pp. 135–146.

17. Ibid.; Thomas E. Buckley, S. J., *Church and State in Revolutionary Virginia, 1776–1787* (Charlottesville: University Press of Virginia, 1977); P. K. Longmore, "'All matters and things relating to religion and morality': The Virginia Burgesses' Committee for Religion, 1769 to 1775," *Journal of Church and State* 38 (1996): 775–798.

18. Leonard W. Levy, *The Establishment Clause: Religion and the First Amendment* (New York: Macmillan, 1986), pp. 38–41, 47–50. For a quite different interpretation of the First Amendment, see Akhil Reed Amar, *The Bill of Rights: Creation and Recon-*

struction (New Haven, Conn.: Yale University Press, 1998), which stresses the freedom of the states to construct their own religious establishments, whatever they might be. If this were the principal intent of the First Amendment, it surely failed because the trend in all the states, including Connecticut and Massachusetts, was toward disestablishment, some earlier, some later.

19. Curry, *The First Freedoms*, pp. 163–188.

20. For some texts of the debates on the First Amendment, see "House and Senate Debates (1789)," in John Wilson and Donald Drakeman, eds. *Church and State in American History*, 2d ed. (Boston: Beacon Press, 1986), pp. 75–78.

21. Edmund S. Morgan, *The Gentle Puritan: A Life of Ezra Stiles, 1727–1795* (New Haven, Conn.: Yale University Press, 1962), p. 451.

22. On Leland, see Curry, *The First Freedoms*, p. 176, and Lyman H. Butterfield, "Elder John Leland, Jeffersonian Itinerant," *Proceedings of the American Antiquarian Society*, LXII (1952), pp. 155–242. Cumberland County petition, October 26, 1785, quoted in Levy, *The Establishment Clause*, p. 56. That most officeholders and, certainly, most members of the federal congress or of the various Continental Congresses were church members does not alter the fact that most of their constituents were not, nor does it suggest that most church members favored government activity in religion.

23. William J. Wolf, *The Religion of Abraham Lincoln*, rev. ed. (New York: Seabury Press, 1963); D. Elton Trueblood, *Abraham Lincoln: Theologian of American Anguish* (New York: Harper and Row, 1973).

An example of the effort to see in the First Amendment only an effort to prohibit a national church can be found in Justice William Rehnquist's dissent in *Wallace v. Jaffree*, 472 U. S. 38 (1985). Rehnquist cites federal involvement in religion after the ratification of the amendment, especially in the nineteenth century, as proof of an "original" narrow understanding of the amendment limited merely to the question of a national church. This opinion does not explain why the First Amendment did not use the term church or why the Congress explicitly rejected language merely outlawing a national church. Rehnquist also cites the history of federal appropriation for the teaching of Christianity among American Indians in support of his view that the First Amendment permits government aid to religion generally, but he understandably does not deal with the coercive elements of federal policy in the Gilded Age, including the blunt suppression of traditional Indian religion on the reservations after 1869. On the situation among American Indians, see Jill E. Martin, "Constitutional Rights and Indian Rites: An Uneasy Balance," *Western Legal History* 3 (1990): 245–270; R. Pierce Beaver, *Church, State, and the American Indian* (St. Louis: Concordia Publishing House, 1966); John Collier, "Do Indians Have Rights of Conscience?," *Christian Century* (March 12, 1925): 346–349; John Collier, "Persecuting the Pueblos," *Sunset Magazine* (July 1924); Elaine Goodale Eastman, *Does Uncle Sam Foster Paganism?* (Chicago: n.p., 1934); P. Girard, "Our New Indian Policy and Religious Liberty," *Catholic World* 26 (1877–1878): 90–108; Robert S. Michaelson, "'We Also Have a Religion'—The Free Exercise of Religion among Native Americans," *American Indian Quarterly* 7 (1983): 111–142.

24. I have not dealt with recent interpretations of the First Amendment that focus on "understandings" that followed its passage in 1791. These include Daniel D. Dreisbach, "The Constitution's Forgotten Religious Clause: Reflections on the Article VI Re-

ligious Test Ban," *Journal of Church and State* 38 (1996): 261–296; Dreisbach, "In Search of a Christian Commonwealth: An Examination of Selected Nineteenth-Century Commentaries on References to God and the Christian Religion in the United States Constitution," *Baylor Law Review* 48 (1996): 927–1000; Daniel L. Dreisbach, *Religion and Politics in the Early Republic: Jasper Adams and the Church-State Debate* (Lexington: University Press of Kentucky, 1996); Michael W. McConnell, "The Origins and Historical Understanding of Free Exercise of Religion," *Harvard Law Review* 103 (1990): 1409–1517; Michael W. McConnell, "Rethinking the Incorporation of the Establishment Clause," *Harvard Law Review* 105 (1992); Stephen B. Presser, *Recapturing the Constitution: Race, Religion, and Abortion Reconsidered* (Washington, D.C.: Regnery, 1994); Ellis Sandoz, *A Government of Laws: Political Theory, Religion, and the American Founding* (Baton Rouge: Louisiana State University Press, 1991).

Index

About the Contributors

John Witte, Jr., is Jonas Robitscher Professor of Law and Director, Law and Religion Program, Emory University Law School.

Thomas E. Buckley, S.J., is Professor of Historical Theology, the Jesuit School of Theology at Berkeley.

Daniel L. Dreisbach is Associate Professor, Department of Justice, Law and Society, American University.

Catherine A. Brekus is Assistant Professor of the History of Christianity, University of Chicago Divinity School.

Mark A. Noll is McManis Professor of Christian Thought, Wheaton College.

Michael Novak is George Frederick Jewett Chair in Religion and Public Policy at the American Enterprise Institute.

Jon Butler is William Robertson Coe Professor of American Studies and History, Yale University.

5037